CITIZENS AND THE NEW GOVERNANCE

International Institute of

Administrative Sciences Monographs

Volume 10

Edited by L. Rouban and the European Group of Public Administration

European Group of Public Administration

Volume 3

Prepared by: EGPA

ISSN: 1382-4414

Citizens and the New Governance

Beyond New Public Management

EGPA Yearbook

Edited by

Luc Rouban

Chargé de Recherche au CNRS, Fondation Nationale des Sciences Politiques,
Centre d'Etude de la Vie Politique Française, France

IOS
Press

OHM
Ohmsha

Amsterdam • Berlin • Oxford • Tokyo • Washington, DC

ISBN 0 9673355 3 1 (IOS Press)
ISBN 4 274 90310 9 C3034 (Ohmsha)
Library of Congress Catalog Card Number: 99-64855

Publisher
IOS Press
Van Diemenstraat 94
1013 CN Amsterdam
Netherlands
fax: +31 20 620 3419
e-mail: order@iospress.nl

Co-Publisher
International Institute of Administrative Sciences - IIAS
Rue Defacqz, 1
B-1000 Brussels
Belgium
fax: +32 2 537 9702
e-mail: iias@agoranet.be

Distributor in the UK and Ireland
IOS Press/Lavis Marketing
73 Lime Walk
Headington
Oxford OX3 7AD
England
fax: +44 1865 75 0079

Distributor in the USA and Canada
IOS Press, Inc.
5795-G Burke Centre Parkway
Burke, VA 22015
USA
fax: +1 703 323 3668
e-mail: iosbooks@iospress.com

Distributor in Germany
IOS Press
Spandauer Strasse 2
D-10178 Berlin
Germany
fax: +49 30 242 3113

Distributor in Japan
Ohmsha, Ltd.
3-1 Kanda Nishiki-cho
Chiyoda-ku, Tokyo 101
Japan
fax: +81 3 3233 2426

Foreword

Ignace Snellen *

Being a citizen is more than a status; it is a quality. So, citizenship is more than a set of rights and obligations; it is an innate orientation on the well-being of state and society. The ancient Greeks realised that, and the polity of Athens institutionalised citizenship through its diverse associations, councils and authorities within the urban framework. In that environment citizenship, in principle, meant participation in the co-production of policies. At the basis of this participation stood a belief in the "happy versality" of man. The Romans in their turn broadened the framework in which citizenship could manifest itself. Roman citizens gave proof of their citizenship by consciously fitting themselves in into the societal order as represented by the state institutions and the authorities of the Roman empire. The medieval citizen, as inhabitant of a city and member of a craft showed his orientation and his solidarity within the confines of parish, guild and neighbourhood.

In modern times the status aspects of citizenship are stressed heavily and the qualitative aspects of citizenship appear to be grossly underestimated. Ideologies, political philosophies, and in their wake public administration as a discipline, were, until recently, more focused on the improvement of the state apparatuses than on the development of citizenship and the involvement of citizens in the making of governmental policies. Some ideologies define a further growth and a more extensive intervention in society as an improvement of the state apparatus; other ideologies, on the contrary, emphasise their slimming down and the suppression of their interventions as such an improvement. Anyway, by those approaches the citizen is left out of the picture. Following this dominant trend, public administration discipline has left the ground, as far as the desirability of citizen involvement is concerned, mainly to administrative lawyers.

The papers in this book, in which also New Public Management as one of the latest re-orientations in public administration is discussed, bear witness to the tension between a focus on improvement of state apparatuses on one hand and involvement of citizens in the co-production of policies on the other. They point at a fundamental change that is taking place in the dominant discourse. The importance of state apparatuses for the development and sustainability of viable societies is being de-emphasised: the attention for "governance" is now taking over the central place, that for so long has been occupied by the attention for "government". By governance is meant an interplay between active (associations of) citizens as primary interested parties on one hand and public authorities in more distanced role of "stage manager" on the other. By choosing arrangements of governance public authorities admit, that they, on their own, are not able to create such provisions as are required by the specific circumstances of the policy target groups, and that they are in such respects dependent on insights, initiatives and activities of those groups themselves. Through the co-production of policies by citizens and governmental authorities together, it is also hoped that "civil societies" will emerge.

---

* Professor Ignace Snellen, President of EGPA, Erasmus University, Rotterdam, The Netherlands

The European Group for Public Administration (EGPA), a branch organisation of the International Institute of Administrative Sciences (IIAS), thinks the *re-invention of the citizen* of such importance for public administrative practice as well as public administration discipline in its support for the emergence of civil societies, in which the citizen's role is re-evaluated, that it decided to devote its annual conference of 1998 to the subject. The expectation is that the studies published in this book will help to bring back in balance the existing unbalanced attention for improvements of state organisations, as opposed to attention for opportunities to revitalise citizenship.

EGPA is very grateful to the French Government and the City of Paris for the hospitality and the support with which they made this conference, which lasted from September 14 till September 17, possible. It was the right environment to re-invent the citizen: the environment in which the "citoyenneté" as a combination of "liberté", "égalité" and "fraternité" was conceptualised.

EGPA is also most grateful to the Ecole Nationale d'Administration, and its Director Mr. Raymond-François Le Bris, and to the Institut International d'Administration Publique, and its Director Mr. Didier Maus, for their logistical and scientific support, their warm welcome and the prestigious activities that were organised for the participants.

This book deserves to find its way to many desks of responsible officials, who try to make public administration more effective as well as more responsive. It may stimulate them to look across the borders of their countries to comparable situations and problems related to citizen participation and to solutions that are tried there.

Contents

About EGPA

Introduction

Citizens and the New Governance

Luc Rouban *

The EGPA meeting held in Paris in September 1998 within the prestigious walls of the Ecole Nationale d'Administration in France provided us with the opportunity to take stock of the political and social effects of the new public management. Simple legal descriptions of the relations between citizens and public administrations or ideological celebrations of the virtues of neoliberal management are no longer in order. Instead, it is time now to conduct a systematic review of the transformations that have changed the face of public management in European countries over the past fifteen years, sometimes radically. This review should take into account the political and sociological dimension not only of public management, which is merely an instrument of government, but also the intertwining relations that develop between citizens and social services. Public management is in fact a part of the set of social norms and practices that define modern or post-modern citizenship, the nature of power relationships, and individual or group capability to inform political decisions.

The nature of relations between citizenship and public management first poses the question of the quality of governance. The right to good governance is not merely a client's right but a broader right with respect to public administrations and government. Governance is the concrete result of political decisions, be they implicit of explicit. It is also the manifestation of two requirements of modern democracies: solidarity and responsibility. The quality of governance should then be conceived not in strictly economic terms but as the result of a constantly renegotiated compromise between effectiveness and democracy. It is, in fact, highly likely that there cannot be quality, or in other words, true effectiveness, without user, or citizen, adhesion or actual participation. Totalitarian regimes have given us the example of false effectiveness, just as ultra-liberal governments have given the example of another type of ineffectiveness, that of a market rationale applied blindly to a variety of human groupings in search of legal or moral norms that, precisely, help create citizenship, meaning a capacity for reciprocal political exchange (which markets cannot offer since they are dominated by unequal information exchanges or oligopolistic situations).

Pondering the relationship between citizenship and public management then leads us to assess the past fifteen years of reforms, modernisations, and transformations that have occurred in European countries. During these fifteen years, neoliberal theories and practices have developed but European societies have also been changing, a dynamic that has created new gaps between fundamental theories and the social practice of reforms. New concepts have developed and have been widely disseminated in academic circles as well as in public administrations, without conducting an appropriate investigation into their true scope or how they are interpreted in countries with different cultures. These concepts are not unequivocal,

---

* Dr. Luc Rouban, Chargé de recherche au Centre National de la Recherche Scientifique (CNRS), Fondation Nationale des Sciences Politiques, Centre d'Etude de la vie politique française, France

and they play on actors' representations. When using them, reformers in various countries do not necessarily speak the same language and do not necessarily have the same goals. Talking about the new governance thus raises a problem of semantics. The term "governance" used by Anglo-Saxon scholars is not easy translatable. In French, for instance, it refers to the idea of the general organisation of public affairs, in other words something that goes beyond the habitual notions of government or public administration, but without translating the underlying idea that social phenomena are autonomous. I believe our English-speaking friends have the same problem with translating the French concept of "service public", which does not only refer to the public nature of a service but to a whole set of historical and political connotations evoking the role of the state in society. In any event, using the notion of "governance" is symptomatic of a sea change in the way relations between citizens and public administrations are perceived, as various chapters in this book attest. Indeed, governance seems to refer to a steering function of societies that have become increasingly complex. But then it is necessary to ponder this "complexity" without simply paying lip service to it. "Complexity" in fact calls up several different evolutions:

- the fact that, first of all, citizens have individual technological resources that allow them to access a great wealth of information that is impossible to control or censure;
- the fact that governance of any sort is the result of collaboration among administrations, interest groups, and networks, and that it is becoming nearly impossible to impose a public policy, even with a comfortable political majority, when a social group vetoes it;
- the fact that the historical confines of territories, be they local or national, are currently crossed by an economic and human flux, and by networks, that destroy administrative borders. A territory is defined as a space that has been appropriated by a social group or an individual. But who can still claim to appropriate a space?
- the fact that the European Union was built without the help of any political or constitutional theory but that it nevertheless produces more and more legal standards. It remains an unidentified political object, but an object that acts and today defines most national regulations of its member states.

It is plain to see, however, that neither governance, nor complexity nor networks suffice to produce citizenship. Contrary to what many post-modern theorists believe, networks are not necessarily democratic and more often create communities than they do citizens. With the benefit of hindsight, it also becomes clear that all the managerial reforms initiated over the past fifteen years have indeed set out to reinforce political power and give it a renewed economic legitimacy. Reducing costs, however, is not enough. We know today that the end of public deficits does not mean the end of poverty and that often the cost of reforms has been transferred onto those who, precisely, are members of neither networks nor pressure groups. Similarly, decentralisation procedures have not always led to more local democracy. In France, for instance, we have seen the strengthening of local elites: mayors have set up highly political cabinets and new screens have been put up between the government and its citizens.

Lurking behind the transformations of public action or governance, the question of citizenship ties is clearly posed. The disaffection for and criticism levelled at the political class in numerous European countries must be taken into account. Voter participation is often low. Political involvement today is more channelled through contact that users have with national or local administrations than by electoral procedures. It is not enough to proclaim that politicians should decide and civil servants should manage. Because users today are demanding more than management. They also are asking for a certain form of equity, they want to be listened to and understood despite their differences, as illustrate the chapters in this book that underline the group benefits of real user participation in implementing political decisions. Between the rigid and blind enforcing of a single norm applied to everyone and the multiplication of economic markets in which citizens can buy services with the only restriction being their purse, there is certainly room for compromise. Such compromise requires original and diversified administrative models.

For the moment there are three theoretical models available. The first, Weber's model, is far from having exhausting all its appeal and usefulness. Many Southern and Eastern European countries are trying to set it up to emerge from clientelism or escape the Mafia. Citizenship is difficult to conceive in the absence of the rule of law. An economic rationale cannot nor should it erase the most elementary political rights. Thus, for what reason should one accept that decisions made by elected political majorities be discarded or transformed because a pressure group or a network has entitled itself the right to veto it? The fact remains, of course, that this model is still a deductive one and only conceives of administration as an extension of the executive power.

The second model is the one proposed by managerialism, which has the theoretical ambition of clearly dividing roles between politicians and managers. It must be acknowledged that this model is adapted to a context of global economic competition, and one can no longer keep spending more and more when the demand for goods and services is only increasing and fragmenting. Still, this model is copied from managerial theories that are applied to corporations and does not provide a means of moving from a "micro" to a "macro" rationale, that is, from an administrative to a political rationale.

The third model, a more sociological one, is that of a partnership between administrative agents and users in the production of social services. It is in the daily interaction of these two categories of actors that public policy is implemented and that political demands are translated into actual services. The public service is reinvented and developed constantly and does not only involve the application of an abstract norm. All those who consider governance from a sociological angle know very well, moreover, that administration is nothing more than a series of exceptions and special cases. This model provides a means of accounting for the specificity of the public sector and expressing what makes administrative tasks unlike any others. It may perhaps be accused of being an anti-model and not exportable easily enough in the name of international administrative co-operation. We could also consider that it is not easily interpreted by the citizens themselves and is better designed for internal use by specialists and scholars.

In the following chapters the reader will find a diverse mix of uses or presentations of these three models, depending on the national situations but also according to the capacity of the various actors to impose common practices or representations and to transform them into new norms of social life.

For two and a half days we discussed the sixteen chapters that make up this book, of which seven of them, it should be pointed out, have been authored by highly qualified young research fellows, which helps to guarantee the future of the EGPA as well as that of administrative research in Europe. It would be presumptuous on my part to claim to convey in a few lines the wealth of our discussions. I will therefore highlight some of the group reflections that came out of our talks.

The first point relates to the fact that the search for a new public management implies taking into account the role of the state. The fact that the state today appears more as an economic actor than a political actor has rather conflicting consequences: on one hand, the possibility of developing the methods and concepts of the new public management with a fairly free hand; but on the other, a crisis of legitimacy that affects the political class as much as it does the administrative structures that are still based on the principle of the rule of law. The tension runs high today between the fragmentation of the services offered and the incapacity of public authorities to make governance meaningful.

The second point, then, has to do with the fact that the identity and political history of each European state must be clearly circumscribed. Where there are managerial models, implementing them depends on adapting them in a way that varies considerably from one country to another. The practices of the new public management have thus proved enriching for Nordic countries whose structures are already characterised by a high degree of decentralisation, by guild-like organisations and by a deep-rooted culture of social pluralism. Outside the Nordic countries, implementing the new public management butts up against or upsets not only the administrative structures but also the representations users and civil servants alike have of them. The impact of the reforms thus depends closely on clientelism in Greece, the role of civil service trade unions in France, on the politicisation of civil service jobs in Austria, the role of political parties in Italy. The new public management, which advocates efficiency and flexibility, is also often contrasted with the cumbersomeness and inertia of the rules of law. But we must not forget that the rule of law is, in most European countries, the sign of a minimum political consensus often reached after considerable conflicts and trials.

One of the main contributions of the work group has been to connect the evolution of public management and the nature of the socio-political environment. It clearly appeared, contrary to what the managerial doctrine claims, that processes matter at least as much as results. Opening up or closing down decision-making systems, taking into account users demands, communication among administrative actors working at the top and those dealing with users at the grassroots level, requires negotiation and mediation more than the standardised application of budgetary norms. This new administrative work is developing mostly on the fringe of the administrative system, particularly in the social realm, where hybrid organisations are proliferating and new professional skills are developing that do not necessarily fit within established occupational grids. All users do not have the same social or economic resources to become clients, and citizens are overwhelmed by overabundant but largely irrelevant information. This situation requires an act of deciphering and organising the demand for public service at least as much as an act of management regarding the supply of public service. Public administrations thus retain an essential function: that of creating or maintaining social ties.

All of the ideas set forth in the various chapters of this book show that we have moved into the second phase of research concerning the new public management. Budget restrictions cannot constitute the ultimate rationale for reforms. The new public management, to be effective in the long term, must not lead to a total disintegration of the administrative system that functions as much on the basis of informal arrangements as on the basis of economic standards. The question of governance is posed today in its broadest sense and is not limited to investigating the financial or organisational instruments that governments have at their disposal. It is not only a question of exploring the limits of the welfare state but much more the legitimacy of the political class or of nation-states as such at a time when the political risk for democracy and citizenship resides much more in social fragmentation and the emergence of independent communities than in the emergence of some Stalinian Big Brother. Postmaterialist values have not yet given rise to clear political recipes but on the other hand cause a new constraint to weigh on European governments. The latter must now define strategies to implement public policies and account for their choices constantly while remaining able to make the decisions that are essential for society. Public administrations are located at the centre of this new tension and the new public management's ready-made formulas do not help to deal with it. Many questions were thus raised at our conference: the transparency of governance is high desired, but does it not enter in contradiction with the need for a strong professional leadership within administrations? It has become commonplace to say that the user should be placed at the centre of administrative action, but is this user always identifiable? We seek to get citizens to participate in governance to improve implementation, but who is going to choose those who participate and those who are excluded from participation? Cooperative public service is a professional reality but how can the individualised relationships between public agents and users be formalised and evaluated?

One of the ambitions of this book is to show that research on public administrations has sparked renewed interest because it is enriched by a sociological perspective that was often lacking in the past. Contrary to what is believed by those who try to sell turn-key new public management in the name of "good governance", administrative action remains dominated by social practices and political power struggles. It also poses difficult theoretical questions. In most European countries, we are witnessing the decline of Weber's model of public administration. With the disintegration of administrative machinery, questions thought to be solved are reappearing: how can one legitimate the existence of a public sector distinct from the private sector? How can a common social rule of the game be defined when the regulating mechanisms of governance overlap?

I would like to thank all of my European colleagues who agreed to participate in this work group and who have demonstrated that we can do intelligent administrative science. I hope that this book will attest to the fact that, in the absence of convergent administrative practices in Europe, there is at least a convergence of scholarship.

What Kind of a Citizen for What Kind of State?

Françoise Dreyfus *

According to the traditional definition a citizen is a person endowed with rights among which political rights are the most prominent, all of them being stated in and protected by Constitution and law. When citizens vote they participate in the election of the Nation's representatives and show their preferences for a political program which will be implemented if the political party voted for wins the elections. However to act as a citizen through political participation does not mean that people express their interest in public affairs only by their votes and the delegation of power they are giving to representatives. A more extended conception of citizenship means that the activities of the State apparatus are under the control of the people who are involved in the decision-making process or at least are informed of the decisions, specially when they are affected by them.

From an abstract point of view such action may be seen as the most democratic solution; the various methods used to promote the "participative State" as well as their limits have been analysed in reference to the almost similar techniques that the supporters of the "market model" propose to apply [1]. The implementation of new public management techniques - whatever the official explanations advanced by Governments - is focused on the citizen - customer - client (the choice of word varies depending on how positively either State or market is viewed).

This chapter discusses whether or not the extended definition of citizen is relevant as long as the key question concerning what is the State and what are its missions is not elucidated or not even posed. Transforming the traditional hierarchical administrative organisation into a decentralised and efficient institution producing measurable results, requires that the meaning and the goals of its action must first be specified.

Political participation [2] may have demonstrated the limits of its effectiveness in the extent to which it legitimates the holding of the power by the representatives. Can we nowadays see the various kinds of citizens' participation in administrative processes and the allocation of new rights as ways to legitimate the change over from a State which has until now been supposed to meet collective needs into a State designed to satisfy individual demands?

If we take the number of conferences, books and articles devoted the relationships between the administration and the customers or the citizens, a good criterion of the scientific interest in the subject, we can say that for the last twenty years or so scholars in France have devoted special attention to this matter [3], [4], [5], [6]. Does this therefore mean that a sound thorough knowledge about the citizens' position vis à vis the administrative decision-making processes and procedures is now available? The answer is negative for a simple reason: most of these academic works have been analysing the reforms implemented by governments in order to improve the relationships between the administration and the citizens, to involve the

---
* Professor Françoise Dreyfus, University Paris I Panthéon-Sorbonne, France

citizens in some decision-making processes, to increase the transparency of administrative action through better information, etc. But most of these analyses are focused, first, on the legal rules which have established new institutions (like the *Médiateur de la République* in 1973, *Commission nationale Informatique et Liberté* and *Commission d'accès aux documents administratifs* in 1978) or which administrative laid down new procedures (among many others, we can cite the Act of 1979 completed in 1986 concerning the requirement to provide formal reasons for administrative decisions, the Decree of November 28, 1983 about the relationships between the administration and its customers, the Act of 1983 regarding the democratisation of public enquiries in the field of building and town planning), and, second, on the public reports on the annual activity of the so-called Independant Administrative Authorities and of the *Conseil d'Etat*. Most of these works are either laudatory or critical towards this legal material and/or the effects it is producing, but do not try to find out what it tells us, from a political scientist's point of view, about the relation between the State and the citizen. The citizen remains an abstract figure endowed with rights. All pluralist democracies must be committed to recognising and protecting them, and those in power may, therefore, establish new rights or modify the contents of the existing ones as expectations change within national and international society. The extension of citizenship (meaning the universal right to vote) arose from a complex process involving both political struggles and social changes during the XIXth century; but we must note that, since the 1970s, citizens have been given new rights, which belong to the so called "third generation of human rights" and which extend the individual's protection against the administration. It is an open question whether it is not the administration itself that has abandoned some of the prerogatives which were the visible signs of its majesty and power.

If these new rights were not given to respond to a social demand the reasons explaining why they have been established must be found. We assume that a renewed concept of the State - whose frontiers must be rolled back - and its relationships with civil society has prevailed for about two decades; it means that we have to look at the current theories the various governments utilise, explicitly or not, when they plan the "State's modernisation" and the switch from a Welfare State to a passive and neutral State able to secure the best possible position in international economic competition.

The implementation of managerial practices within the administration is generally considered a natural tool for the process of transforming the State's role, but it may be questioned whether it has positive consequences for citizens.

1.   Good governance

In order to cast a new light on the philosophical grounds of the third generation of human rights, it may be useful to examine the current requirements imposed by the international financial organisations on developing countries asking for grants.

Good governance is a term whose appearance in the World Bank vocabulary dates back to the end of the 1980s [7]; good governance is mainly defined "as the manner in which power is exercised in the management of a country's economic and social resources for development" [8]. For the World Bank the nature of the political regime does not matter, it is only concerned that States' policies are capable of making markets work efficiently. To do this, and organise a stable legal framework upon which economic actors can depend, States must promote participation that "enables the public to influence the quality or volume of a service through some form of articulation of preferences and demans" [9], accountability that means holding public officials responsible for their actions" [10] and transparency of administrative decisions and rules. According to neo liberal economic theories [11] believing "in the market system and voluntary exchange as the most efficient and most widely equitable modes of organising human activities" [12], the World Bank postulates that State must confine its role "to provide an enabling environment for the private sector" [13], for free economic exchanges and for the protection of property rights.

The implementation of good governance principles is imposed nowadays on those countries in which authoritarian regimes have been replaced by democracy; for instance, the constitutional recognition of these rules by the constitution of Republic of South Africa in 1996 may be interpreted as responding to the World Bank's prerequisites [14]. This is not the place to discuss the validity of this concept of good governance, nor the relevance -in relations to the goals pursued - of the actions it has lead to in the developing countries [15]. This detour via the World Bank merely provides the opportunity better to understand how the dominant ideology about the relationships between State and economy is determining the rules to be followed by public administration.

The ideas developed by neo-liberal theorists over the past thirty years or more could have been seen as empirically confirmed by the crisis of the world's economy in the 70s. This crisis demonstrated that in rich countries the State was unable to deal with the consequences and above all to prevent increasing unemployment; doubts regarding the State's capacity to play an efficient role could therefore justify a questioning of its policies in social and economic fields and the restriction of its interventions when public resources were shrinking.

The theories which advocate reference to the market model and the limitation of the State's action have been used, consciously or not, by governments when they have found it necessary to reform their administrations and their modes of operation in order to attract investments and savings. Insofar as globalisation means that States themselves are competing as actors on the international market, their capacity to attract capital depends on the degree of legal security and of freedom of action which they offer to investors. In consequence, public management, following the example of the private sector, must be economical and strictly oriented towards value for money, efficiency and performance.

It is quite naïve to believe that the traditional distinction between public and private may be obliterated only as far as managerial methods are concerned; in fact, it is public action and its purposes as a whole which are brought in question. The attainment of the public interest (or common good) which has traditionally legitimated the State's role and justified the particular legal status of civil servants is loosing its symbolic value. The market is now, *de facto* fulfilling the public interest if we hold, as the neo liberal theorists do, that individuals act according to rational choices in order to maximise their profits and that free competition promotes a balanced distribution of resources; the State merely has the limited duty of insuring the rights the individual needs to exercise their economic freedom in the best conditions. The State's power even partially to reduce inequalities is being replaced by illusory improvements of the rights of the citizen seen as *homo oeconomicus*.

The recent use of the term good governance must not hide the fact that its content has been established for a long time and was the methodological reference for the British, American and Canadian governments who started to reform their public administration at the end of the 70s. In France, the extension of the rights of citizens in relation to the administration can be traced back to the presidency of Giscard d'Estaing, the first of the presidents of the Vth Republic to seek to implement policies based on liberalism; previously, the will to rationalise the management had appeared within the administration itself[1] as well as in public enterprises At the same period, the drafters of the National Planning document considered that "the VIth Plan must tend to establish or re-establish the conditions of a true market everywhere they are not yet wholly secured" [16].

2.   Towards the triumph of the client

The various measures taken in France, over the last twenty or more years, to simplify the citizens' relationships with administration, to reduce the extent of the secrecy surrounding administrative decisions or to organise preliminary consultations with the public in urban and environment fields [17][18] were far from being insignificant although they were not revolutionary. On the one hand, the opportunities they give to the citizens are actually taken up by quite a few people, essentially those who are aware of the existence of these new rights and who have the social attributes which allow them to use these rights [19]. On the other hand, we may remark that, as time goes by, governments are not renewing their policies in this field. The government's communication of February 14, 1990 concerning the relationships between administration and customersis significant in this respect: "the aim of the policy regarding the public service renewal started up by the Government is entirely oriented towards the service to the consumers. All internal reforms currently performed are working towards them... The Government's action will give priority to three subjects during the next months: better inform and welcome people, simplify the official texts, procedures and formalities, associate the consumers to the renewal of public service" [20]. If these are compared with the actions which were given priority in the framework of the governmental campaign against bureaucracy in 1982-83, no substantial change or innovation is apparent [21].

Such transformations in the administration's relationships with the citizens may be seen as an enlargement of the rights each citizen is entitled to in a democracy. In this respect to be informed of the administrative action is a way to implement the principle stated by section 15 of the Declaration of rights of man and the citizen, which provides: "Society has the right to call every public agent to account for his administration"; and to be consulted in a decision-making process simply means that the exercise of freedom of opinion is extended. The difference with the past lies in the fact that administrative secrecy is no longer the general rule and that in some precise cases the citizens' involvement in a decision making process

---

[1] Modern methods of management have been introduced in 1968 with RCB and since 1971-72 with pilot experiments concerning "direction through objectives" which prefigured in many ways the "service's projects" implemented in accordance with the Public Service Renewal stated in the Prime Ministrer's circular of february 23, 1989.

provides an opportunity to redefine the content of the public interest and to defuse potential conflicts between the administrative authorities and the citizens [22].

It may, however, also be asserted that transparency is to a large extent an illusion [23] and, like participation with which it is often linked, it mainly helps to legitimate administrative actions. Above all, it must be pointed out that the traditional patterns in which the State-citizens relationships were molded is being loosened in parallel with the State's privatisation policy; although less visible in France than in other countries such as Great-Britain, such a policy is being pursued.

By using the word "customer" in preference to "citizen", official speeches and texts clearly indicate that all the tasks performed by public administration can be seen as services whereas traditionally, the term customer designated only the client of public enterprises like the French Railways (SNCF) or French Electricity (EDF). But in fact the distinction between citizen and customer is not always clear; for instance in January 1983 the then Prime Minister P. Mauroy said: "The citizens, facing administrative activity, must as well as the civil servants have rights and this rights must be protected. In this purpose, we are elaborating under the responsibility of the Minister delegated for Civil Service and Administrative reform a charter concerning the relationships between administration and consumers" [24]. Later, another Prime minister, Alain Juppé, wrote in the working document, *Réflexions préparatoires à la réforme de l'Etat*, following his circular of July 26, 1996, that he intended "to put again the consumers at the centre of administration" and "put the citizen at the core of public service" [25]. It is clear that the two words are used as synonyms, but even if the precedence given to "consumer" is purely rhetorical, it is also symptomatic of a real change when it applies to a person dealing with a tax-collector or with the judiciary [26].

Giving substance implicitly to the idea that all public activities are undifferentiated, the extended reference made to the consumer contributes to the blurring of the frontiers between the State's specific functions and its other activities which, because they belong to the market sector, can be transferred through contract or privatisation into private hands. The references to the consumer may undoubtedly be interpreted as a means to assert the permanent prerogatives of the administration vis à vis the consumers. But we may also think that the choice in favour of this term rather than "citizen" characterises a transitional step towards a time when the client will have replaced the client-customer; and it has been clearly demonstrated that a client does not have the same kind of protected rights as a citizen or even a customer [27].

The rights to be informed and to transparency, the right to participate in decision making processes and the simplification of administrative formalities may be tools strengthening democracy; the citizens exercising these rights are no longer simply subject to administrative decisions. To some extent they become actors, provided they take the opportunity to control public action which is, after all, in fact the concrete expression of the political choices they have articulated through elections at national and local levels.

But if the State abandons any of its activities and allows them to be performed by private agents; if it intends to shape the public management in accordance with the management of economic units in competition on the market, this also means that it will no longer enforce the principles of equality and neutrality which are the basis of public actions . In consequence, the new rights will not help to strengthen the citizen's position as an active actor of public life; on the contrary, they will be used as strategic resources by rational people concerned by the maximisation of their own benefits.

In conclusion, the goals to be achieved by the implementation of the rules of good governance are not directed towards the citizen, as a member of *polis* empowered with the right to know and control what the government is doing; rather, they tend to give *homo oeconomicus* access to the information which is useful for operating in the market .

The meaning of the policies on new rights for citizens is well exemplified by the British Citizen's Charter. It has been shown that John Major did not intend to give new rights to the citizens but wanted, on the one hand, to improve the civil servants' efficiency and, on the other hand, to use consumers to monitor the performances of the privatised enterprises. The whole policy is build on the following principle: citizens are clients and must be satisfied as such; at the same time, the government's legitimacy will be sustained if both the enterprises it has privatised and the public services are providing better and cheaper services.

Finally a new type of citizen is emerging, constructed by the governments themselves; to make sense this new citizen must correspond to a new kind of State, the minimal State, whose organisational features and role are still far from being precisely defined. Moreover the creation of this new citizen-client may be seen as a way to depoliticise public issues and actually to increase the power of governments.

References

[1]   B.G. Peters, The Future of Governing: Four Emerging Models. University of Kansas Press, 1996.
[2]   J. Leca, Réflexions sur la participation politique des citoyens en France. In: Y. Mény (ed.), Idéologies, partis politiques et groupes sociaux. Presses de Sciences Po, Paris, 1989, pp. 43-70.
[3]   C.U.R.A.P.P., Administration-administrés. PUF, Paris, 1983.
[4]   C.U.R.A.P.P., Information et transparence administratives. PUF, Paris, 1988.
[5]   C. Wiener (ed.), L'évolution des rapports entre l'administration et les usagers. Economica, Paris, 1991.
[6]   I.F.S.A., Administration: droits et attentes des citoyens. La Documentation française, Paris, 1998.
[7]   B. Campbell, Quelques enjeux conceptuels, idéologiques et politiques autour de la notion de gouvernance. In: Institut africain pour la démocratie, Bonne gouvernance et développement en Afrique. Editions Démocraties africaines, Dakar, 1997, pp. 66-94.
[8]   World Bank, Governance and Development. World Bank, Washington D.C., 1992, p.1.
[9]   World Bank, Governance and Development, *op. cit.*, p. 22.
[10] World Bank, Governance. The World Bank's Experience, *op. cit.*, p. 13.
[11] M. Friedman, Capitalism and Freedom. University of Chicago Press, Chicago, 1962.
[12] W.J. Samuel (ed.), The Chicago School of Political Economy. Transaction Publishers, 1993, p. 9.
[13] World Bank, Governance. The World Bank's Experience. World Bank, Washington D.C., 1994, p. 56.
[14] F. Dreyfus, Le saut de l'ange, *Revue française d'administration publique* 85 (1998) 7-14.
[15] B. Hibou, Banque mondiale: les méfaits du catéchisme économique. L'exemple de l'Afrique subsaharienne, *Esprit* 8-9 (1998) 98-133.
[16] P. Nora, Rapport sur les entreprises publiques. La Documentation française, Paris, 1968.
[17] J.B. Auby, Y. Jegouzo, La cas de l'urbanisme et de l'environnement. In: I.F.S.A., Administration: droits et attentes des citoyens, *op. cit.*, 37-49.
[18] X. Piechaczyk, Les rôles des commissaires enquêteurs et l'intérêt général, *Politix* 42 (1998) 93-122.
[19] C. Blatrix, Vers une "démocratie participative"? Le cas de l'enquête publique. In: C.U.R.A.P.P., La gouvernabilité. PUF, Paris, 1996, pp. 299-313.

[20]　Ministère de la Fonction publique et des Réformes administratives, *Le renouveau du Service public, Les rencontres 1990,* Sélection de textes officiels, Paris, p.91.

[21]　Secrétariat d'Etat auprès du Premier ministre chargé de la Fonction publique et des réformes administratives, Administration portes ouvertes. La bureaucratie en question. La Documentation française, Paris, 1984, pp. 14-18.

[22]　P. Lascoumes, J.-P. Le Bourhis, Le bien commun comme construit territorial. Identités d'action et procédures, *Politix* **42** (1998) 37-66.

[23]　J. Chevallier, Le mythe de la transparence administrative. In: C.U.R.A.P.P., Information et transparence administratives, *op. cit.*, 239-275.

[24]　Administration et société, *Revue française d'administration publique* **28** (1983).

[25]　J. Chevallier, La réforme de l'Etat et la conception française du service public, *Revue française d'administration publique* **77** (1996) 195-196.

[26]　L. Dumoulin, T. Delpeuch, La justice: émergence de la rhétorique de l'usager. In: P. Warin (ed.), Quelle modernisation des services publics?. La Découverte, Paris, 1997, pp. 103-129.

[27]　J. Pierre, La commercialisation de l'Etat: citoyens, consommateurs et émergence du marché public. In: B.G. Peters, D. J. Savoie (eds.), Les nouveaux défis de la la gouvernance. Les Presses de l'Université de Laval, 1995, pp. 49-70.

Transparency and Citizen Participation

Stefan Sjöblom [*]

1.   The problem

On a general level, the structure of modern decision-making systems can be described as a mix of several models of governance, which has been changing rapidly over time. The development during the 70's emphasised the relationship between the bureaucratic model and corporatism. During the past years, the change has been to the direction of a market model of governance, supplemented by an increased dependence on professional employees. It can be argued that the reform efforts within the public sector - especially on the local level - are inclined to increase rather than decrease the tension between various decision-making structures. Looking at the local government reforms in the Nordic Countries, one can find at least three prominent features [1]: a more distinct bottom up approach, a shift towards New Public Management and an increased importance attached to economic considerations.

Although the recent administrative policy in the Nordic Countries has been successful in many respects, the development is plagued by many problems. One major problem has to do with legitimacy. Increased legitimacy has, of course, been the comprehensive goal of the reform policies. The problem lies in the way in which various dimensions of legitimacy have been handled and interpreted. As Rose [2] points out, two norms within the concept of legitimacy are especially relevant in the Nordic context. One norm is that of democratic control; the ability of residents to influence those decisions made at the local level that affect their daily lives. The other norm is that of efficiency or effectiveness, particularly the effectiveness of local government authorities in mastering the challenges with which they are confronted. Especially from a Finnish point of view, one could argue that the primary driving force behind most of the recent reforms has been a concern with efficiency rather than democracy.

The potential consequences of this development are many, some of them are highly problematical. As far as the relationship between various social groups and organisations is concerned, promoting governability from a bottom-up approach can increase the freedom of action of the groups but at the same time cause conflicts between various actors, thereby reducing governability as well as access to the agenda. New arrangements can result in fragmented responsibility and complexity, which can weaken perceptions of government legitimacy. Finally, a system relying on one single source of legitimacy is always a vulnerable system. A situation in which the authorities are justifying their decisions in terms of efficiency or effectiveness and the citizens have no or little control of the agenda is failing one of the central criteria for procedural democracy.

As these examples show, the crucial question when judging the reforms pursued in terms of NPM concerns the relationship between the values and instruments they contain. Depending on

[*] Stefan Sjöblom, Associate Professor, Swedish School of Social Sciences at the University of Helsinki, Finland

whether various values, goals and instruments are consistent or conflicting, the reforms have various implications for the administrative design and, consequently, for the role of the citizens. Transparency is one of the crucial goals in the NPM oriented reforms. It has been widely discussed in relation to various modes of governance and management principles. In this paper, I am not so much interested in governmental features promoting transparency in general. My perspective is another: If we assume the management to be transparent or to act transparently, how do we expect the citizens to benefit from such a situation and how are they likely to react in relation to the policy-making processes? In other words: what kind of implications does transparency have in terms of participation?

2.   On New Public Management

As often declared, NPM is a label containing a broad range of administrative doctrines, values and instruments which have been characteristic for the reform agenda in all OECD countries during the last decades, although the main emphasis may vary from country to country. NPM is a comprehensive label or term, not a theory or a theoretically integrated concept [3]. Within a Nordic context, at least the following general features of NPM have been of special relevance regarding the reform agenda:

A shift in focus of the steering systems from process to output

As in other countries, an output or performance orientation has been considered a major prerequisite for increasing transparency and accountability in public organisations. Performance orientation contains several instruments that operate as performance indicator systems: performance budgeting, benchmarking procedures and quality assessments [4] [5]. Transparency is seen as a meta-goal - rational decisions and actions are possible if goals and means are adequately transparent. Although transparency can be related to several administrative values (such as responsiveness), it has - at least from a Nordic point of view - primarily been associated with efficiency and effectiveness, i.e. promoting fiscal and political, but not necessarily public, accountability. Moreover, the technical aspect has been of a greater importance than the political one. Transparency is more a question of making goals, means and budgets clear and distinct than about the implications the transparency may have for the interaction between various actors on the political stage. In this sense, one could argue that a greater emphasis has been laid on efficiency than effectiveness.

A shift toward privatisation and semi-marketisation and away from government institutions in the service provision [6]

A wide range of market solutions constitute another "mega-trend" within the NPM relating to an administrative reform doctrine built on ideas of competition, users' choice and incentive structures. These have, for instance, led to a radical reorganisation of municipal administration. The core idea is to improve administrative efficiency and guarantee individual rights by offering citizens the right to choose among different providers of public services. Whether these tasks are performed by public or private bodies is of secondary importance as long as the most efficient solutions are chosen. The central government is responsible for the general rules of the game to ensure efficient local bodies [7]. The legitimacy of the political system is closely related to public accountability through freedom of choice and the citizen's role as a consumer.

There are, however, considerable differences in the implementation of market solutions in the Nordic Countries between municipalities and sectors. Usually the efforts are concentrated on specific types of service provision [8]. In some respects, it seems that the discussion about market solutions has been more intensive than the implementation of concrete market strategies.

Business-type managerialism and professional leadership

NPM has also given rise for radical changes in the conceptions of leadership emphasising professional skills, managerial qualities adopted from the private sector and a vision of the "chief as leader of reforms" and requiring a high degree of discretionary power. Again, at least in a Nordic context, it is disputable to what extent such changes in leadership really have occurred [9]. On one hand, it is indisputable that the "visions of leadership" have undergone changes to a managerialistic direction, but on the other hand, the old routines and management styles are still present functioning as filters while the authorities are adopting the NPM principles. There is evidence, which shows that the leaders are confronting even stronger tensions between the expectations of the politicians and the bureaucrats than before [10]. The question of loyalty, as well as the relationship between the principles of administrative versus political accountability has become more problematic.

Market control rather than democratic control

Generally speaking, it is clear that these conceptions of NPM rest on the idea of 'economic man' both regarding the role of the individual and regarding the key factors promoting good and efficient government (the market model) [11]. However, the political system needs to counterbalance the weaknesses of the market, particularly regarding the mechanisms for aggregation of preferences and support. Various user or consumer control devices often serve to decentralise and desegregate control, diminishing opportunities for influence by those who are not users [12]. It is still an open question to what extent political and public accountability can be reached by emphasising the individual's role as a consumer, thereby perhaps diminishing her role as a political citizen.

I shall not continue the discussion on to what extent the various elements of NPM actually have been realised and implemented in the Nordic Countries. Several such studies have been undertaken [13] [14]. Instead, I shall take the general characteristics of NPM that were briefly referred to above, as a point of departure for discussing the relationship between the key values and goals that NPM reflects and particularly the implications these relationships have on the role of the citizen.

Among the arguments in favour of NPM, one is of a special interest in this context. At least in the beginning of the NPM era, it was frequently claimed to be a universal and neutral conception - an apolitical framework in which many different values could be pursued effectively [15]. Consequently, different political priorities could be accommodated in the NPM framework by altering the design of the management principles of the political system. The counter argument to this assertion of universality would be that different administrative values have different implications for fundamental aspects of the administrative design. However, as Hood [16] has pointed out, this incompatibility argument should rest on a "plausible case that an all-purpose culture either does not exist or cannot be engineered into existence. Unless it can do so, it risks being dismissed for mechanically assuming that there is a particular set of administrative design-characteristics which goes with the ability to achieve a particular set of values." Hood also seems to be right in the assertion that a prerequisite for establishing the proper scope and the historical room for NPM is to test its limits in terms of relatively narrow administrative values [17].

My point of departure here is that this contradictory argument is one of the more severe counter-claims against NPM. In any case, the implications of this argument are clear: the values, goals and instruments related to NPM should to a greater extent be analysed in relation to each other to detect conformities as well as contradictions. Otherwise, it seems impossible to understand the final impact of the reforms in relation to the citizens and the legitimacy of the political system in general.

3.   Administrative values and the citizens

As Yates [18] has shown, each administrative value - may it be legality, accessibility, accountability or responsiveness - has a procedural and a substantive meaning. In the procedural sense, and from the citizen's point of view, the values implicate greater communication and interaction between citizens and public officials. The substantive aspect concerns the question of what kinds of decisions are made. The central criterion is whether those affected by the decision feel that the right decision was made. In addition, there is a distinction between strong and weak constructions of the process values. The values are weak when they provide only mild possibilities for the citizens to address the decision-makers and strong when they go towards changing the nature of the proceedings or the resulting policy [19].

The problem with promoting an administrative value through the reform instrument related to it is that it may have direct or indirect consequences or no effects at all on the role of the citizens, depending on which relation between the key actors of the political system is supposed to be affected. As stated before, transparency is one of the major goals of NPM reforms. It is perhaps primarily associated with efficiency but can, as well, be related to effectiveness, responsiveness or democratic decision-making in general [20]. Depending on what kind of accountability we want to pursue through improved transparency, the efforts may or may not affect the citizens' possibilities of influencing decision-making.

3.1.   Transparency and efficiency

To a considerable extent, the discussion about transparency has been related to efficiency, which is one of the two central principles of administrative accountability. Since public bureaucracies do not work according to the principle of maximising profits, they are expected to minimise costs and to use their resources carefully. On a micro-level, it is usually argued that decentralised systems are more likely to increase efficiency than centralised systems, because individual agencies have more information according to which the operations of the agency can be changed [21].

The instruments for promoting efficiency are numerous: performance indicator systems, performance budgeting, benchmarking procedures and so on. I shall not discuss these instruments in any detail. However, ideally speaking we expect the bureaucracy to provide clear and distinct information of their performances. We expect that the performances can be operationalised into clear measures and indicators, providing that goals and targets are equally operationalisable [22]. If we expect the efficiency related transparency to have any effect on the citizen's behaviour, we also expect her to be able to make use of this information and that her choices of services, attitudes towards the bureaucracy etc. primarily rest on economic considerations. She is supposed to act like a consumer and her role is close to the one in the market model. To act responsively, the bureaucracy should register the consumers' behaviour and if necessary, and possible, adjust the performances in a more efficient direction.

As we know, none of these assumptions are necessarily true. There are considerable problems concerning the operationalisation of public sector performances and considerable variations regarding the implementation of performance management in the public sector. There may be strong incentives for actors in public organisations to provide misinformation and non-transparency rather than transparency and, finally, the evidence that the individual makes her choices regarding public sector performances primarily on economic grounds are not convincing. If we, however, stick to the ideal type of reasoning concerning the connection between efficiency related transparency, it would be the one outlined above.

3.2. Transparency and effectiveness

Fiscal accountability or efficiency in a narrow sense is rarely regarded as the only accurate criterion when evaluating public performances. It can be accurate in exceptionally specialised agencies, but the more policy oriented the agency is, the more its activities cut close to the main public values, the more important measures of effectiveness are usually considered to be in order to achieve political accountability. In a narrow sense, effectiveness concerns the relationship between intended policy goals and goal achievement. However, even the achievement of formal goals does not necessarily guarantee the achievement of intended impacts, which is the argument for more extensive frameworks including needs, problems and preferences of the citizens [23]. Such a definition broadens the perspective in the direction of responsiveness.

In general, it can be said that performance measurements primarily contribute to administrative accountability and only secondarily to political accountability [24]. The reasons for this are manifold. When the criteria are extensively defined the measurement problems increase rapidly. There is a greater risk for ambiguous results and difficulties in reaching an agreement on the implications of the results among relevant actors. Moreover, there is evidence that politicians have the tendency to avoid clear and transparent decisions for tactical reasons [25]. However, if we again ignore the difficulties and follow the "logic" of performance management based on an extensive conception of effectiveness that presumes that such a management should affect the citizens' possibilities of influencing the performances, we find that compared to a more narrow sense of performance management the expectations are slightly changed.

We would expect the bureaucracy to have as clear and distinct performance and quality indicators as possible and information on the needs and preferences among the citizens. Seen from the citizens' point of view, one would expect there to be mechanisms by which they can address the authorities when needs and preferences are changing. The interaction between the bureaucracy and the citizens is based on exchange of information. These characteristics are related to the service state model [26] where the citizen's role is that of a client and the organisations, again if they are acting responsively, are supposed to react as needs and preferences change.

3.3.   Transparency and responsiveness

In terms of transparency, the limit between effectiveness and responsiveness is a bit vague, but from the citizen's point of view, there is an important difference. If I argue, as above, that the conditions of responsiveness are satisfied when the definition of political accountability includes attention to the needs, problems and preferences of citizens as members of target groups [27], the argumentation follows a weakly defined procedural conception of responsiveness, requiring only mild forms of redress for citizens or mechanism for exchange of information [28]. If we, on the other hand, rely on a strong substantial conception of responsiveness we would presuppose that there are mechanisms making it possible to intervene directly in the policy processes and, at the extreme, that public officials might be required to do exactly what the citizens wish.

This of course means that the bureaucracy would face the classical risks of governmental overload and problems in handling partisan interests. If we again neglect these problems at the heart of the existing tension between representative and direct democracy, it would presumably mean that we should be ready to accept an increased political function of the bureaucracy. In a decentralised system, the bureaucracy would have a stronger responsibility for the compromises of collective bargaining at the policy level. This follows the same argument as Yates' [29] statement that as the bureaucrats play a highly significant role in decision-making and value-choosing they should also take the lead in the clarification of values and alternatives and to a larger extent participate in an open debate. This would mean that the bureaucracy acts as a moderator in handling the diverse interests of the participant organisations, groups and citizens. The implications that a high transparency regarding efficiency, effectiveness and responsiveness have on the roles of the bureaucracy and the citizens are briefly summarised in figure 1.

As it is frequently noted, efficiency, effectiveness and responsiveness represent different principles of accountability, or: "a magic polygon without hierarchical order, so that none of them can be maximised without restricting the fulfilment of the other ones" [30]. The idea of a balanced equilibrium is not possible - in practice, one principle is always promoted at the expense of the others. Similarly, various types of transparency can be more or less compatible. This does not mean that the dilemma cannot be solved. One of the dominant features of western bureaucracies is a joint combination of several modes of governance. Consequently, the public manager has to combine politics and production and reflect upon conflicting values and demands at the same time protecting the operational code of the organisation [31]. There is evidence showing that such a combination can be made effective [32].

Figure 1 - The roles of the bureaucracy and the citizens when given a high transparency of the political system in relation to the values of efficiency, effectiveness and transparency.

Value	Role of the bureaucracy vs. citizens	Role of the citizens vs. bureaucracy	Type of participation
Efficiency	Adjustor	Consumer	Choice
Effectiveness	Reactor	Client	Dialogue
Responsiveness	Moderator	Active citizen (Participant)	Intervention

It is, however, important to remember that at the same time as the citizen is acting according to different roles it is not necessarily so that she, in trying to influence the management, chooses a role or a strategy which is congruent with the management's conception of its own role. For instance, a hypothetical organisation showing an extremely high level of transparency in terms of efficiency is not necessarily especially open to a citizen who for one or another reason is not satisfied with her consumer role, but instead tries to intervene in more direct ways. The active citizen is likely to confront the professional code of the bureaucracy. I shall not discuss all the possible tensions between transparency and various principles of accountability. I will restrict myself to transparency as a prerequisite for participation, primarily from the citizen's point of view.

4.   Transparency and participation

4.1.   *The citizen as a consumer - transparency and choice*

In theory, the relationship between transparency and the citizen's role as a consumer is simple. In the above discussion, we concluded that if we expect efficiency-related transparency to have any effect on the activities of the citizen, we expect the organisation to provide clear and exact information on its performances. This helps the citizen to make her choice based on, if not solely on economic, then at least on utilitarian grounds. Regardless of whether the choices are made on utilitarian grounds or not, the condition is that a market situation exits, which enables the citizen to choose between different alternatives and at the same time functions as an incentive for the organisation to act transparently. A pure consumer role is highly apolitical. The citizen is participating by choosing among available alternatives. If, however, a market situation does not exist, but the organisation is still acting according to the principles of performance management, the professional code is likely to be of a great importance in deciding what is to be considered as 'good' performance. This increases the risk of non-transparency *vis-à-vis* the citizens.

It is, of course, a fact that one of the core ideas in public administration reforms in all the Nordic Countries has been the improving of administrative efficiency and guaranteeing individual rights by offering the citizens the possibility to choose among different providers of public goods and services. According to Rose, there is also evidence showing that the NPM related reform efforts are widely accepted [33]. However, the extent to which the market-like mechanisms have been created in the Nordic Countries varies. Real market situations are still relatively rare compared to the traditionally organised service provision. Undoubtedly, situations where the management is trying to implement performance management without elements of competition are much more frequent.

Nevertheless, the ability of individuals to exercise consumer sovereignty may be viewed as a form of democracy - a situation in which individuals decide and express their choices by means of consuming or not consuming the services offered to them. However, as Rose [34] has pointed out, individual decisions regarding the consumption of specific services are of an entirely different scope than decisions related to an aggregate set of goods and services, which is characteristic of decision-making on the political arena. Even if service arrangements related to NPM may increase consumers' choice and efficiency, they may also limit the scope of democracy, or the sphere in which the citizen is able to act politically. This may also be the case when the principles of the performance management are implemented without elements of competition. In such a situation, technical and professional considerations are likely to gain in importance. We run the risk of creating what has been called the trap of "democracy without politics" [35]. In this respect, the tension between efficiency related transparency and participation is crucial when reflecting upon the possibilities of pursuing public accountability.

4.2.   The citizen as a client - transparency and dialogue

As discussed earlier, a high level of transparency in terms of effectiveness would implicate that there are, between the bureaucracy and the citizens, mechanisms for an exchange of information on the different needs and preferences. This means that there, at least in a procedural sense, should exist relatively strongly organised channels for participation, i.e. forms of redress for citizens, that may affect the proceedings of the bureaucracy or the outcomes of the policy in question. The conditions for a high level of transparency are: a) that the bureaucracy is characterised by a strong service orientation and b) the willingness and capability of the clients to act as 'enlightened' citizens in relation to government performances. Improving accessibility of services by means of decentralisation, obligations of giving citizens information about services and various forms of consumer-feedback systems have been regarded as important instruments for improving transparency in this sense.

It seems evident that transparency in terms of effectiveness could be achieved in a highly decentralised system in the relationship between street-level bureaucrats and citizens. Such a system would come close to some aspects of the communitarian ideal relying on small-scale service provision and user democracy [36]. In a less decentralised system, the potential risks would be a politicisation of the information on preferences and performances due to imperfect measurement systems, which would be counterproductive in terms of efficiency. Moreover, information asymmetries in the agent-client relationship and the inclination to produce non-transparency, thereby protecting organisational interests, are likely to increase in a less decentralised system.

4.3.   The active citizen - transparency and intervention

Transparency in terms of a strong conception of responsiveness is deeply rooted in the tradition of participatory democracy and can be achieved only by providing strongly organised means of intervention in the policy processes. It is also closely related to the self governing state model [37], according to which the citizens not only have impact on the services offered by the administration but also take part in the production processes as co-producers and as citizens deciding what is to be produced. Control can be carried out by establishing user group representation or by transferring grants to the citizens who organise the production themselves [38].

If we do not believe that the self governing state model can be fully implemented but still think that responsiveness should be pursued through extensive participation, we face the problem of how to avoid governmental overload and achieve cohesiveness and capacity to act when the people is split into factions and groups of special interests. The civic or republican tradition has one answer to that problem. Applying the republican view on local government, Baldersheim [39] argues that the central objective is to distinguish more clearly between the municipality as a producing organisation and the municipality as a political arena with the general responsibility for the community. The government plays a role as the enabling authority which is focused on citizen autonomy, leadership, political education and involved citizens. This view is clearly more political than the conception of a service state and would allow extensive participation at the same time stressing the role of the government as a moderator of diverse interests.

Such a conception, as well as demands for extensive participation in general, rely on the assumption that the citizens are politically interested, willing to participate and that their civil competence and qualifications are, if not high then, at least sufficient. As relatively collective and egalitarian orientated as the Nordic states still are, some recently published research results justify the question to what extent those qualifications exist. These results are even alarming in parts. A recent Swedish study [40] shows that the citizens' inclination and resources to participate are diminishing, regardless of whether participation means engagement in political parties, attending political meetings, participating in demonstrations or addressing the decision-makers. Studies in Finland indicate that the citizens' knowledge about local politics is relatively poor and that the willingness to engage in for instance party politics is weak [41] [42]. A study on participation yet to be published [43] shows that the interest to participate, when it exists, is primarily directed towards relatively conventional and transitional activities. The cleavage between the politically poor and the politically well situated is still considerable, although it, in the Finnish context, is impossible to say whether the cleavage has been increasing or diminishing over the past years. Although an Norwegian study shows that there seems to be a correspondence between the citizens' expectations and the primary thrust of recent local government reform activity, the study comes to the conclusion that there is reason to be cautious in emphasising the individual's role as a consumer without underlining the possibilities for the individual to act as a political citizen [44].

I am not saying that the recent development is similar in all three countries, for instance, Norway may in many respects be a deviant case compared to Sweden and Finland. However, considering the results and indications referred to above, it does not seem realistic to expect dramatically increased participation that is solely based on a model of extreme decentralisation, regardless of whether that model is the market or the self-governing state model. If we want to increase citizen participation it has to be achieved with, not without politics, as well as bureaucracy, which turns us back to the conception of an enabling authority and indeed underlines the importance of transparency and the code directing management activities.

5.   Conclusions

Some prerequisites for transparency that are related to various types of participation are summarised in appendix 1. Figure 2 is an attempt to outline some hypothetical relationships between transparency, participation and the effects concerning the legitimacy of the decision-making system.

Figure 2 - Hypothetical relationships between transparency and participation

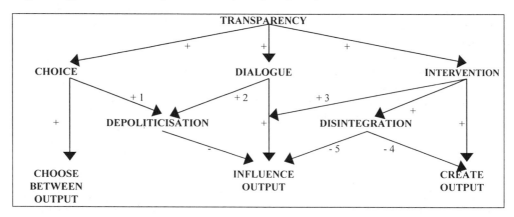

Figure 2 illustrates a presumed ideal type of situation in which a system attempts to promote transparency in terms of efficiency, effectiveness as well as responsiveness, or in other words choice, dialogue and intervention. As far as the legitimacy of the system is concerned, these attempts are expected to improve the citizens' possibilities to choose between outputs, to influence outputs and to create outputs. However, referring to the line of argumentation I have been following in this paper, the possible dysfunctional effects are perhaps the most interesting when judging the relationship between transparency, participation and the legitimacy of the system as a whole. Some of the conceivable dysfunctional effects are numbered in the figure and can be briefly summarised as follows:

1. A crucial question is to what extent performance management, especially in non-market situations, which are still the most typical ones, contributes to depoliticisation, thereby reducing the sphere in which the individual is able to act as a political citizen.
2. On the same grounds, it is possible that transparency, in terms of effectiveness, will promote depoliticisation, provided the position of the professional bureaucracy is strong when deciding on the implications of the information concerning citizen needs and preferences. Such situations of information asymmetries have been discussed particularly in highly specialised fields of knowledge such as medical services. The opposite situation might, however, be even more frequent. Goals, means and targets are politicised due to imperfect information and measurement problems, by which the policy-makers' capacity to act is reduced.
3. In practice, the primary function of interventionist means and channels for participation has so far been to provide means for influencing rather than creating output, which means that the participatory arrangements are complementary in relation to normal decision-making procedures. To be effective in terms of responsiveness, such a system would have to be

characterised by a relatively high level of citizen autonomy and a management code accepting extensive participation. Disintegrative effects (5) of participation and limited possibilities of managing diverse interests, tend to restrict such characteristics.

4. The possible disintegrative effects of participation in relation to the creation of output have to do with the differences in political resources among the citizens. Especially in a mixed system, which does not rely only on one mode of governance, such risks tend to increase.

Although I have mainly been dealing with the perceivable problems in the relationship between transparency and participation, it is obvious that a high level of transparency in general terms is crucial in trying to reinforce participatory arrangements. However the relationship contains several problems caused by the mix of models characteristic for modern decision making systems and the confrontations between various management ideals. As I argued before, from a Nordic perspective it is highly unlikely that the future development will be towards one pure model of governance. A joint combination of several models with an imperfect balance between values and interest will remain as a dominant feature. This requires stronger moderating mechanisms than before, and it might be well founded to agree with Lennart Lundquist [45] on the assertion that we still have to rely on the civil servants as the guardians of democracy. At least it seems reasonable to emphasise their role in the discussion on consistent and conflicting public values.

References

[1]   L. Rose, Reform Activities and the Legitimacy of Local Government. Reflections on the Nordic Experience. In: V. Helander S. Sandberg (eds.), Festskrift till Krister Ståhlberg 50 år den 31.5.1997. Åbo Academy Press, Åbo, 1997.
[2]   L. Rose, *op cit.*, p. 144.
[3]   K.K. Klausen, Indikatorer på NPM:s gradvise men begrensede gennemslag i Danmark. In: K.K. Klausen and K. Ståhlberg (eds.), New Public Management i Norden. Odense universitetsforlag, Odense, 1998.
[4]   *Ibid.*
[5]   C. Reichard, The Impact of Performance management on Transparency and Accountability in the Public Sector. Paper presented att the Annual Conference of EGPA, Leuven, 1997 (manuscript).
[6]   K.K. Klausen and K. Ståhlberg, New Public Management. In: K.K. Klausen and K. Ståhlberg (eds.), New Public Management i Norden, *op. cit.*
[7]   H. Baldersheim, The problem of Legitimacy in Local Government. Roots Choice or Virtue? In: V.Helander and S.Sandberg (eds.), Festskrift till Krister Ståhlberg 50 år den 31.5.1997. Åbo Academy Press, Åbo, 1997.
[8]   K. Ståhlberg, Utvecklingspolitiken i finländska kommuner. Vad, var och vem? In: K.K. Klausen, and K. Ståhlberg (eds.), New Public Management i Norden, *op. cit.*
[9]   A. Bergström, Från försiktig byråkrat till handlingskraftig ledare.Nya management ideer i svenska kommuner och landsting. In: K.K. Klausen and K. Ståhlberg (eds.), New Public Management i Norden, *op. cit.*
[10]   N. Ejersbo, Nye ledelseformer i danske kommuner. In: K.K. Klausen and K. Ståhlberg, (eds.), New Public Management i Norden, *op. cit.*
[11]   K.K. Klausen and K. Ståhlberg, *op. cit.*
[12]   L. Rose, *op. cit.*, p. 157.
[13]   *Ibid.*
[14]   K.K. Klausen and K. Ståhlberg, *op. cit.*
[15]   Ch. Hood, A Public Management for All Seasons? *Public Administration* **69** Spring 1991, p. 8.
[16]   Ch. Hood, *op. cit.*, p. 10.
[17]   Ch. Hood, *op. cit.*, p. 16.
[18]   D.T. Yates, Hard Choices: Justifying Bureaucratic Decisions. In: J.L. Fleishmann *et al.* (eds.), Public Duties: The Moral Obligations of Government Officials. Harvard University Press, Cambridge, 1981.

[19]   D.T. Yates, *op. cit.*, p. 42.
[20]   C. Reichard, *op. cit.*
[21]   P. Uusikylä, Agency Discretion and Public Accountability. In: New Trends in Public Administration and Public Law. EGPA Yearbook, Budapest, 1996.
[22]   C. Reichard, *op. cit.*
[23]   W. Wirth, Responding to Citizens' Needs - From Bureaucratic Accountability to Individual Co-production in the Public Sector. In: F.-X. Kaufmann (ed.), The Public Sector. Challenge for Coordination and Learning. Walter de Gruyter, Berlin, 1991.
[24]   C. Reichard, *op. cit.*
[25]   C. Reichard, *op. cit.*
[26]   T. Beck-Jörgensen, Modes of Governance and administrative Change. In: J. Kooiman (ed.), Modern Governance. Sage, London, 1993.
[27]   P. Uusikylä, *op. cit.*, p. 211.
[28]   D.T. Yates, *op. cit.*, p. 42.
[29]   *Ibid.*
[30]   W. Wirth, *op. cit.*, p. 74.
[31]   T. Beck-Jörgensen, op. cit., p. 231.
[32]   *Ibid.*
[33]   L. Rose, *op. cit.*
[34]   *Ibid.*, p. 151.
[35]   S. Montin & I. Elander, Citizenship, Consumerism and Local Government in Sweden. *Scandinavian Political Studies* **18** (1995).
[36]   H. Baldersheim, *op. cit.*, p. 139.
[37]   T. Beck-Jörgensen, op. cit., p. 223.
[38]   *Ibid.*
[39]   H. Baldersheim, *op. cit.*, p. 137.
[40]   O. Petersson *et al.*, Demokrati och medborgarskap. SNS förlag, Stockholm 1998.
[41]   S. Borg, Puolueet ja edustuksellinen kunnallisdemokratia. Tampereen yliopisto. Kunnallistieteiden laitos, Tampere, 1998.
[42]   S. Pikkala, Eikö kunnallinen demokratia ansaitse valtuutetun luottamusta? Meddelanden från Ekonomisk-statsvetenskapliga fakulteten vid Åbo Akademi. Ser A:486, Åbo, 1998.
[43]   S. Sjöblom, Kuntalaiset ja vaikuttaminen. In: K.-P. Mäki-Lohiluoma, M. Pekola-Sjöblom and K. Ståhlberg (eds.), Kuntalaisten valta ja valinnat. Finnish Association of Local Authorities, Helsinki 1998.
[44]   L. Rose, *op. cit.*, p. 157.
[45]   L. Lundquist, Demokratins väktare. Studentlitteratur, Lund, 1998.

Appendix 1 - Transparency and participation - some prerequisites and possible consequences.

Transparency related to:	Code of the bureaucracy:	Conditions:	Organizational alternatives	Possible counter effects
Choice	Efficiency	• Competition • Clear and distinct knowledge	• Market • Market-like mechanisms	• Depoliticization • Suboptimization under non-market conditions
Dialogue	Service-orientation	• Interaction	• Decentralized service production (public/private)	• Asymmetric information
Intervention	Citizen autonomy	• Participatory arrangements • Civic competence, readiness for participation	• The enabling authority • Individual co-production	• Disintegration • Inequality

Citizens and the Quality of Public Administration in Greece

Calliope Spanou [*]

Introduction

Citizen-administration relations present universal as well as aspects particular to specific socio-political contexts. The first have to do with the unequal relationship between the two parts and the "bureaucratic insensitivity" or insufficient responsiveness. These constitute universal aspects of bureaucracy - citizens relations and are found at various degrees in practically all bureaucracies. This first set of parameters does not explain, however, important aspects of the relationship; it lacks specific reference to those features that are peculiar to a given bureaucracy, and concern the socio-political context and its influence upon it. A second set of parameters relative to these aspects has to enter into account.

"Quality" of administration may therefore take different meanings. The aim of the paper is to draw a picture of the possible meaning of quality of administration in Greece, i.e., from the point of view of the citizen. The interest of such an endeavour is twofold. First, it could serve as a basis for the subsequent improvement of policies. Second, its wider significance lies in testing the universality claim of "quality" - by supporting, countering or relativising it - in light of the peculiarities of a specific policy context.

The discussion that follows is based upon the opinions expressed by citizens and civil servants concerning their mutual relation. Given that the general feeling towards public services in Greece is commonly perceived as negative, it is important to start putting together the pieces of the puzzle in order to identify the various dimensions of a generally unsatisfactory relationship.

The empirical data were provided by a survey conducted in Greece, between 1993-1994. More specifically, it was an inquiry into the mutual perceptions and the way they possibly relate to each other. Questionnaires addressed to citizens and civil servants contained partly similar or identical questions. A daily newspaper - *Eleftherotypia* - published the citizens' questionnaire while the civil servants' questionnaire was distributed on the occasion of training sessions. Despite the methodological limitations of the data, there are reasons to believe that the answers reflect some general trends[1].

---

[*] Professor Calliope Spanou, University of Athens, Department of Political Science and Public Administration, Greece

[1] The research was based on a similar one concerning citizens' perceptions, conducted by the Research Center of the University of Picardie (France). See [1].

The profile of the respondents[2] to the questionnaires is undoubtedly biased given the centre-left position of the newspaper (that accepted to collaborate) and the rather educated public that spontaneously responded to the questionnaire[3]. This bias is, however, taken into account when and where it matters: this is basically the case when politically sensitive questions are addressed. For the rest, it can be claimed that the results reflect in a rather accurate way the general perceptions on the issue. These perceptions form the framework of daily contacts between citizens and public services; they express the general experience and pre-disposition that guide concrete contacts with public administration. A central hypothesis of the paper is thus that they constitute the *implicit conditions of the encounter*, and may therefore determine in large part its outcome and mutual attitudes.

Given limitations in the space available, this contribution cannot reproduce in detail the results of the questionnaires. Reference has to be made only to a limited number of parameters that illustrate the thrust of the argument in the paper.

1.   General perceptions

Among citizens, the image of public administration and civil servants is clearly negative. This extends to general expectations, competence, expertise, and attitudes towards the public. More specifically, respondents declare a low degree or no satisfaction of the service provided (55% and 34%, respectively, while only 0,2% consider it as very satisfactory). The time responsiveness of public administration is assessed as "excessively slow" in 80% of the answers, and "normal" in 20% of the answers.

For citizens, public administration is mainly characterised by its *phobia of responsibilities* (82%), impersonality (64%) and complexity (64%). The first answer is proportionally linked to the educational level, while the two latter are inversely linked to the educational level. Public administration is also seen as authoritarian (43%) and scholastic (30%).

---

[2] More specifically the profile of the citizens who responded to the questionnaire is the following:
The total number of citizens who answered the questionnaires was 471. Divided by gender 71% were men and 29% women. 31% were employed in the public sector, 58% in the private sector, 9% not employed. In terms of age: 36% were 25-34 years old, 33% 35-44, 12% 45-54, 10% 55-64, 7% under 25 years and 2% over 65 years old. In terms of education, 58% had higher education and post graduate degrees, 17,6% higher technical education, 21% secondary level and 3% compulsory education. 59% come from big cities, 18% from cities of over 50.000 inhabitants and 33% from cities of less than 50.000 inhabitants. Last but not least, in terms of political sensitivity, 62% positioned themselves left of centre, 21% centre and 17% right of the centre. Seen differently, the centre positions account for 61,5%, while the two left positions account for the 33,5% and the two right positions for 5% of the respondents.
    The total number of civil servants was 400, of whom 57% were men and 43% women. In terms of age, 22% were between 25-44, 52% between 35-44, 24% between 45-54 and the rest under 25 or over 55 years old. In terms of educational level 70% had higher education degrees, 11% higher technical education and 19% secondary level education. 40% of the civil service respondents worked in the three big cities (Athens, Pireas, and Thessaloniki), 23% in cities of over 50.000 inhabitants, and 37% in cities of less than 50.000 inhabitants.
[3] This research does not claim to represent a fully-fledged opinion poll. The methods used present advantages and disadvantages. The value of the data lies, among others, in the fact that there are comparable questions in both cases and the answers can thus be cross-checked. Besides, this has to be seen within the context of general absence of such studies.

All positive qualifications (understanding, helpful, fair, objective, disciplined) do not even reach 2% of the answers! Moreover, public administration does not exhibit impartiality (87%), but treats more favourably those who have the "connections" (87%) or "wealth" (10%). Citizens equally distrust its presumed political neutrality (97%). Public administration obeys the government of the day (75%) rather than applying the rule of law (9,6%), or acts as it suits itself (15%). The public seems to acknowledge political responsibilities in the way Greek administration operates (see also infra).

Citizens do not hold civil servants' expertise in high esteem. Access to public employment is seen as based mostly on political (52%) or other personal connections (18%) and much less upon merit such as capacities (22%) or educational qualifications (8%).

On the other side of the relationship axis, *civil servants have an equally negative image of public administration.* They agree with citizens that in terms of time administrative responsiveness has "its own rhythm" (59%), followed by the "urgency of the case" (23%) or "similar" independently of the content of the case (18%). General responsiveness to citizens' needs is seen as "mediocre" at 90%, against 8% as "non-existent" and 2% as "full"! These perceptions are particularly interesting since they come from the civil servants themselves. They can be seen as self-criticism but also as a form of victimisation of those who serve within such a negatively perceived environment. In any case, the picture adopted by civil servants is practically identical to the one citizens have about public administration.

Civil servants choose the same qualifications to describe public administration: *phobia of responsibilities* (lack of initiative) 65%, impersonality 45%, complexity 62%. Again, positive qualifications rate below 12%, "scholastic" is accepted at 30% (like in the citizens' responses), and only "authoritarian" is lower than the comparative rate in the citizens' sample by almost 50 percent.

What appears as rather revealing is civil servants' self image which is by-and-large negative. Merit (studies and individual capacities) is seen as having the same importance as non-merit factors (political and personal connections) in career development. This shows the weak trust in the role merit plays in the overall civil service system. Only slightly more than half the respondents believed that their talents are adequately used by the service (54%). Their status compared to other employees (private sector) is rather seen as worse (48%), than better (28%) or similar (24%).

2.   The public encounter

The manner in which civil servants treat citizens on the occasion of the public encounter is "not satisfactory at all", or only "a little" (39% and 46% respectively), while 15% consider it as "rather good". Civil servants are seen as trying to "get rid of citizens as soon as possible" (74%) and as being "impersonal" (25%). Only 2% of the answers see them as "understanding and helpful". The image of the civil servant is predominantly authoritarian, symbolised by the "person behind a desk" (74%), or the tax officer (50%). The usual public service employees like policemen, teachers, doctors, postmen follow with 16%, 15%, 5%, 2% and 0,6% respectively. Dominant representations of public services and civil servants do not focus upon the service provided (education, health, etc.). On the contrary, they emphasise distance, authority and the separation of the two worlds.

Interestingly enough, citizens' responses tend to show a preference for written information (77%), as opposed to face to face contact and oral information (23%). The latter is, however, seen as "mediocre" in terms of intelligibility, clarity and simplicity (69%), as opposed to 9% "fully intelligible" and 22% "incomprehensible". This assessment is very similar to the one concerning written information (77%, 9% and 23%), respectively. The preference for written information may seem rather difficult to interpret. Any hypothesis should therefore be connected to the attributes (perceived advantages and disadvantages) of the direct or indirect relation which the public service implies. The contradiction has to be seen in the light of the possible lack of security of oral information (see for example, low estimation of competence and expertise), but also the negative expectations from a personal encounter.

Indeed, as shown by a different set of answers, personal contacts provoke in citizens feelings of uneasiness, anxiety, insecurity (63%) and impatience (22%). Respondents of all educational levels shared these emotional reactions. They can be considered as a common feature, inherent in the relation with public services.

Despite the preference for written information, in most cases, citizens go themselves to the public service (79%) instead of using the telephone (21%). The latter is relatively more preferred by persons of higher educational levels. The limited use of the telephone may be explained by the low responsiveness of civil servants in telephone contacts and the low expectation on behalf of citizens of possibly getting accurate information in this way.

Citizens generally expect negative treatment or behaviour from civil servants. When this expectation is confirmed, they tend to adopt a "combative" attitude (71%), rather than be "patient and optimistic" (15%), or "give up" (14%). Addressing the hierarchically superior is the most frequent reaction (93%). Others do give up (35%), while fewer refer to the *Body of Administrative Inspectors* (11%), the media (20%), or a politician (7%).

Seen from their side of the coin, *civil servants* regard citizens as having a preference (in order of priority) for personal contact (48%), written information (40%) and much less for the telephone (12%). Clearly, however, the telephone is the least used means of contact, which has to be explained in the context of the limited communication capacity, the impersonality and the potential for encountering even more indifference from the other end of the line.

The actual contact is acknowledged as *emotionally loaded* by civil servants as well. They are aware of the "anxiety and insecurity" (62%) of citizens, but they also sense "aggressiveness" (61%). Aggressive behaviour from citizens (68,4%) as well as "arrogance and impoliteness" (63,4%) and "insistence on exceptional treatment" (69%) particularly disturb them. On the contrary, civil servants seem to mind less the reference to the superior or the incapacity of the person to formulate clearly the question. Still, what they perceive as "aggressiveness" and "arrogance" cannot be dissociated from the dominant feelings of insecurity and anxiety on the other side of the relationship.

In their responses, civil servants accept the existence of discretionary power in the performance of their duties. Though they are irritated by insistence upon exceptional treatment, they seem to consider such claims at a high rate, mainly on their own (60%), but also by referring to their superior (20%).

Insistence on exceptional treatment is often linked to a loose perception of the binding character of the law, as a result of the experience of frequent political interference. But it seems particularly irritating for an additional reason: it puts pressure on the sphere of discretion of the civil servant who is very keen on preserving it against the hierarchy but also the public [2] [3]. Discretion is the more or less extensive margin of manoeuvre that, independently of hierarchical position, a civil servant - and any bureaucratic organisation agent - tends to secure. It may consist in personalising the contact, being more or less helpful, taking initiatives or not, and, generally, making the extra bit when performing his/her duties. It can be viewed as the "re-humanising" of the "de-humanised" (in the Weberian sense) bureaucracy. At the same time, *discretion is an important dimension of the power relation* between the civil servant and the citizen; this power relationship is anyway perceptible in the emotionally loaded atmosphere it takes place (anxiety, insecurity, aggressiveness, negative expectations). Invading this sphere of discretion is probably perceived by civil servants as an attitude contesting the power relation and the distance they try to establish as an expression of separation between themselves as part of the administrative machine on one hand, and citizens on the other.

This interpretation seems to be confirmed by other sets of answers. "Politeness and respect" by far predispose positively civil servants (90%). This type of attitude is perceived as a sign of citizens' acceptance of the power relationship. It then takes the form of a pre-condition of a "good" relationship. Besides, a "clear situation of need" has also a positive influence on their responsiveness (42%) towards the public; this is to be linked to the legitimising potential of public services as "helping those in need".

Civil servants are aware that citizens are irritated by attitudes of indifference (71,8%) and incompetence (40%). While both can be seen as an acknowledgement of certain behaviour patterns within public services, they equally constitute severe criticisms of civil servants against their own human environment. More specifically, indifference corresponds to the above-mentioned perception of citizens that civil servants try "to get rid of them as soon as possible". Against this, the public is seen as "holding prejudice" against public administration in general (74,3%) and the civil servants (77,4%).

3.   Problems and responsibilities

What is the origin of these problems and who is responsible? The problems, according to citizens, stem more from administrative inadequacies (64%) than from the complexity of laws (36%). In other words, the problem lies in public administration itself more than in factors independent of it. Legal complexity (44%) is, however, aggravated by the lack of initiative on the part of civil servants (44%), while political interference accounts only for 12% of the answers. Furthermore, "readiness to take initiatives" is the attitude almost unanimously recommended to civil servants (98%) rather than applying the law "in the letter" (2%).

Civil servants, from their side, see as a primary source of administrative problems legal complexity (64%) rather than administrative inadequacies (36%). It is interesting to notice that the priority is *inverse* compared with the citizens' responses, which attribute more importance to administrative inefficiencies. That could be seen as an attempt to limit the collective responsibility of civil servants. Still, "lack of initiative" accounts for unsatisfactory performance (46%) practically as much as the "absence of discretionary power" (47%), - which refers to the restrictive character of laws. These two apparently contradictory answers show civil servants' ambivalence towards the question. At the same time, however, almost unanimously (98%) they consider "taking initiatives" as a way to serve the public better.

From the civil servants' point of view, factors accounting for unsatisfactory encounters between citizens and public administration include (in order of priority):

a) Complexity of legal rules and procedures (52%); b) prejudice of the citizens (47%); c) insufficient inter-service coordination (43%); d) educational level of the citizens (35%); and e) organisation of contacts with the public (28%). The causes chosen in priority seem to be equally distributed between matters concerning public administration (a, c, e) and characteristics of the citizens (b, d). In other words, *citizens have their share of responsibility in the unsatisfactory situation*. This can be seen as an attempt for civil servants at collectively defending their position and role.

When grading their own responsibilities, civil servants appear to be self-critical. Their responsibilities are assessed as of medium importance: in a scale from 1 to 7, the three centre positions account for 79%. Still, civil servants consider responsibilities as falling *more into the political sphere*. In a similar 1 to 7 scale, according to civil servants, the share of political responsibility concentrates mostly in the last two positions of high responsibility, accounting for 68% of the answers, while the three centre positions account for 28% of the answers. Indeed, severe criticism against public administration imputes the causes of administrative inefficiency to the "instability of the general policy framework" (70%), "political interference" (66%), "organisational and technological inadequacies" (65%) and "interference from various interests" (55%). Though at a lower rate, it is interesting to note their view of the human factor: 30% consider public personnel as "inappropriate".

4.   The role of public administration

But *what is expected from public administration*, in terms of its role in society? Legitimising values can be detected through the "mission" public administration has to fulfil according to respondents. Among citizens, the majority refers to the "public interest" (appealing to the traditional values of impartiality and neutrality) (58%) as well as to "social justice" (56%); these two core missions - and consequently, the underlying values -are practically put on an equal footing. In this case, the centre-left political sensitivity of the respondents (as readers of this particular newspaper but also as shown in the way the position themselves in the political left-right continuum) is to be taken into account. While the "public interest" answer presents a very limited variation according to the political position, the "social justice" answer is clearly linked to a centre and left of centre position: it is preferred by 53% of the centre, 67% of the left and 30% of the right. For the rest, "citizens' satisfaction" only comes third (46%), followed by "ensuring economic development and full employment" (27%) and, further, by "ensuring security of people and property" (8%) and "providing jobs" (2%).

Despite the unsatisfactory performance in terms of service delivery and the current importance of economic and employment policies, these aspects of public administration's role seem to come later. They could be seen as a normal outcome of a public administration that operates according to "public interest" and "social justice". They could therefore be interpreted as a *demand for public administration to simply play its role* - coloured by the political sensitivity of the respondents towards social justice.

This hypothesis may be supported by an additional set of answers. While the number of civil servants is mostly considered as "excessive" (86%, as opposed to 13% considering it as "adequate" and 1,5% as "small"), there is an equally important separate demand for increasing the personnel in two particular fields: education and health services (both rate at about 86% of the answers). This can be seen as a clear demand for improvement of welfare services that are insufficiently developed and for a stronger service orientation of public administration.

An interesting discovery of the survey is the social and political sensitivity of the civil servants. Given that it is delicate (and difficult) to have a direct answer concerning their position on the left - right political spectrum, this can be approximated by their position towards core political values. More specifically, using the "economic efficiency - social sensitivity" continuum (from 1 to 7), the data show that civil servants position themselves mostly at the centre and towards the higher social sensitivity end. Positions from the middle of the continuum until the social sensitivity extreme reflect 90% of the respondents! Seen differently, the centre position accounts for 31% and the three last positions for 59% (social sensitivity), while the three first positions account for 10% (economic efficiency). Given that there is no apparent reason to believe that these data are biased (even if the sample is not statistically tested as representative), this could be seen as a more or less accurate picture of a general feeling in the civil service. In a similar continuum describing the preferred extent of the scope of government (from mere private initiative to full state intervention), most of the positions taken are located at the centre (32%), with a clear pending towards the interventionist state (43% against 25%). These general trends seem to be linked to the civil servants' status and are possibly independent from party-political preferences.

This remark seems to be confirmed by the legitimizing values civil servants refer to. They appear in the same order of priority, like in the citizens' responses: "public interest" (78%), "social justice" (60%) "citizens' satisfaction" (44%). These are by far the preferred answers, the others falling below 10%. Though the high rate of "public interest" is not surprising, because it represents the dominant legitimising ideology of the public service, it is interesting to note the high rate of "social justice", which brings the general trend closer to the one detected in the citizens' responses. A rather convincing hypothesis would therefore be that ensuring "social justice" is generally seen by civil servants as an important administrative mission in the Greek context, which at the same time legitimises administrative intervention.

5.   Power distribution

Who has influence on decisions and, perhaps is, indirectly, responsible for this situation? According to citizens' answers, public administration does not act in view of its own interests neither civil servants are considered to be influential (96,6%). Decisions are not influenced by trade unions either (91,3%). On the contrary, they are influenced, mostly by powerful economic interests (66,5%), the political personnel (57%) and organised interest groups (44%). It is, though, interesting to notice that the answers concerning the question "who influences" present a much lower degree of certainty (illustrated by a high rate of non-responses), compared to the certainty about "who does not influence" decisions. This could be the expression of citizens' perplexity vis-à-vis the complex and insufficiently intelligible or transparent political-administrative world.

But civil servants do not have a very different perception of the situation. They assess their own influence on decision-making as the least important (12%), followed by trade unions (35%), with an impressive rate of non-responses (46 and 42% respectively). Most influential appear politicians (85%) and the various interest groups (63%) and economic interests (57%) and "well connected" persons (53%). Politicians' influence presents a high degree of certainty, while the latter have to be seen in the context of high rates of non-responses (between 35 and 42%).

The above perceptions - as well as their self-image (supra)- describe a low degree of satisfaction from their status and work and low self-esteem. This is a factor that has to be taken into account as part of the general framework of the relationship to the public. To put it differently, these perceptions may explain the tendency (as shown before) to emphasise power when facing citizens. At the end of the day, civil servants, as a group, do not present a high degree of differentiation from other social groups and their social prestige is generally low in the Greek context. Instead of qualities, expertise and social prestige, what is left to justify their different social position is their bureaucratic power resources vis-à-vis citizens.

6.   Improvements

For citizens, the menu of improvements includes "simplification of procedures" (86%), followed by "equal treatment" (47%), "better information" (37%), and "better reception of the public" (16%). 70% among them believe that citizens should have a say concerning the improvement of public services. "Simplification of procedures" is also a priority for civil servants (72%), followed by "better information to the citizen" (48%) and "better information for themselves" (33%). "Equal treatment" is less important (19%), followed by "better reception of the public" (16%). Consulting citizens for improvements is accepted at a rate of 65%.

In terms of the characteristics of the public encounter as such, it is meaningful to note the relatively low insistence of external features on the configuration of the citizen-administration relationship (reception for example). It is, however, clear that these are far from satisfactory. A possible interpretation is that there are other priorities, and that part of what is a reception problem is included in claims formulated in a different way (information, equality of treatment etc.).

7.   Tentative conclusions: citizens, quality and the new public management

The above analysis aimed at providing only a general framework of citizens'-administration relations in Greece. It certainly needs to be refined. However, civil servants and citizens share almost the same perceptions of public administration and its agents. Though in some cases civil servants tend to defend their different position vis-à-vis citizens, they agree with them on virtually all important criticisms. On the other hand, it is important to keep in mind that these perceptions *tend to emphasise the negative collective experience* and expectations that may not always be confirmed in practice [4]. For our purposes, however, they describe the backbone of an ambiguous and conflict-prone relationship. They potentially undermine the credibility of the public services and their role in serving the citizen.

To summarise some important features of the situation in the Greek context, it is worth mentioning the following points. Public administration presents a rather feeble legitimacy as the agent that implements law. This applies at the different levels of service provision, competence / expertise and neutrality /impartiality. These features may be linked to inadequacies of Greek administration with regard to defining aspects of the Weberian model of bureaucracy [5]. The negative image seems to concern the *service provided* as well as the *conditions and external aspects* of the relationship with public services. Neither administrative efficiency nor civil servants' behaviour renders the relationship easier. The legitimacy deficit leaves the scope open to power aspects, emphasising the distinction between those belonging to the administrative world and the "others", who are condemned to experiences of anxiety and insecurity.

How could "quality" then be defined in such a context? If wholesale improvement is undoubtedly needed, how can quality -as a specific component- be distinguished?

Any attempt at defining "quality" needs to distinguish the different analytical levels of the citizen - administration relationship. The first is the macroscopic level of *legitimacy*, e.g. the normative foundations (grounds) of expectations vis-à-vis public administration. Democracy is the core value here. The second one is the meso-level of *organisational* factors, e.g. within the individual public service organisations and the civil servants as a collective actor facing the citizens. This is equally the management level. The third one, is the microscopic level of *interpersonal relations* taking place in the framework shaped by the two previous, e.g. the concrete conditions of the public encounter, the respective attitudes of citizens and civil servants and their interaction within a given political and administrative setting. These three analytical levels appear clearly in the way citizens and civil servants view each other and their relationship.

Where does quality stand? What is "quality"? "Commonly, service quality relates to the more *direct or immediate aspects* or impact on the client of any service". It refers to "*quality of service delivery* rather than of service *outcomes*". Components of service quality include "timeliness of service, amount or volume of service, accessibility and convenience, availability or continuity of service, accuracy, safety, appropriateness or suitability (meeting the needs of the client, choice...)", but also, pleasantness, simplicity etc. These components are inter-related and trade-offs take place between them [6].

From this definition it appears that quality considerations primarily concern the second and third levels of analysis. Still, some of its components are determined by the limited resources available and the criteria that prevail in the way they are used (e.g. to ensure spatial distribution as well as maintenance of certain programs to meet citizen's needs). How citizens' needs and the way to satisfy them are defined? And who defines them? These questions re-introduce the political element in the apparently "de-politicised" issue of quality. But, as the OECD report puts it, "fairness, equality, neutrality and confidentiality... as higher level issues, are best kept separate from service delivery components. In general, these aspects of a different order are principles used to ensure that citizens are not discriminated against because of social status, race, colour, origin, sex etc. They thus serve a different purpose from service quality components, whose objective is to ensure the best possible services at all times for the resources available for the target group" [7].

It thus seems obvious that quality is a *partial approach to* the relations between bureaucracy and the citizens (as well as to policy formulation). This new catchword in administrative science contains a particular view of "administration as service and the public as client" [8] and maintains a rather unclear - if not confusing - relation to other important aspects of citizen - administration relations.

The perceptions and interpretations presented above have therefore to be seen in context. Socio-economic, political as well as internal administrative factors account for them. The weakness of expertise, efficiency and the low social prestige, the limited welfare state and the tradition of clientelism (that conditions behaviours even when it is not practised) are important peculiarities of the Greek administration. Even more, a weak private sector and civil society, the experience of political authoritarianism are equally part and parcel of the general picture. All this influences expectations, values of reference and the meaning of "quality" or "improvement". A policy aiming at improving quality cannot be dissociated from such considerations.

These factors have to do with *the legitimacy* of public administration in general. Their by-products, (e.g. low esteem for and self esteem of civil servants, emphasis on power aspects in the relationship to the public as well as management inadequacies and lack of human as well as technical resources), surface as the more pressing problems. They result in problematic service quality, which is only partly improved through the methods usually suggested. Structural as well as cultural changes need to accompany any technical improvements (organisation of work etc.). Otherwise, an unfavourable environment will soon neutralise them.

Greek public administration has inherited from clientelistic traditions its introverted character, the low competence level and insufficient emphasis on merit. In short, achieving results was not a primary concern. These features have been reinforced by the experience of political authoritarianism, which tended to emphasise a top-down, commanding approach and show little interest in citizens' needs. Citizens had obligations rather than rights vis-à-vis bureaucracy. The private sector was traditionally hardly more competitive. It put very little pressure on public administration. Connections with government ensured immunity from or alleviated market pressures. Civil society, while active around political cleavages, did not develop autonomous structures to counter administrative authoritarianism. The exclusion on political criteria and inclusion via clientelistic networks regulated in a rather clear-cut way relations between citizens and public administration.

Other aspects, like the use of discretionary power or the legal complexity etc., refer to universal problems associated with bureaucracy. Still, the specific way they appear in the above framework, is the result of their interaction with the peculiarities previously described. The heavy presence of politics on public administration worked against developing initiatives that are not rewarded within such a system. The phobia of responsibilities therefore reaches beyond the prevailing routine aspects of any bureaucratic organisation. It is indeed difficult to clearly separate the different factors accounting for the unsatisfactory situation in citizens-administration relationships.

In a context like the one described above, what is meant by improvement of "quality" is a necessary and important objective but not sufficient one, unless quality is defined in a way that incorporates the wider architecture of the citizen-administration relationship. But it would then loose its specific meaning. The universal ambition of "quality" thus needs to be moderated. This equally applies to the more general approach to administrative reform that is expressed by the "new public management". The contribution of NPM has to be seen in relation to the different levels of analysis. The following questions need to be asked:

(i) The legitimacy issue. Does the NPM change the foundation of expectations vis-à-vis the bureaucracy? In other words, does it affect democracy as its legitimacy basis? The rhetoric and assumptions of the "customer" or "client" and of the centrality of his/her desires are already questionable in the private sector from which they are borrowed. What do they add to the relationship between the citizen and the public services?

(ii) The organisation of public services, the service provision and management. At this level, managerialism introduces uniform methods and proposes one-size solutions (decentralisation, fragmentation, delegation etc.). Its contribution -without reference to its validity- lies principally at this level. It has, however, the ambition of embracing the whole range of citizen-administration relations and representing a comprehensive alternative view, while at the same time it reduces them to a "service" relation, one that is external to the actual process of government.

(iii) The actual interpersonal encounter between a civil servant and a citizen. To what extent can the power relation, the impersonality and the use of discretionary power (forming part of personal strategies in the organisational context) be eliminated by NPM techniques?

Improving the terms of the unequal relationship between the citizen and the administration means strengthening the relative position of the citizen vis-à-vis public administration. This involves more than a mere "service relation". Changing the terms of the encounter does not only concern the external aspects of the relationship (time, accessibility…). It has also to do with the substance of the service provided while it depends on the *type* of service itself (regulatory policies vs. re-distributive ones, for example). Can borrowing models from other fields (e.g. the market) possibly have an influence on the normative foundations of expectations and demands vis-à-vis the bureaucracy? The risk of a double confusion between means and objectives and between normative and real should not be underestimated. The borrowing only shows the malaise and the lack of imagination in redefining the public - private relationship within a context of clashing ideological references.

References

[1]   CURAPP, La communication administration - administrés. PUF, Paris, 1983.

[2]   M. Crozier, Le phénomène bureaucratique. Seuil, Paris, 1963.

[3]   M. Lipsky, Street-level Bureaucracy. Dilemmas of the Individual in Public Services. Russell Sage Foundation, New York, 1980.

[4]   C. T. Goodsell, The Case for Bureaucracy. A Public Administration Polemic. Chatham House, Chatham NJ, 1994.

[5]   C. Spanou, A la recherche du temps perdu. La réforme de l'administration en Grèce, *Revue Française d'Administration Publique* **75** (1995) 423-439.

[6]   OECD, Responsive Government. Service Quality Initiatives. PUMA, OECD, Paris, 1996, pp. 23-25.

[7]   *Ibid.*, p. 25.

[8]   OECD, Administration as Service. The Public as Client. PUMA, OECD, Paris, 1987.

The Improvement Policy of Services to the Users in France in the Face of Equity Requests

Philippe Warin *

Introduction

A traditional request for quality public services (accessible, fast, efficient) exists as well as a steady confidence of the French in the Public Service. Opinion polls have always underlined it. Efforts to satisfy the citizens are noted; but progress remains to be done, especially regarding information to the users, administrative simplification, rapidity of dealing with the requests[1].

But from the point of view of *ordinary* users[2], the quality of the public action (services offered by the public services) is not only a matter of satisfaction or dissatisfaction according to measurable criteria of accessibility of the services, simplicity of administrative steps, rapidity of dealing with the file, reliability of services, etc. For the individual users, the question of the quality of the public action also refers - and may be above all - to a *feeling of justice or injustice*, i.e. to the perception of having been treated *fairly or unfairly*. That is what the results of recent research carried out into the service relations between service providing operators and users show [1].

What these chosen expressions of justice or injustice emphasise is the fact that the users expect the operators and the services to take into account the specifities of their personal situations when they are *victims of circumstances* (impediment to use certain rights and authorisations) or when they are *victims of damage* linked to the activity or intervention of public services. In these different cases, users expect the administrations to apply the principles of social solidarity and equity, of precaution and responsibility[3]. We can imagine the complexity of these expectations that refer to the tricky problem of the adaptation of individual preferences to collective choices.

When users are interviewed, we notice that the disillusion sometimes expressed towards the public services results from the discrepancy they observe or feel between the management logics they think they recognise in the behaviour of the operators on the one hand and the general principles they support and they consider to be (or to have to be) the ones of the public service.

---

* Philippe Warin, Chargé de recherche au CNRS, Institut d'Etudes Politiques de Grenoble, CERAT, France

[1] This is the brief summary we draw from the analysis of the opinion polls relating to the public administrations published in the past fifteen years (analysis carried out by the *Revue Française des Sondages*).
[2] Different from "institutional" users (firms, local administrative units, other administrations).
[3] We have also developed this point in our contribution "La citoyenneté de guichet. Quelques éléments de définition et de discussion", symposium at the French Institute of Administrative Sciences, *Service public et lien social*, Lille, October 1997 (forthcoming in a collective book edited by Gérard Marcou and Séverine Decroton).

These *basic expectations* which require all the administrations to determine their actions in relation to reasserted principles, do not necessarily elude the administrations. Here we can refer to the operators who have contacts with the public and who are daily facing these expectations and thus often manage them in a discretionary way relying on rules and norms of application. Some measures of the administrative modernisation sometimes put operators in tricky situations. For example, a coordinated follow-up of certain personal files has been developed between several services and give the operators information about some aspects of the situation of the claimant they ignored: that might lead them to deal with the case in a more restrictive way whereas they used to look for a more conciliating solution while making do with the rules. In other cases, after the development of appeals to the court against the administration or because of the integration of new rules and organisations of the services, the grant of certain administrative authorisations becomes harder and makes the explanation of the decision to the applicants more difficult.

Other examples would also confirm the fact that the services are not inattentive to these basic expectations[4]. But the question consists in knowing if it also means that the latter can be reconciled with the approach aiming at improving the quality of the services performed to the users. In particular are these expectations taken into account by the central administration that gives impetus to and organise the policy of quality, as an important condition of the administrative activity and its modernisation?

The elements of answer put forward below come from a survey in progress in the central administration[5]:

– within the General Department of the Administration and the Public Service (DGAFP), with "the network of ministerial correspondents for the improvement of the services to the users", i.e. operational executives of the ministries responsible for conceiving and leading this approach within the central administration and towards the territorial devolved administrations of the State.

> This network was constituted on May 20th, 1996 under the aegis of the DGAFP as a continuation of the interministerial works about the reception of the user in 1994. Today it concerns all the ministries and also involves the Commission for the State Reform.
> It is coordinated by the office responsible for leading the modernisation at the DGAFP and designed as an authority of mutual information and work, of proposals aiming at transforming the orientations of the State Reform into concrete actions. Its mission also consists in developing communication between ministries concerning the sector of the relation to the user.
> It works in the form of regular exchanges, of study days, of work in sub-groups on themes in common interest (listening to the users, quality indicators, durability of the measures of quality improvement).

---

[4] We could make a list of many public or official declarations of the successive ministers of the Public Service. Other expressions are also significant such as the book of Paul Legatte, Ombudsman of the Republic, concerning the principle of equity. We should also take into account the contributions made at an international level in this matter as it is shown by the recent symposium about the ethics in the public service organised by the Organisation for Economic Cooperation and Development in December 1997. The synthesis issued by the OECD/PUMA talks about "an infrastructure of ethics" and proposes a list of references. The problem of corruption and the question of transparency that are at the core of this initiative seem to be a bit far from the general basic expectations exposed in the present paper; but for this type of concern it could be of interest in the long run to prepare mechanisms of responsibilities and consultation.

[5] Survey carried out within the framework of a research concerning "The performances of justice in the public services" for the General Department of the Administration and the Public Service.

Concrete initiatives of ministries and territorial devolved administrations are presented and discussed there. In two years this network enabled to deepen the actions launched in terms of methodology in order to meet the expectations of the actors in the field.

Ministerial correspondents work on an official assignment to design operational tools based on the directives received from high-ranking government officials of each ministry who conceive the global strategies of modernisation.

– with official representatives of the Commission of the State reform (CRE) created by a decree of September 13, 1995 for a temporary length of time (until June 1998). The Commission led actions to support other networks and working parties gathering together high-ranking government officials

Among the important works of the State Reform there is the purpose to "place the citizen at the centre of the service public". The aim consists in "better taking into account the needs and the expectations of the citizens", this purpose constitutes the first priority of the State Reform, as the circular of the Prime Minister of July 26th, 1995 stipulates it.

Two main working lines were favoured: simplifying the relations between the State and the citizens; increasing the quality of the service performed to the public [6].

In order to reach the first goal the CRE elaborated a bill and presented it at the French Parliament. It mainly fixes new rules enabling the citizens to benefit from a quick and effective treatment of their requests or claims. Moreover a tally of the systems of prior administrative authorisation enabled to suppress or to reduce the number of formalities (450 out of the 4000 systems of this type are or will be concerned in the short run). At the same time the CRE favoured the experimentation of procedures enabling the accelerated issuing of documents (car registration papers, passports in prefectures) and the development of credit card payment in public services (850 centres were equipped with computers in 1997: prefectures, sub-prefectures, general public revenue office, tax offices, courts of law, higher education schools, etc.). The CRE also tried to strengthen the fact that the structures should offer varied services and should be close to the public (supporting experiences of "houses of public services").

In order to reach the second goal, the CRE worked out methodological tools making the implementation of new systems possible such as the "contracts of service", "quality charter" and "commitments to service" (see glossary annexed). This also means actions to facilitate a coordinated follow-up of individual file between the different services, to accelerate the payment of money owed by the State, to develop procedures before public decision making (in case of negative decisions, of construction of a collective building that is not concerned by the consulting regulation already in force), to strengthen the transparency of decision (harmonising the existing provisions and considering them a law) and to facilitate the search for non-contentious solutions (strengthening of the powers and the means of the local mediation).

The first interviews conducted with both levels of the central administration show that at the moment the expectations of social solidarity and the requirements of precaution or responsibility of the public action do not influence the initiatives taken by the centre. These basic expectations are neither integrated nor really perceived [2].

This observation is simple but it questions the very meaning of the policy of administrative modernisation enforced in France and raises the question of the relevance of references to efficiency and public performance.

This obvious discrepancy results from several factors. It seems interesting to us to examine them here, even rapidly, insofar as it enables us to explain certain conditions in which the administrative modernisation is presently carried out in France and thus to point out some

---

[6] See the 95/96 and 97 activity statements of the Commission of the State Reform, published by the Documentation Française.

aspects that do not necessarily make the development of "a public action of quality" easy, i.e. according to Luc Rouban a public action that better respects the needs expressed by the citizens".

1.   A central administration far from individual users

1.1.   Individual expectations that escape the quality improvement policy

These basic expectations partially concern organisations included in the sector of the public administration without being included in the one of the Public Service for all that (it is the case of the social security scheme, of the unemployment benefit scheme, of the public body of social housing or of the large public utilities firms etc.) or in the one of the local city services. These expectations are scattered among a variety of administrations so that the basic expectations we are dealing with here do not only - and even sometimes not mainly - concern the network of ministerial correspondents and the CRE. Other actors (especially boards of directors and executive authorities of the other administrations) are then involved but on whom the DGAFP and the CRE do not necessarily have influence.

At the same time, the request for improving the access to the services and the rapidity of the services are more easily perceived by the administrations for many reasons. This tends to occult those basic expectations that are not so well represented or that are more difficult to identify and to deal with.

1.2.   Improvement measures of the public services that do not directly aim at individual users

In the ministry of Industry the users are the firms, the elected members, the local representatives of the State concerned by questions of reliability and industrial security and industrial and technological development. The individual user does not appear directly or if he does it is as a result of it, as the *final beneficiary* of the steps taken to improve the quality of the installations and vehicles and the prevention of industrial risks (beneficiary of a safe environment), the reliability of measuring tools (beneficiary of better quality products), and the conversion of small and medium size firms (beneficiary of new possibilities of economic activities).

The case of the ministry of Equipment is different because it deals with publics of individual users. Nevertheless the decentralisation, while emphasising the fact that the services of the Equipment are at the disposal of local administrative units and are marketed, leads to consider the improvement of the services performed to the users in terms of relations between institutional client / supplier so that the relations to the individual users turn out to be a more indirect concern.

At the same time, the fact that both ministries (Industry and Equipment) emphasise the principle of transparency as well as the steps taken towards the security of risky installations probably means that this contributes to come up to the requests for information and precaution. But this does not meet the expectations of justiciability of the administrative action and of public responsibility that were exacerbated over the last years by a certain number of *affairs* and that can just be settled from a political and legal point of view thanks to a review of the law concerning the liability.

1.3. The weight of legal references and of the political constraints

In kingly administrations such as the ones of the Tax or of the Interior, the constitutional and legal base of the administrative activity makes it difficult to conceive these needs of solidarity even if these administrations make considerable concrete efforts to increase the rapidity and the reliability of the services.

The improvement measures of the service to the users to which they try to give impetus today concern the way how to deal with massive applications for administrative authorisations or for documents (prefecture) or for tax returns (tax offices) and aim at increasing the security of the service performed and to commit oneself to better delays. But they cannot or do not have to compromise over anything; it is also an essential condition of the government officials and administration's neutrality. The publics must be considered in a uniform way according to a relation of absolute equality; making agreements can also reduce the area of the possibilities regarding the improvement of the services to the users. The same thing occurs to the activities of control in other administrations. This point of view is also criticised; the present example of the way the prefectures deal with the "paperless" (foreigners in "irregular situation") well explains the very relative character of the notion of "absolute equality".

The movement of "devolving and decentralising" the services of the State that develops today and that is based on the idea of the territorial administration of the State can contribute to partially changing the representations especially by adapting the principle of equality to the needs of social and territorial differentiation. But it first concerns services in the social domain (taking into account such notions as *priority geographies* or *positive discriminations* that do not have any legal reality yet), whereas the kingly services will hardly be able to depart from the principle of citizens' equality all over the territory of the Republic in dealing with most of the applications for authorisations.

The perception of the users is more political in an administrative sector such as the one of the Social Affairs that has been recently created and constituted as a nebula that varies according to the governments and the economic orientations from the largest scattering to the strongest concentration.

In this respect the ministry of Labour represents an interesting example. Today this ministry substitutes a more global strategy aiming at improving the relations with the wage earners and the job seekers for an approach aiming at improving the services performed which used to favour actions towards the integration of disabled workers. The aim is to make the relations between long term unemployed and agencies for the unemployed and between wage earners (especially wage earners in small and medium size firms) and factory inspectorates easier and to contribute in this way to coming up to the political choice consisting in putting the action of the ministry back in the defence of the labour law and the right to work.

But this does not mean that the ministry of Labour is willing to take into account any type of expectations expressed by the wage earners and the job seekers, neither does it mean that the Department of the General Administration of the Modernisation can be particularly influenced by the pressure and the mediatisation of such topics as *exclusion* and *social justice*. As far as employment is concerned, the answer is clear and also refers to the principle of equality before the public service: standardisation of the treatment, no priority publics nor any positive discriminations.

2.   A policy subjected to internal strategies and budget logic

2.1.   *Internal obstacles linked to the administrative working*

- Legitimacies to construct

Ministerial teams who succeeded each other over the past years understood that the purpose of quality was one key element enabling both the defence of their means in the global budget regulation and the assertion of their orientations in the face of the category interests relating to the different departments of their central administration.

The integration of this purpose supposes its control, i.e. it should be asserted at the highest level as a priority and all that it implies regarding the missions that must be determined, assigned and endowed with means and legitimacy. In such conditions, it is clear that the persons responsible for the missions aiming at improving the services to the users at the ministerial level (this concerns the network of ministerial correspondents led by the DGAFP) had first to find a place within the ministries before stabilising and strengthening their position and their function.

Nothing is easy in this matter especially at a time of stagnation and reduction of means. Other central departments, offices or services are inevitably worried about the emergence of new priorities that may deprive them of a part of their resources and powers. Therefore a large part of their efforts devoted to the organisation and the spreading of a quality policy at the central level first consisted for the persons responsible for these missions in normalising their exchanges at an internal level.

The first ministries involved in such actions have now managed to settle most of the conflicts of legitimacy and to stabilise their approach. It seems to concern the ministry of Interior (regarding the territorial administration of the prefectures) and of the Equipment and Industry. But the present example of structural reform in process at the ministry of Economy and Finance shows that nothing is ever really taken as settled. The creation of departments of common services forces the new department in charge of the public relations and communication to precisely define its domain of competencies especially towards another department responsible for the personnel, the modernisation and the administration (one of its present concern is to keep the control of the central computer service of the ministry and through it the tool and the policy relating to economic, financial and fiscal information intended for the services and the publics; moreover the internal as well as the external communication is at the core of an administrative interconnected organisation, this is one of the priorities recently expressed by the Prime Minister [7]).

- The coexistence of competing strategies

The multiplication of the systems of action between the inter-ministerial networks led by the DGAFP and the working groups of the CRE has also led to emphasise the questions of legitimacy. Without detailing the relations between central actors, we can say that two logics co-existed in the last years:

- one of them is based on the idea of the sharing of experiences, the support of the decentralised innovation and the operational support brought to the development of managerial solutions adapted to each administrative context on the DGAFP's side, which was impelled by the policy of the personnel management at the end of the eighties and based on the principles of involvement and responsibility of the territorial devolved services (with the "quality circles" and "projects of services");

- the other one is supported by the CRE and characterises a return to a centralised action aiming at massively simplifying the administration and at introducing new systems of general organisation of the public administration according to a more budget and economist's vision of the modernisation (see below).

This more or less easy and productive juxtaposition is now coming to an end. It cost energy on both sides to validate both logics. In a nutshell, the strategy of competition prevented from debating crucial political aspects such as the one of the revaluation of the place and role of the users in the production of the public action. Until recently no new proposals have been made relating to the direct participation of the users; things seem to change. Indeed, the Higher Committee of the Public Service examines the reform of the Commission of the modernisation of the public services [8].

- Working in "closed network"

Central services responsible for leading the steps aiming at improving the service to the users are not only entangled in the ministries' mysteries. Neither do they only aim at strengthening their legitimacy. Their first function consists in helping territorial devolved services develop quality measures according to their own constraints by giving them tools and methods. Thus regular exchanges with the territorial devolved administrations represent an essential requirement for the achievement of their mission.

In the ministries that led the way in the matter of the policy of centres of responsibilities and in the contracts of service now (Industry, Equipment, Interior, Finance, etc.), such services

---

[7] The circular of the Prime Minister of June 3, 1998 devoted to "the preparation of programmes of modernisation of the administrations which last several years" defines the development of new information and communication technologies among the five great themes to be dealt with.

[8] The reform is going towards an increased participation of the users in the Commission of modernisation. Trade unions suggest that departmental committees of modernisation should be reorganised which could be a way to organise a larger consultation with the users at this level.

often have systems of regular exchanges with the territorial devolved services. Contacts with regional and departmental services (Interior and Industry) or sometimes the use of more institutionalised information or consultation systems ("centre of observation" at the Ministry of Finance and at the ministry of Equipment, "territorial information centre about the public expenditure" at the ministry of Interior) enable these exchanges to occur; such relations are part of the recommendations of the DGAFP which advocated the creation of places of exchanges at different levels. It is not yet the case everywhere among others because of the difficulties to find receptive executives.

Such exchanges should enable better mutual knowledge of the services as well as a capitalisation of experiences and favour the search for global ways to solve the problems faced by the users. At the same time, they make a regulation of the local initiatives possible in order to avoid too many variations from one service to the other, from one place to the other as well as the disappearance of equal citizen rights all over the territory.

However the way the networks work shows that they particularly contribute to making the learning of the management tools proposed by the central administration easy. These tools must be used all along the successive stages of the modernisation (from the projects of service to the contracts of service). This comes up to the pragmatic concerns of the participants (how to organise the reception in the services? how to dispatch the workforce in an optimal way? how to introduce tools of forward-looking management? how to create commitments to the service? etc.).

But when non-executive operators are absent and when there is nobody representing users' associations (that is not compensated by other forms of direct relation as far as these central actors are concerned) such exchanges do not enable detailed feed-back information regarding the basic expectations as the latter are expressed at the counters. Inevitably the organisational learning implemented in that way can only be partially achieved and quite largely drops the reality of the supplying service.

2.2.   *The predomination of the budget logic*

Over the last years the stagnation or the decrease in the public budgets led each ministry to require their territorial devolved administrations to define how necessary the presence of the state is according to the local situations and the priorities regarding the purposes and the means resulting from it. The aim is to get a territorial devolved administrative unity with self-managed budget.

This innovation is supposed to be intended to reduce the burden of the central services, to accelerate the administrative procedures, to bring users closer to the decision-making centres[9]. Nevertheless it aims at reducing the state expenditure, since this system enables the budget regulation to be inverted; the services no longer give information to the central level about their budget needs, which means a lot of complex arbitrations, but they now receive a pre-

---

[9] That is the way the circular of the Prime Minister of July 28th, 1995, relating to the preparation and the implementation of the State Reform and the public services, presents it.

determined global budget off which they can no longer get[10]. In order to respect it they must define priorities in their missions within projects of service or target contracts.

Compared to this macro-economic stake, the modernisation within the ministries more and more consists in organising a better adapted administration. The latter must enable to reallocate the means and the workforce of the State to activities or priority sectors while trying at the same time not to weaken the administrative system all over the territory.

The development of the contracts of service (Interior, Equipment, Education) constitutes the financial approach of the modernisation. This procedure aims at totally mixing the means at the territorial devolved level; which also implies to sign contracts concerning target results. The aim is to make the supplying services more sensitive to the budget evolution and to give the (central and territorial devolved) management services the possibility to make means' savings (the expression is significant, we then talk about "returns on investment").

At the same time, the aim still consists in improving the quality of the services while trying to serve the logic of territorial devolvement. Thus even if the various actions towards administrative simplification impelled at the top of the government today (lifting of systems of prior administrative authorisation, implementation of computerised exchanges of data, creation of partnership between services within structures responsible for varied services...) can improve the service to the users, they also aim at helping the autonomous services to increase their profitability and to reallocate their means.

Ministerial services responsible for improving the service to the users are directly involved in achieving the organisation of better adapted administrations. It especially concerns the ministry of Industry and of Equipment, the services of which are also in charge of helping territorial administrations (prefectures, departmental offices of equipment) to define and plan their priority missions with the help of management tools (management control, indicators of activity, reference workforce etc.) and of new principles of budget (contracts of service) and territorial organisation (structures responsible for varied services).

With the constraint of budget savings, the purposes of quality or of improvement of the service to the users are in turn directly concerned. The objective is not only to better meet the users' requests but also to improve the efficiency of the administrative services especially regarding the standardised mass processes (administrative authorisations, documents, declarations, technical controls etc.) so that it could result in rooms for manoeuvre that could be "reinvested" at once in new tasks ("green label", certificates of accommodation in the case of prefectures, transposition of European regulations etc.).

In such circumstances, the reorganisation of public services based on priority purposes, on a logic of means and obligation to get results raises practical crucial questions to the users.

Especially does this reorganisation enable to maintain the contents of the services? Does it leave the operators in contact with the users with this discretionary power when they deal with

---

[10] The move to systems called "quality charters" and "commitments to service" confirms the predomination acquired by the budget logic (see glossary annexed) [3].

the request, which to the users' mind represents the *social value added* of the public service[11]? This type of problem becomes collective and raises a question of justice for example when a service closes, when benefit schemes change, when a service is reorganised and prevents the operators from keeping on coming up to the requests occurring at the periphery of the basic service etc.

The quality actions that are associated with the reorganisation of the services try to implement new rules of action in order to increase the guaranties brought to the users ("the silence passes for an approval", the acknowledgement of receipt is generalised, the operators are obliged to forward a misdirected request etc.). Though necessary and important as they may be, these concrete answers do not correspond to the basic expectations of the users. With these additional guaranties the users get new rights that are unilateral rights, i.e. *rights of claims[12]*. But they cannot directly solve the divergent conflicts of interests between the citizens, the local administrative units and the economic actors on the one hand and the State and its services on the other hand that arise with the reorganisation of the services.

In other words, even if the improvement of the services to the users enlarges the individual or statutory rights, it does not enable to come up either to the contradictions or to the conflicts brought about by the rationalisation of the administrative activity. The very conception of it leads to consider the users as third parties able to set their own rights against it; but this is achieved through a unilateral command (what is proposed is what seems to be good to the administration) which makes it possible to keep on dealing with the question of modernisation in an instrumental (efficiency of the administration and the counters) and quantitative way (reducing public expenses) and not in a fundamental and qualitative way (which social expectations must the State meet and how can it do it?).

Conclusion

The aim of the previous remarks was to explain some of the conditions for the implementation of the improvement policy of the service to the users at the level of the central administration in France. This examination, even if incomplete and may be partially inaccurate finally arouses the attention on aspects that make it probably difficult for the central administration to recognise and to take into account the basic expectations expressed by the users. We simply would like to synthesise them without organising them into a graded order.

Insisting on such aspects does not in any way detract from the considerable efforts achieved to offer a public action of quality; the results obtained and the positive opinion of the public concerning them largely justify the fact that they should be carried on. This enables only to

---

[11] This aspect was emphasized in France at the beginning of the nineties by sociological works dealing with the service relations between operators and users: see the minutes of the seminar (1989-1990) "The service relation in the public service" jointly organised by the City Plan, the Department of Research and Innovation of the ministry of the Equipment and the prospective mission of the Paris city transport authority, published in 1991.
[12] The bill prepared by the CRE regarding the citizen rights concerning their relations with the administrations is the symbol of this option which is part of the liberal mode of thinking in the matter of citizenship (which is conceived in terms of rights to the person). Some persons have observed a development of the rights of claims in European countries [4].

remind that the requests are really "complex and diversified" as Luc Rouban underlined it and that this reality eludes the preparation of the improvement policies of the service to the users.

We can draw two observations from the previous remarks:

– The observations concerning the way French administrative networks that are involved in the preparation or the operational implementation of actions aiming at improving the services performed work, show that the work between the different ministries which is aimed at, does not produce a total break in the traditional working mode of the administration which is organised into a hierarchy (the CRE constituted an example of this model).

Therefore there are systems of operational support to the central departments and to the territorial devolved departments that have an important power of screening information. They only take into account concerns coming from the management services relating to the implementation of managerial solution but generally they drop the concerns of the supplying services although they are directly facing the basic expectations often aroused by the changes induced by the reorganisation of the services.

From that point of view, the non-existence of an open pragmatic approach, that integrates the opinion of the users and the one of the supplying services, is likely to be one of the specificities of the way the French administration works which prevents a consultation regarding all the needs. In this respect, we must note that the various initiatives aiming at improving the service to the users had always to avoid forcing the services to apply the *procedure* in a more important way, i.e. a working way that brings to light, discloses and obliges the actors involved (government officials and users) to express their opinions and their interests so that they can be confronted with each other. Although other European countries are used to other participatory practices, they tend to take this orientation towards accountability [13]. Such practices are difficult to implement in France (we can mention the failure of the creation of users' associations supported by the circular of the Prime Minister in 1989 concerning "the revival of the public service"); but we can still wonder if a more important territorial devolvement is of interest concerning the preparation of the implementation of the improvement measures regarding the service to the users which implies that the regional and departmental offices of the administration would have to be involved.

– Secondly, we can also observe that the administrative modernisation which is always limited by the budget constraints, the increasing number of legal regulations (the abundant European regulation is one of the main example), the technological innovation try to adapt the organisations and the activities in a realistic way by confirming the solutions devised by the professionals. Doing so, it only favours the "*value of achievement*" (that explains the

---

[13] Great Britain gave an important role to the powerful consumer associations in the process of modernisation of the public services and thus enforced a State Reform in its own way which inspired France [5]. For example, the Wolf report about the reform of the access to the English justice delivered a few months ago proposes to integrate a certain number of intermediary bodies such as tenant associations or associations of victims of bad medical care.

importance given to the issue "public performance") to the detriment of general principles emphasised by the users.

The operational level (DGAFP and CRE) is not concerned here, it keeps on going forward according to the purposes set to it. But this remark raises the question of the political will likely to use the improvement of the service to the users as a real subject of general policy which would enable to discuss the principles of justice and responsibility that should prevail in a modern administration. The question of a new public management more focused on the requests of the citizens is not only a question of management but also and at first a political question that is worth a public debate.

References

[1]   J.-M. Weller, La modernisation des services publics par l'usager: une revue de littérature, *Sociologie du travail* **3** (1998), 365-392.

[2]   P. Warin, La performance publique: attentes des usagers et réponses de ministères, presented at the 9th international symposium of the journal *Politiques et Management public*, Aix-en-Provence, June 1998, 15 p.

[3]   R. Gaillard, Les citoyens au coeur du service public?, *Revue Française d'Administration Publique* **80** (1996) 695-699.

[4]   A. Lyon-Caen, Le service public et l'Europe. Ronéoté, Institut International de Paris - La Défense, Paris, 1995.

[5]   G. Jeannot, Peut-on faire de l'usager un client? Retour sur l'exemple britannique. In: P. Warin (dir.), Quelle modernisation des services publics? Les usagers au coeur des réformes. La Découverte, Paris, 1997, pp.287-307.

Appendix

GLOSSARY

(Based on the document of the Commission of the State Reform, Développer la qualité, Paris, La Documentation Française, 1997).

- The "centres of responsibility" came from the experience of the "projects of service" and were formalized in 1995 by a standard convention. They subject the increased rooms for manoeuvre given to the managers to the implementation of tools to know the cost and to measure efficiency (the service must draw up a yearly budget; the central administration must draw up ratios enabling the different services to compare their activity and their expenses; the service must draw up a management report). When the management tools are set up, the service benefits from interchangeable credits that should enable it to increase its efficiency by reallocating expenses. This way of working was progressively extended to all the territorial devolved services.

- The "contracts of service" introduced by the policy of State Reform result from the observation that the management methods of the means became obsolete. Thus in 1997 contracts of service were launched for three years linking central administration to some of their territorial devolved services. These contracts extend the centres of responsibility experimented from 1990 on; their novelty consists in placing the users at the centre of their purposes by realizing the idea of internal commitment and by giving the services quite extended rooms for manoeuvre both for the preparation of the yearly budgets and for the management of their means during the year. Today some administrations begin to work out commitments to service especially based on experiments carried out in public utilities firms (French Electricity Board - French Gas Board, French Telecommunications, French Rail, Paris Public Transport Authority).

- The "quality charters" are used today as framework of consistency and of guide to implement quality steps or even commitments and actions that all contribute, at their respective level, to improving the service performed to the users. They are organised according to a logic of project and specify the aims and purposes, the principles, the actions, the methods and the means for the implementation of quality steps. They are worked out by the ministries and concern both the central services and the territorial devolved services.

- The "commitments to service" contribute to placing the user at the centre of the concerns of the public services. They are designed as sources of legitimacy and legibility of the services performed by the administrations. They can constitute the structuring main line of the quality charter and in that case they are the result of it. They can also constitute only one of the elements of the charters (improvement of the critical processes, systems enabling the listenig to the users...). They can concern the results or the means, the basic service or the joint service and types of publics; they can specify a certain level of quality and be accompanied with a compensation in case of non compliance.

Municipal Democracy and Citizens' Participation. Citizens' Views on Municipal Decision-Making and Possibilities to Affect Local Social Policies

Vuokko Niiranen *

1.   Introduction: The Actuality of Citizens' Participation

Public administration, and in particular, changes to the Nordic welfare state are linked to the emphasis on the citizen's point of view. The commitment of citizens to administration is connected to the legitimacy of public administration. Particularly in the Nordic context, it is a question of how to combine professional municipal management, municipal political decision-making and the active commitment and participation of citizens, i.e. how to find a space for the people living in the municipality. The citizen government, which supports political rationality, has been put forward as a continuation for new public management [1]. Until present, in municipal administration, interest has concentrated on the development of the effectiveness of the administration, not on the development of democracy. In the 1990's, citizen's have not been very interested in the selection of ideologies. Political party activities do not receive support at municipal level. In any case, the people living in the municipalities are not particularly interested, and, for example, in Finland in the 1996 local elections, the voting per cent was 61. This lack of interest and commitment can easily lead to the domination of decision-making by a small group, made up of municipal citizens in elected offices and politicians, and a reduction in the authority of public administration. For this reason, the participation of citizens and the commitment that arises from this and the growth of municipal membership are central issues.

In municipal decision-making, representative democracy has been the foundation of the political system and the dominant form of democracy. Citizens' own participation has primarily referred to their right to elect the people who make political decisions concerning them and their possibility to act as political decision-makers themselves. In addition, citizens can try to have an impact, especially on those decisions which concern them.

Democracy also includes a content-related dimension. The decisions made by elected officials should represent the citizens' will, and the local municipal government should produce or arrange such services which citizens need. In other words, citizens expect both democratic forms and efficiency from local government. Representative democracy is no longer enough, and new forms of direct participation are needed to supplement, diversify and sometimes also to replace it. These new forms of direct participation are especially justified, firstly, by the fact that citizens are not interested in political participation, secondly, elected officials are estranged from citizens, and thirdly, the credibility of the representative system is becoming weaker.

---

* Vuokko Niiranen, Researcher, University of Kuopio, Department of Social Sciences, Finland

The background policy which emphasises the direct participation of the citizen has some conflicting aims. These include rectifying the weaknesses of representative democracy and targets for savings, improving the responsiveness of municipal provision of services and general issues concerning the increased sharing of responsibility with municipal citizens or their immediate community. By increasing the direct participation of citizens, an attempt is made at the improved legitimacy of justification of the representative system, and through this the strengthening of municipal autonomy. These objectives seem to reflect the idea of pluralistic democracy, the interaction of those active in local administration, the groups holding the power, organisations and citizens.

Does municipal decision-making genuinely have room for pluralism, and if so, what kind of changes can take place and how quickly? The significance that people give to a phenomenon and their comprehension of it are also concretely reflected in their actions. The citizens' own experiences and impressions of municipal decision-making affect the degree to which they themselves are willing to participate and commit themselves. Changes in the way of doing things, for example, the increase of citizens' rate of participation or the procedures by which those in elected offices and workers give the citizens space and support their direct participation, require change in ideas relating to these. The significance, channels and form of the municipal political decision-makers' notions of citizens and citizens' participation create preconditions, such as how the participation of citizens will be used and how efficient and effective citizens' participation will be.

2.   Local Administration, Democracy And Citizens' Participation. Some Background Ideas for this Research

2.1.   Municipal Autonomy as Citizens' Autonomy

Finland is divided into 452 self-governing municipalities. Municipal autonomy is guaranteed in section 51 of the Constitution. Because Finland has no intermediate level self-government with the power to legislate over municipal affairs, all municipalities are governed by a uniform set of rules independent of their size or geographic position within the country. The central government defines the general principles of municipal self-government by legislation. This includes defining the general and specific mandates of local government, tax legislation and state supervision, under which local authorities carry out their functions. The general mandate of local authorities outlines the general powers of municipalities. It defines the scope of functions that municipalities are free to take upon themselves. These include, for instance, the provision of many cultural and educational institutions, maintenance of sport facilities and some commercial activities. The range of functions under the special mandate of local authorities has been growing ever since independence in 1917. The most important statutory functions performed by local authorities are educational and cultural services, health care, social welfare services, planning and building, and fire and rescue services. The highest authority at the local level resides with the municipal council (in cities, the city council). Candidates are put forward by political parties and voter associations [2].

For purposes of central government administration, the country is divided into 5 provinces, headed by governors appointed by the President of Republic. The provincial governments are, properly speaking, administrations without democratically elected organs. The main purpose of State supervision is to ensure that local authorities carry out their statutory obligations. However, the state supervision and the scope for control has been pared down by new legislation. In spite of this, in some areas the legislative control (e.g. individual rights) is strengthening, too. The conventional municipal functions of social welfare, health care and education account for over half of local authority expenditure. The rest of spending goes towards numerous administrative functions. Finnish municipalities differ greatly from one part of the country to the other, and not just in terms of revenues and expenditure but also in population density, economic structure, geographic and climatic conditions.

Municipal autonomy can be divided into two aspects, the aspect of municipality and that of the citizen (Figure 1).

Figure 1. The situation of citizens' participation

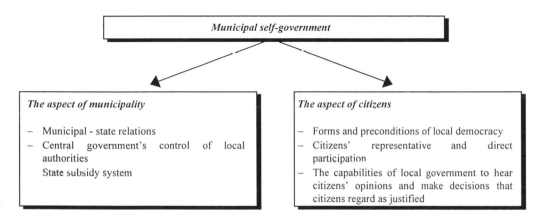

The aspect of municipality examines the autonomy of the municipality in relation to the state. The municipality understands the aspect of the citizen as co-operation based on the autonomy of members, that is citizens' representative and direct participation, and this is considered as an important form of autonomy and a prerequisite [3, 4].

Usually, municipal autonomy is regarded as a form of administration which represents democracy and the effective participation of citizens is linked to this. Autonomy can also be examined as a societal phenomenon which is construed, realised in the interaction between people. This being the case, municipal autonomy is a cultural phenomenon which shapes itself in the social relationships between citizens, in different events, activities and speech. The citizens' point of view emphasises the capabilities of the municipality. These include the local decision-makers' ability to hear the points of view of the citizens, the sensitivity to acknowledge the citizens' experiences of the local system of operations, and the skill to make decisions which to the citizens' mind are just.

Municipal autonomy is more than just another form of organising public administration. One can ask what is municipal autonomy in relation to the autonomy of citizens, and what does a democratic system of decision-making really mean to citizens, and how do they understand this. Examined from the point of view of citizens, municipal autonomy, i.e. the autonomy of members of the municipality based on co-operation, is in many ways a different thing to municipal autonomy in relation to the state.

Citizens' participation is also supported by law. According to the Finnish Constitution, officials are to support citizens' possibilities to affect matters concerning themselves. Social and health service legislation requires that the client has the possibility to have an impact on decisions concerning himself and, for example, decisions concerning his residential area or prevention and management of social problems. The Finnish Local Government Act was reformed in 1995, and now contains a whole chapter on citizens' participation. In democratic issues, it has been the legislative aim, on the one hand, to strengthen the position of representative democracy, i.e. the position of the Local Council, and, on the other hand, to develop new forms of citizens' direct participation along with it. These aims are also supported in the European Charter of Local Self-Government by the European Council ratified by Finland in 1991.

2.2.   The Development of Municipal Administration and Citizens' Participation

Citizens' direct participation and impact are related to a wider development of society. The focus of the Finnish municipal government system has increasingly moved towards a weakening of representative democracy, i.e. the number of political decision-makers is decreasing. On the other hand, the matters politicians decide upon have become increasingly wide-scoped. Decision-making power has been given to professionally trained and qualified municipal officials. The number of issues to be decided on in municipalities and, for example, the number of services offered by them has increased. Also the self-governmental right of municipalities, for instance, in social and health services, has increased and state control decreased. Municipal services are developed to meet citizens' needs according to each municipality.

Figure 2. The citizen as a user of public services and as a community participation

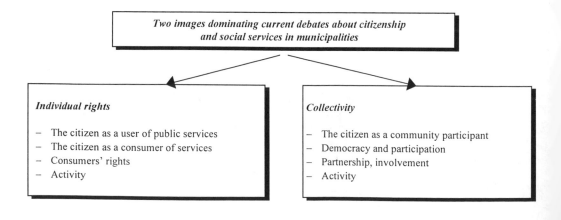

Local autonomy has increased differences in municipalities in a positive way, but according to some studies, it has simultaneously strengthened differences which increase inequality among citizens and municipalities. Citizens are unequal in different municipalities. Municipal decision-makers' political leanings and economic-political conditions have an effect on this. However, in Finland, it is the responsibility of the municipalities to organise educational, social and health services and make them available to each citizen. The discussion on citizen participation is placed in the aspect of individual rights - collectivity (Figure 2). This seems to dominate two different ideas: the citizen principally as a consumer, as a public service user and secondly, the citizen as a member of the community [5].

Participation can be justified as the service user's right to participate by using the service (or potentially using the service) as a client. Experience of having an effect on the content of the service, its quality and availability increases the belief that one can have an impact on affairs in the municipality and especially, that one has the right to participation in the state of services. The question remains as to whether or not the consumer wants to develop municipal democracy, or is his or her interest limited to participation which is needed only when the aim is to improve the responsiveness of the service? Community membership and participation in community matters can promote the feeling of belonging to the community.

3.   The Theoretical Framework of the Study. The Aspects of Democracy Theories in Citizens' Participation

Political participation emphasises the realisation of the rule by the people, i.e. democracy. Democracy can, for instance, be evaluated on the basis of the contents of democracy, or the form of democracy, i.e. how decisions are made. In the latter point of view, in the process aspect, democracy can mean, for example:

* participation in the election of those who make or execute decisions;
* participation in decision-making itself;
* having an impact on the contents of decisions.

Recent democracy discussion and studies have emphasised the responsiveness, or the ability of the political system and the people working within it to reach conclusions which meet citizens' needs and requirement. Who makes citizen-related decisions and how well can they represent citizens' opinions, bearing in mind that it is impossible to meet citizens' needs perfectly, are important factors. Along with needs and values represented by citizens, such issues as equality, justice, civil rights and the financial coping of the municipality and its citizens should be taken into consideration [6, 7]. The legitimacy of local political decision-making is considerably influenced by citizens' opinion about the reasonability and justification of elected and municipal officials' decisions and methods.

Democracy is often assessed according to the significance given to citizens' participation. On the basis of views on participation, classic models of democracy can be divided into elitist theories, participatory theories and pluralist theories that combine elitist and participatory theories [5, 8, 9, 10, 11] . In fact, the contents of the theories and their differences of meanings are more complex than described in the following simplified division used in this study.

According to elitist theories, only few citizens can and want to use decision-making power in a municipality. Democracy is realised in elections through voting. Elected candidates represent the common interests of all citizens in a municipality and they can achieve good decisions when using their decision-making power. Citizens' own active participation in government is not needed; it is enough, that their reaction in elections can act as a measure of how well they consider the decision-makers to have succeeded. For this reason, for politicians, elections also mean a threat, the possibility of losing the attained position of power.

Figure 3. A simplified division of theories on democracy

Elitist theories	Pluralist theories	Participatory theories
☐ Only few know how to use power.	☐ Democracy contains both elitist and participatory networks.	☐ Participation develops and brings up citizens' personality and feeling of responsibility.
☐ Elections as a form of participation.	☐ Direct and representative democracy acting together.	☐ It is efficient.
☐ Representative democracy sufficient.	☐ Participation develops and brings up citizens' personality and feeling of responsibility.	☐ Aims at wide-scale and direct participation.
	☐ It is efficient.	
	☐ Aims at wide-scale and direct participation.	

According to pluralist theories, power is divided unequally among citizens and not used by one elite alone. Several elitist groups fight for power. Democracy can also contain several dominant elitist groups, in which case, one elitist group uses power in one matter and another elitist group in another. The pluralist form of democracy includes the idea that citizens also have the opportunity to use power through a group. Society consists of networks based on various elitist groups and citizens' direct participation and impact on the elitist groups.

Along with changes in society, forms of participatory democracy theories, which emerged later, represent developed views on citizens' own participatory skills. In the participatory theoretical trend, participation has both an absolute and an instrumental value. There are no objective decisions which would be good for all citizens in municipal decision-making. Furthermore, politicians' skills and knowledge have their limits. In order to produce multifarious points of view and reach decisions, citizens' large-scale participation is needed. Therefore, participatory theories emphasise each individual's own capability, will and talent for participating in decision-making related to himself or his closest community.

In modern municipal democracy, there are two elements influencing simultaneously [8]. Only the elites make decisions, not all citizens. The decisions will, however, remain meaningless and the elitist groups without public acceptance of their position if the participation is not large-scale. Therefore, decision-making requires elites, and also participation. One reason for the crisis of representative democracy and estrangement from citizens can be found in the fact that representative democracy excludes or fails to provide room for citizens' own active participation. In a simplified form, participation is merely activity in connection with voting on election day.

4.   Some Empirical Results

4.1.   Research Data and Method

The study examines citizens' own views on the efficiency of municipal democracy, their experiences of participation and having an impact on local municipal decision-making and their view on how and where they receive the information on local issues needed for participation. The study investigates the whole local government, paying special attention to social and health services in municipalities. The results are based on comprehensive studies carried out at the University of Kuopio in Finland during 1995-1996. The studies comprise in all 54 small or medium-sized municipalities and cities in Central Finland. A questionnaire was distributed to a random sample of 12 962 citizens aged 16 to 70. The response rate was 66%.

The same questionnaire was also distributed to a group of decision-makers and workers, i.e. to a sample of 485 municipal politicians and social and health service workers in the same 54 municipalities. The group of decision-makers consisted of the city mayors and municipal heads and the chairmen of the municipal councils and committees for social and health services. The group of workers consisted of municipal social and health care directors, social workers, doctors and public health nurses. The response rate was 60%. The studies were carried out mainly by questionnaires and the data were analysed by means of quantitative analyses, i.e. factor analyses, combined variables, and the reliability of combined variables was analysed with Cronbach's alpha.

4.2.   The Availability of Information is a Prerequisite for Participation

Citizens' possibilities to receive information, participate and have an impact are deficient. Participation always requires the availability of sufficient information. The study demonstrates that municipal ways of providing information are deficient. It shows clear and surprising differences in the views of citizens, elected officials and municipal officials on citizens' possibilities to receive enough information on social and health services. For instance, elected officials consider that citizens receive information on social and health services very well, whereas citizens themselves assess that they receive information insufficiently.

The attitudes towards providing information about social and health services in municipalities are contradictory. A good half of elected officials and about a fifth of social and health service workers believed that citizens are fully satisfied with the information they receive about social and health services. Problems with citizens' possibilities to receive information refer especially to social services. However, workers in social and health services or municipal decision-makers often fail to recognise these problems. Citizens want to participate and have an impact on local affairs, but the channels or ways of participation offered to them lack credibility. A person participates when he considers the issue important to him and when he can trust that participation is worthwhile [11].

4.3.　Respondents' Views on Municipal Democracy

Respondents were asked to clarify their views on decision-making in their own municipality. The questions were based on classifications of democracy theories of the relation between citizens and decision-makers and the significance given to citizens' participation. Answers show that citizens form an inconsistent group (Table 1). Some citizens are satisfied with representative democracy and have confidence in their own politicians, whereas other citizens are disappointed with the possibilities of participating because matters change slowly or because there is not enough money to meet citizens' needs. However, almost an equal number of citizens believe in participation and think that trying to have an impact on joint affairs is important. One group that can also be distinguished is a group I call "the distanced". The distanced are not interested in municipal politics, they do not believe in participation and consider having an impact as not worthwhile. This group does not have trust in the political decision-makers of their municipality either.

The results of the study reveal that citizens' confidence in their elected officials is weakening. Decisions reached by elected officials often have far-reaching consequences on the everyday life of citizens. It is important that decision-makers are informed about the consequences their decisions have, and citizens should already know the possible consequences at the preparation phase of decision-making in order to improve the quality of services and increase the responsiveness of workers in individual organisations who have to be aware of clients' experiences. Listening to clients' opinions and assessment of services form a part of the services' responsibility in citizen participation and having an impact [12]. However, decision-makers are not always informed of clients' experiences. The study reveals that the interaction between elected officials and clients is minimal. Collecting feedback from citizens who use social and health services is increasing, but collection of feedback has not yet become a natural part of the system. The organisational structures of provision of services give room to workers, their leaders and persons responsible for financing, but fail to give it to clients.

Table 1. Respondents' (citizens') views on municipal democracy (%).

Claim	Agree %	Do not know %	Disagree %
Local politics is interesting	45	16	39
Citizens' having an impact is useless, because municipal activity is ruled by law	37	18	45
Citizens' having an impact is useless in the present economic situation	42	16	42
Citizens' having an impact is useless, because changes occur so slow in municipalities	38	22	40
Elected officials in my municipality do not have enough knowledge about the everyday life of the citizens	52	24	24
I know at least one of the decision-making elected officials in my municipality personally	64	10	26
Elected officials can take care of the matters	40	25	35
The citizens' opinion of services is asked for in my municipality	30	23	47
Municipal officials listen to citizens more than elected officials do	21	49	30
The opinions that citizens have are of no significance in decision-making	45	19	36
Participation in joint municipal affairs should be learned at a young age	82	13	5
Participation teaches citizens to take responsibility for others	85	10	5
Citizens should be offered new forms of participation	84	14	2

(N=8559, p=.000)

5.   The Functional Value, Display Value, Instrumental Value of Participation

There are different values also in citizens' participation. To put it briefly, increasing citizens' direct participation is not merely a question of participation as an absolute value. Furthermore, the idea is that through participation other aims will be reached, which provide extra value, more good for something else [13]. Different aims from very different view points and with various interests have been accredited to participation and increasing participation. The "other good" which comes about through participation may, by the implications, be contradictory to the idea of participation. Citizen participation and its development processes and aims can be seen in different ways depending on the examination standpoint and the purpose attributed to participation (Figure 4).

Figure 4. Different areas of examination of the direct participation of citizens

Active body	Process	Objective
☐ The citizen ☐ The service-using customer	Own personal way of learning. The right to self-determination and subjective approval. Satisfaction with participation. Things affecting whole or specific points.	Recognition of own existence and legitimisation of own objectives. Having an impact on things near to or important to oneself.
☐ The municipal service provider ☐ Professional	Follows the professionally desired principles. Professional satisfaction from work done well. Assessing the quality of the services and feedback.	Improving the outcome of one's own work. Improving the responsiveness of the service. Widening the point of view.
☐ Administration	Participation in the development of channels. Participation in the "display value". Participation in the development of operations.	Widening the decision-making point of view. Making savings.
☐ Municipal political decision-maker	Rating political decision-making. Assembling support groups. Caution and fear of competition.	Public support and the legitimatisation of political decision-making. Increasing supporters. Making savings.

Where the profession develops the client's participation in order to improve the quality of its own work, as regards the client, the participation may last their entire life. To the citizen, participation may mean making their own existence apparent, whereas for the worker, the same thing means one activity among a range of others. Improving the citizens' opportunities for participation may mean an increase in the responsiveness of operations, making savings, and a means of showing one's own improvement and development. The attitude of elected officials towards an increase in citizens' participation seems to be an area of conflict. The relationship between direct participation and representative decision-making requires the redetermination of the role of elected officials.

If the structures and modes of action of municipal administration do not provide a space for citizens, their participation also remains ostensible. The development of participation implicated by pluralism does not simultaneously further the mode of practice, the culture of the organisation, or the formal structures on which the assumptions of elitist democratic theory are based. A mere theme of discussion, and the fact that citizen participation is only for municipal administration display, may lead to a kind of delusion for both public and citizen participation. Knowledge without the possibility of using that knowledge leads to public delusion, and ostensible channels of participation can bring delusion to citizen participation, providing a distorted picture of the citizen's own possibilities to participate and to have an impact.

Stefan Sjöblom [14] draws our attention to the existing, often implicit aim for efficacy behind the claim for an increase in direct democracy. Municipal administration and its structures are not at all developed rationally. Earlier attempts have been made to improve the legitimacy of decision-making, for example, using professional or market-oriented models. New aims regarding citizen participation are realised only when they logically meet other various aims in the municipal system of decision-making. In participation, or wanting to participate as a client, citizens meet municipal administration and its operational and political system of services, as well as the influence and exercise of power mechanisms linked to these. At the same time as they are citizens, elected officials, officials or users of a particular service, people form the municipal system of services. In the everyday life of municipal administration, citizen participation signifies a change both in the relationship between political decision-makers and professional workers, and the values which guide the activities behind these two categories.

6.   Conclusion: Is There Space in Municipal Democracy for Pluralism?

There are problems in the interaction between citizen residents in the municipality, the municipal decision-makers (politicians) and workers in social welfare and health care. The rapid changes in service structures, changes in people's problems and the fact that these have become more complicated, the small amount of interaction between decision-makers and citizens as well as the economic difficulties encountered by the municipalities, form a complicated tangle of problems. Basically citizens do want to have an impact on things close to them, but blocked channels are not always credible and this reduces the effect of and will to participate. If the receiving of information necessary to participation and interaction is missing, the situation cannot be rectified unless the municipal workers, elected officials and the citizens first acknowledge the lack of communication. Discussion about the weakness of citizen participation may in itself strengthen and renew current users, unless we also stop to think about the reasons for weak participation and possibilities for participation. At the same time, thought should be given to whether or not practice should be created through which the citizens can claim their right to services merely by being an adequately active and participating citizen. What if the citizen does not have enough time or energy? The citizen's personal interest in participation often comes about when the matter, for example, the organising of a particular service, is current and important the him/her. If, prior to this, participation has been seen in a negative or frustrating light by the citizen, it can be hard work to change this and get the citizen to adopt a participating role.

Citizen participation requires a different form of discussion and culture of activities than the traditional representative democratic model. In this study, elected officials did not consider the forms of participation represented by dialogue in the pluralist model to be as important as ways of having an impact based on sharing or collecting information. There are many characteristics in the problems surrounding direct citizen participation and in the increase of direct democratic dialogue which can only be from the neopluralistic point of view [15]. Several groups do not use power at the same time, rather they compete for it. Part of resources for the participation of citizens, the municipal clusters and organisations are insufficient, starting with the notification and willingness to have an impact on formal and informal networks. Despite the great amount of information and the fairly good amount of channels through which citizens can have an impact, administration and decision-making are not open. This limits the participation of some groups and allows others greater access than before to decision-making. Participation groups are unequal among themselves.

Participation having an impact requires a sufficient amount of information. Problems accumulate and skills for having an effect become weaker. The study indicates that less-educated citizens and citizens who were unemployed had the weakest channels of participation and having an impact in municipalities. These citizens also noted a lack in the availability of information. They were not interested in municipal issues and they regarded participation as insignificant. These citizens are active users of social and health services, but feel that they cannot influence the services themselves and that social and health care workers fail to listen to them. The problems they are confronted with - alcohol problems, mental problems or problems related to child welfare - are not considered as politically interesting, and these citizens themselves lack the channels of influence or connections to political decision-makers in their municipalities. This group also included an alarming number of young people. Adolescents have no political contacts, and they are not interested in municipal decision-making. The ways of participation offered to them are more adapted to adults than young people. If young people feel that their opinions are insignificant in the official decision-making system, they may become even more distant. Young people are also a likely group for society-hostile extremist groups.

In order to participate and influence mutual affairs, citizens need information. Information means power. In connection with information, power means the possibility to contribute to providing information and channels and forms of providing information. In municipal decision-making, power also refers to the possibility of deciding what kind of and whose information is important. For citizens, information means power in that only when they are informed about their possibilities to influence. Only then can they decide whether or not to use these possibilities open to them. The strengthening of the foundation of municipal democracy requires that citizens believe in decision-makers' and important municipal officials' ability to make fair decisions. Also, as changes in society are increasing rapidly, extremely subtle political-ethical orientation is needed to make citizens accept the services and other activities intended for socially deprived people.

From the perspective of municipal administration, it is important that reforms are not cosmetic; they must be real, believable. The citizen participates when the matter in question interests him/her, when he/she feels that his/her immediate circle will really benefit from it, and when participation is credible [16]. Discussion on the increase of participation was scheduled during the time of the economic crisis. At the same time, administration was principally emphasising efficiency and results. For the most part, municipal administration is based on the bureaucratic administration model. Political decision-making has greatly rested on the elitist theory of democracy. New municipal decision-making models, for their part, implicate the model of the pluralist theory of democracy. When citizens also have little experience of impact participation, a slow process of learning and conscious teaching can be expected. Attitudes and values towards expectations and citizen participation must first be changed. In general, values change very slowly.

References

[1]   P. Ahonen and A. Salminen, Metamorphosis of the Administrative Welfare State. Peter Lang Publications, Frankfurt am Main, 1997.

[2]   The Association of Finnish Local Authorities, Local Government Vocabulary, Helsinki, 1995.

[3]   A. Niemi-Illahti, Itsehallinnon ja ideaalimallin kehitys ja reaalimaailma. Ideaalityyppimetodi kunnallisen itsehallinnon käsitteen ja pohjoismaisen hyvinvointivaltion itsehallinnon tulkinnassa. Vaasa University Publications. Studies No 163. Hallintotiede 11. Vaasa, 1992.

[4]   V. Niiranen, The Multidimensional Management of Social Services. *Finnish Local Government Studies* **4** (1995) 21.

[5]   V. Lowndes, Citizenship and Urban Politics. In: D. Judge, G. Stoker and H. Wolman (eds), Theories of Urban Politics. Sage Publications, London 1995, pp.160-180.

[6]   L.H. Staples, Powerful Ideas About Empowerment. *Administration in Social Work*, **2** (1990) 29-42.

[7]   F. Twine, Citizenship and Social Rights. The Interdependence of Self and Society. Sage Publications, London, 1994.

[8]   L. Lewin, Folket och eliterna. Almqvist & Wicksell, Stockholm, 1970.

[9]   R. A. Dahl, Dilemmas of Pluralist Democracy. Autonomy vs. Control. Yale University Press, London, 1982.

[10]   C. Pateman, Participation and Democratic Theory. Cambridge University Press, Cambridge, 1989.

[11]   K. Bohm, Med-och motborgare i statdsplanering: en historia om medborgartagandets förutsättningar. Stockholm, 1986.

[12]   C.A. Rapp, Charles and J. Poertner, Social administration. A client-centered approach. University of Kansas-Longman, 1992.

[13]   G.H von Wright, The Varieties of Goodness. Bristol Thoemmes Press, 1963.

[14]   S. Sjöblom, (1997): Demokrati och effektivitet som organiseringsvärden i offentlig politik. (Utg. av) Voitto Helander och Siv Sandberg: Festskrift till Krister Ståhlberg. Åbo Akademi University Press, Åbo, 1997, pp 89-105.

[15]   D. Held, Models of Democracy. Polity Press, Cronwall, 1995.

[16]   C. Pollitt, Democracy and Bureaucracy. In: D. Held and C. Pollitt (eds.), New Forms of Democracy. Sage Publications, London,1994.

Recent Legislative Innovations in the Greek Administrative Institutions: The Example of the "Citizen's Advocate" Institution or the Greek Ombudsman

Panagiotis E. Poulis *

Introduction

The role of institutions is to interpret contemporary needs and supervise the functions and acts of Administration [1]. However, when institutions do not respond to social needs they have to be altered so that they can satisfy these needs.

Since Greek Administration is a chronic invalid there has been a need to reinforce its administrative institutions so as to cure or improve and confront "the phenomena of misgovernment, ineffectiveness, low production and low quality of its services" [2].

Greek Administration in order to become more effective has recently introduced the institution of the Citizen's Advocate [3], known as "Ombudsman" in Europe and many other countries of the world [4].

It is obvious that the roots of this institution in European and other countries' history of Administration are old and deep. It first appeared in Sweden in 1776 and was established under Constitution in 1919, in Denmark in 1953, Germany in 1956, Norway in 1963, the US in 1966, Great Britain in 1967, France in 1973, Portugal in 1976, Spain and Holland in 1981, Cyprus in 1991, Belgium in 1992 etc. It is known that the institution was established in the European Union in 1992 with the Maastricht treaty and has also been put into practice in many Eastern European countries [5].

In Greece, many efforts have been made to introduce this institution. Its realisation has been delayed for many years and some forms of it that have appeared through the years were very different from the internationally established institution of the Ombudsman [6].

Very important is the fact that the only institution for the control of the Greek Administration has been the "Body of Inspectors", which came into existence in 1987 and was in use until 1997. Later, the institution of the "Citizen's Advocate" and the "Inspectorate of Administration" appeared [7].

The Inspectorate of Administration, despite its problems and weaknesses has offered a lot to the Greek Public Administration and its operation is still necessary.

The purpose of my introduction is not only to display the provisions of the law which enact Citizen's Advocate in Greece and its detailed comparison with similar institutions in other

---

* Professor Panagiotis E. Poulis, Democritus University of Thrace, Greece

countries, but mostly to examine and analyse several characteristic elements which activate the institution.

My present introduction will focus on sections which deal with the organisation and status of the Citizen's Advocate (1) his authorities (2), the characteristics of its activation (3), and finally some conclusive comments.

1.   The Organisation of the Institution

The Citizen's Advocate has recently been established in Greece under Law 2477/1997 in order to protect the citizens from arbitrary or illegal administrative acts, and the delays and negligence of bureaucracy. According to article 1, paragraph 1 of the above referenced law the Citizen's Advocate's main mission is to act as mediator between citizens and civil services, Local Authorities, legal entities and social services in order to protect the citizens' rights, to fight against misgovernment and maintain law and order [8].

The Citizen's Advocate was named "Law Guard" or "Law Fighter" in ancient Greece, where we find the roots of its modern name. Nowadays, in Europe and other countries of the world like America, Canada etc. he is called "Mediator", "People Protector", "People Defender", "Citizen's Attorney", "Citizen's Protector" [9].

It is obvious that the status of this recently appeared institution is an Independent Administrative Authority. However, its legal approach does not agree with the model we encounter in the European countries like the "Autorités Administratives Indépendantes" in France [10].

We shall analyse the framework and function of this independent Administrative Authority. According to the adjustments of law 2477/1997 the Citizen's Advocate is assisted by four assistant Advocates who enjoy personal and functional freedom while on duty. It is clear through the provisions of the law that the Citizen's Advocate and his four Assistants cannot be examined and prosecuted for their opinions and acts while performing their duty. Prosecution is permitted only when there is a case of slanderous defamation, insult or failure to preserve secrecy.

The above law adjustment apparently tends to establish the independence of the Citizen's Advocate and his four Assistants and give them prestige and respectability. The Citizen's Advocate has to be protected from malicious, misleading and unjust accusations that would make his task difficult and would oblige him to spend more time in defending himself in court rather than controlling civil services.

Another provision of the law defines that "the Citizen's Advocate and his Assistant Advocates must be persons of high respectability, scientific knowledge and social acceptance" [11].

The selection is made by the Council of Ministers/Cabinet after the proposal of the committee of Institutions and Transparency. The Citizen's Advocate is appointed after a Presidential decree and with a five year tenure of office.

As to the Assistant Advocates and the deputy of the Citizen's Advocate, they are appointed for five years with a decision of the Minister of the Interior after a proposal of the Citizen's Advocate. Moreover, the same person is not permitted to stay in the post of the Citizen's Advocate after he has been in office for five years. Additionally, the term of office of the Assistant Advocate ends whenever the Citizen's Advocate's tenure of office stops. Inability to perform their duties, illness or physical or mental disability are reasons for the replacement of the Citizen's Advocate and his Assistants, while insufficiency in the discharge of their duties is an additional reason for the Assistant Advocates to be relieved of their duties [12].

Moreover, the Independent Administrative Authority is staffed with 30 specialised scientists and 40 seconded employees, who have the qualifications of a specialised scientist [13].

The legislator in order to ensure the smooth running of the Independent Administrative Authority provided for the establishment of a Secretariat, where the Head is chosen by the Citizen's Advocate. The organisation of the Secretariat and all the matters concerning its function are settled according to the rules and regulations of the Authority.

Currently, the budget of the Authority, is taken from the annual budget of the Ministry of the Interior, Public Administration and Decentralisation, but a new government agency will be established to deal with the required appropriations.

In conclusion, the Independent Administrative Authority consists of five members, i.e. the Citizen's Advocate and four Assistant Advocates. However, these members do not form a collective organ [14].

Furthermore, the Citizen's Advocate exercises neither hierarchical nor disciplinary control on the Assistant Advocates, because, as it has already been mentioned, they enjoy personal and functional freedom [15].

Another significant point on the validity of this Independent Administrative Authority is that this Authority according to the provisions of the law 2477/1997, article 1, paragraph 1 is not amenable to control either by an Administrative Authority or a Government Office. It is understandable that this Independent Authority cannot be submitted to any kind of hierarchical control or state supervision while performing their duties. The Citizen's Advocate exercises "an intermediary control", and as professor Spiliotopoulos indicates, this control is "of limited effectiveness, since it does not refer to possible malpractice of Ministers and Under-secretaries. It is therefore possible, because of the persistence of the Administration, that this will not lead to a positive effect" [16]. At this point it is worth underlying that the best form of control for the protection of the citizens against possible breach of the state organs is the principle of the judicial control which characterises law and order [17].

2.   The Authorities of the Institution

As already mentioned, the primary mission of the Citizen's Advocate is to protect citizens' rights and fight against misgovernment. What is more, the main goal is to uphold the law.

First, we should identify the limits of his jurisdiction and particularly the services within his authority.

The relevant adjustments of the constituent law provide that the Citizen's Advocate must have a wide field of authority, which is meant not only for the civil services but for the Local Authorities of 1st and 2nd degree as well, the rest legal entities of the public law, and for the public utility services like telecommunications and electricity services. It should also be pointed out that the law establishing the Independent Administrative Authority narrows the limits of its jurisdiction. In particular, according to the provisions of the law, under its jurisdiction do not come "the Ministers and Under-secretaries as to the conduct of public affairs, the religious bodies corporate under public law, the judicial Authorities, the military services concerning matters of national security and defence, the Intelligence Service, the Ministry of Foreign Affairs with regard to the foreign policy and the international relations of the country, the State Legal Council and the Independent Administration Authorities as to their basic function" [18]. Moreover, the Citizen's Advocate cannot intervene in cases concerning National security or in matters that have an effect on the status of the staff of civil services.

Furthermore, the Citizen's Advocate's control focuses on individual administrative actions or omissions of the civil services which encroach upon people's rights or infringe upon legal interests of natural persons or legal entities.

He specifically examines the cases where a civil service organ either individual or collective:

1. violates by act or omission rights or interests protected by the Constitution and the Law.
2. refuses to fulfil a specific obligation which is imposed by final judicial decision.
3. refuses to fulfil a specific obligation which is imposed by a provision of law or an individual administrative action.
4. acts contrary to the principles of decent administration and transparency or abusing his position of power [19].

Moreover, the Independent Administrative Authority does not look into legal cases which are still pending [20].

The Citizen's Advocate after receiving a signed report from a legal entity or a natural person or an association of persons must take action. He can also ex-officio see to matters which attract the public interest [21].

It should be noted that the Independent Administration Authority does not undertake cases where the administrative proceedings have born rights or have created a favourable status for third persons, which can be reversed only by judicial decision, unless there is violation of the law or there is some connection of the matter with the protection of the environment [22].

As to the control process, according to the relevant provisions of the law, it starts as soon as a signed report of a particular matter reaches the Citizen's Advocate. The report must be submitted to the Citizen's Advocate within a period of six months after the person involved has been informed of the actions or omissions which he turned to the Independent

Administrative Authority for. It should be noted that the report is independent of the hierarchical appeal or legal redress and does not interrupt or suspend the time that is provided by the law for the exercise of legal means. In case legal redress is sought the Citizen's Advocate does not undertake the case before the official body reaches a decision or before a required three month period passes without any action taken after the report [23].

The Citizen's Advocate as an Independent Administrative Authority has the right to communicate with the rest civil services who are obligated to accommodate the proceedings in any way. They can be asked for information, documents or other probative evidence for a case. They can also be questioned, demand autopsies, and ordered to provide expert opinions. On examination of documents or other probative evidence which are at the disposition of civil services, nothing can be characterised as confidential unless it concerns national defence, public security or the international relations of the country. If a civil service does not comply with the Citizen's Advocate, the latter can report to the competent Minister [24]. Refusal of an employee, a civil servant or member of the Administration to collaborate with the Citizen's Advocate on an investigation is considered as breach of discipline and violation of duty, while for the members of the Administration it can be a cause for their replacement.

At the conclusion of an investigation the Citizen's Advocate draws up a report of the findings addressed to the Minister appropriate to the matter, and makes every attempt to assist in a solution of the citizen's problem.

In addition, the Citizen's Advocate has the obligation to draw up an annual report accounting for the work done throughout the year, highlighting the most important cases with the proposals for improvement to the civil services. Finally, the findings are discussed in a special plenary session of the Parliament and published in a special edition of the National Printing House Office.

In summary, the Citizen's Advocate has auditing and supervisory duties. Annual findings must be presented with full transparency to the appropriate government body, with the goal of improving the relationship between government and citizens. Additionally, opinions and proposals must be presented to ensure the smooth running of the civil services.

3.   The Characteristics of the Institution

The institution of the Citizen's Advocate has the following characteristics:

a. It is an Independent Administrative Authority, although as previously mentioned, it does not wholly border on the foreign model. The Citizen's Advocate, according to the relevant adjustments of the law, is not subject to control by a government office or Administrative Authority. This means that independence is the corner stone of the Institution when all the prerequisites which characterise an Individual Administrative Authority exist [25].

b. Post requirements of the Citizen's Advocate include: recognised respectability, high scientific knowledge and social acceptance. Final selection which is made by the Cabinet, represented by the Government party, is not characteristic of an Independent

Administrative Authority. The first Greek Ombudsman has already been chosen. It's professor Nikiforos Diamantouros of Athens University.

c. According to the constituent law the Citizen's Advocate and the four Assistant Advocates enjoy "personal and functional freedom" while performing their duties. Members of the Independent Administrative Authority are obliged to act according to their conscience as the Constitution and the country's laws ordain, without any dependence on obligations or possible orders and instructions by the members of the government. The personal independence of the members of the Authority is based on the fact that during their term of office they can only be relieved of their duties on rare occasions as it has already been mentioned [26].

d. This independent Office has its own Secretariat and independent budget. These are positive elements for the smooth running of the newly-established institution. Moreover the appointment of a Head for this independent Secretariat, who is chosen by the Citizen's Advocate himself according to the provisions of the Greek laws, strengthens the independence of the Administrative Authority.

e. No control either hierarchical or disciplinary is exercised on the Assistant Advocates as is specified by the relevant provision of the law. This is characteristic of the independence of all the members of the Authority.

f. Full transparency of the Citizen's Advocate's work is secured with the annual report and the plenary session of the Parliament.

Conclusion

From the above detailed account of the provisions of the law for the Citizen's Advocate, which has recently been voted into existence, the following conclusion, can be drawn.

The recent introduction and establishment of the institution of the Ombudsman in the Greek law and order is important because it will solve crucial problems of a "weak" public administration. The mission of the Citizen's Advocate is "the protection of the citizen's rights, the fight against misgovernment and the maintenance of law and order".

Therefore, the Greek Ombudsman, in order to be useful and effective should operate objectively without any intervention or dependence on the Executive, leading not only to distrust and dispute in the work and authority of the institution, which is introduced for the first time, but its independence as well.

A critical assessment of the Independent Administrative Authority can not be made as it is not as yet fully operational. However, the adoption of this institution is a great step towards the modernisation and progress of the Greek Administration.

Time will reveal the strengths and weaknesses of the Citizen's Advocate, as well as the validity of its proposals for improvement and better operation of the Institution.

References

[1]   Th.N.Vegleris, To Symboulio tis Epicratias, Meletes Dimosiou Dikeou, Athens 1929 (in Greek).
[2]   Isigitiki Ekthesi tou shediou nomou gia ton Ombudsman kai to soma Epitheoriton - Elegton tis Dimosias Diikisis (in Greek).
[3]   See L.2477/1997 "O Ombudsman kai to Soma Epitheoriton - Elengton Dimosias Diikisis" (in Greek).
[4]   N. Haralambous, O thesmos tou Epitropou Diikisis stin Kypro, Epitheorisi Dimosiou kai Diikitikou Dikeou, vol 2, p. 5, (in Greek); D.C. Rowat, Pourquoi un Ombudsman Parlementaire?. In: Mediateurs et Ombudsman, *Revue Francaise d'Administration Publique*, **64** (1992) 571.
[5]   O. Gohin, Institutions administratives, 2e ed., L.G.D.J, Paris 1995, p. 207; O elenhos tis kakodiikisis stin Ellada, Ant. Sakoulas publications, Athens 1096, p.31 (in Greek). Besilla- Makridi, O Ombudsman, os neos thesmos elenhou tis dimosias diikisis stin Ellada, Epitheorisi tis Apokentrosis tis Topikis Aftodiikisis kai Periferiakis Anaptixis, vol.6 (1996), p. 7 (in Greek).
[6]   A. Makridimitri, To Elato stin ammo i o Ombudsman stin Ellada (in Greek).
[7]   I. Anastopoulou, To Soma Elenkton tis Dimosias Diikisis, Efarmoges Dimosiou Dikeou, 1992, p. 375 (in Greek). Poulis, I prosfates nomothetikes Exelixis sto thesmo ton Elengton tis Dimosias Diikisis, Diikitiki Diki (1995), vol.1, p.1. (in Greek).
[8]   Article 1, par.1, L 2477/1997.
[9]   Ikonomikos Tahidromos, December 12, 1996, p. 48 (in Greek).
[10] Antonopoulou, I Anexartites Diikitikes Arhes, Ant. Sakoulas publications, Athens 1995 (in Greek); J. Chevallier, Les Autorités Administratives Indépendantes et la régulation des marchés, *Justices*, **1** (1995) 82; R. Drago, Le Conseil de la concurrence, *J.C.P.* (1987) I.3300; Gaudemet, Les pouvoirs des autorités administratives indépendantes: réglementations et sanctions, *Le courrier juridique des Finances*, **77** (1997). Legrand, Ombudsman Scandinave, Préface Roland Drago. Bibliothèque de Science Administrative, tome 2, L.G.D.J., Paris, 1970.
[11] Article 2, par.1, L.2477/1997.
[12] Article 2, par.2, L.2477/1997.
[13] Article 1, par.4, L.2477/1997.
[14] P. Daltoglou, Geniko Diikitiko Dikeo, Fourth edition, Athens 1996, p.467 (in Greek). Spiliotopoulos, Enhiridio Diikitikou Dikeou, Eighth edition, Ant. Sakoulas publications, Athens 1997, p. 394, footnote 7 (in Greek).
[15] Council of State 872/1992.
[16] E. Spiliotopoulos, Enhiridio Diikitikou Dikeou, p.392 (in Greek).
[17] *Ibid.*
[18] Article 3, par.1, L.2477/97.
[19] Article 3, par.2, L.2477/97.
[20] Article 3, par.3, L.2477/97.
[21] Article 4, par.3, L. 2477/97.
[22] *Ibid.*
[23] Spiliotopoulos, Enhiridio Diikityikou Dikeou, p. 397 and bibliography (in Greek).
[24] Article 4, par.5, L.2477/97.
[25] N.D. Koulouris, "i Anexartites Diikitikes Arhes", Ta Allodapa protypa kai ta imedapa kakektipa. Diikitiki Diki, **5** (1993) 140 (in Greek).
[26] Council of State 872/1992.

The Experience of France's "Family" Welfare Office: Lessons in the Search For New Management Techniques

Michel Chauvière *

France's Social Security system exhibits the particularity of encompassing a separate section for family welfare matters. This component today accounts for roughly 10% of total social security expenditures, down from the 40% it represented at the time of its creation in 1946, at the end of the Second World War. For historical reasons, this division, which serves to ascribe as great an importance to the family as to work, is not encountered elsewhere [1].

The National Family Welfare Office ("CNAF") along with the 119 local offices ("CAF"), operating as public and private legal entities, respectively, represent the organisations which have been assigned to oversee some twenty different types of welfare disbursements, in addition to implementing a complementary social policy intended for families and infant care. Some of these disbursements are not necessarily family-oriented in nature, as exemplified by the financial assistance granted to handicapped adults, instituted in 1975, or the minimum insured income since 1988. In all, some 280 billion francs of public monies are spent by these offices, with their revenue stemming from employers' withholdings as well as from a portion of a general tax fund ("CSG") created in 1988. This considerable financial effort benefits over 7 million welfare recipients, both those enrolled in specific programs and the needy, who also happen to be families with dependent children, young members of the labour force, handicapped adults and the elderly.

The complexity of the system has become such that the quantity of information required to cease disbursements is continually increasing. In keeping with the French notion of citizen participation, this information is first obtained by means of simple declaration and then meticulously corroborated, in conjunction with the Tax Office in particular. A welfare recipient on average writes to his CAF office 6 times a year, over which period he receives an average of 19 letters, including a news bulletin featuring the title: *"Bonheur"* (*Happiness*).

As with any Social Security system, the nation's various social service agencies jointly manage both the CNAF and CAF offices [2]. Yet, the CNAF/CAF's unique history, along with the special support they have received both from associations and the political arena, set this system apart from the nation's basic social security functions. The Ministry for Social Affairs is normally responsible for exercising oversight authority; however, regulation has been emanating from the Prime Minister's Office and the Economy and Finance Ministry to an increasing extent. In June of 1997, the decision was taken to subject CAF welfare payments to family income criteria and, six months later, to tie this program's disbursement scheme to a simple indicator of household taxable income [3]. Is the functioning of this institution actually becoming transparent, devoid of its own policy-making capacity, despite the equal representation considerations or any of its substitutes within the various oversight boards?

* Michel Chauvière, Directeur de recherche au CNRS, GAPP - ENS de Cachan, France

The CNAF's relative autonomy also provides the opportunity for developing an independent research activity, as well as a consistent incentive-based policy, by virtue of the widespread dissemination of calls for tender in the field of social sciences. These practices have, in essence, introduced a kind of third power, held by a group of experts, whose supervision and influence have become key issues. In this vein, the journal *Recherches et Prévisions* (*Research and Forecasts*) regularly discusses the relationships between the CAF organisation and its users, or modernisation efforts; its reports are based on studies and experimental programs conducted in-house. The small paperback collection *Espaces et familles* (*Family space*) showcases the results obtained from this work. A third journal, *Informations sociales* (*Social policy news*), is aimed at disseminating the findings of external research in the field to a broad audience of professionals and decision-makers (with a circulation of some 13,000 issues). Despite their heavily institutional bent, these various documentary sources do provide a wealth of information not only on the organisation's transformations, but on social protection issues and the work of professionals in the field as well.

1.   The Welfare Recipient's Spatial Perception

Several processes impact the "user's space", to use the expression coined by Isaac Joseph and Gilles Jeannot [4]; this notion refers to the space within which the user (recipient) can or cannot enter into contact with the organisation, either on his own or as part of an assembled group.

The development of modernisation strategies, based to a great extent on a managerial model. This development happens to coincide with a period of lesser emphasis on social democracy and social policy issues, as well as with a strengthening of the hold exercised by the State, which has been noticeably involved ever since the decrees issued in 1967. Such a push for modernisation has incited a feeling, on the part of the system's most virulent supporters, that the bold values being championed by France's Social Security policy, and even more so those of the CAF welfare programs of the 1940's-50's, have not just been eroded but abandoned entirely. To the contrary, the welfare recipients themselves have certainly gained from improved reception conditions and better treatment.

The effects of renouncing systematic entitlement payments. The universality of granting disbursements to all families remained a bold and symbolic feature of the program up until 1997, and it has now been reinstated. In reality, the public authorities and the welfare agencies themselves jointly decided early on to expand the number of entitlements and to set public policy priorities (with respect to large families, single-parent families, etc.) or policy focuses (housing, fighting poverty, etc.), most often in conjunction with the introduction of variable income-related criteria from one entitlement to the next and from one situation to the next. This entitlement-specific rationalisation has contributed to separating the institution from members of the workforce, welfare recipients or the needy. Furthermore, it has inserted a more selective terminology into the service, geared towards the public, users and even customers, along with establishing other types of relationships for all service beneficiaries.

The effects of an increasingly precarious social status. With increasing frequency, as recipients' transfer payments rise considerably in comparison with their work-related income, many among them, particularly large families either in a precarious situation or with low household incomes, have now entered into a relationship of dependence and vulnerability with respect to their welfare offices. This tendency is also true of handicapped adult entitlement beneficiaries or guaranteed minimum-income recipients. Herein lies the importance of the interaction transpiring at the office's reception desk, in terms of both the quality of service provided and the enhanced satisfaction of users. In this perspective, the CAF institution implemented a survey strategy and initiated image-building programs, as if seeking to attract actual customers. However, the risk remains of uncontrolled and sometimes violent demonstrations, especially at the reception desk. In December 1997, a group of unemployed demonstrators protested in front of the CNAF headquarters... they didn't miss their mark!

The consequences of the so-called "social management of family entitlements" program. Recently, CAF offices have been launching several operations for seeking out potential beneficiaries for housing subsidies, assistance to young families, guaranteed minimum income support or even for parent education financial aid. "Program participants and welfare recipients, protect your rights" read the title of the first issue of the Paris CAF journal called *Vies de familles (Family living)*, released in February of last year. While the effectiveness of this action has not been fully determined, the internal memoranda being circulated have already revealed an attitude of over-dependence and rejection on the part of the recipients concerned.

2.   Modernisation and the Image of Welfare Recipients

On the basis of a multitude of recommendations and experiments, the CAF has been seeking to develop a user-oriented strategy. In reality however, it's the new style of public-sector management which has provided the CAF with the tools for upgrading the value of the services provided, particularly in improving the environment in which the service user / agent relationship is developed. An exhaustive search through some ten years of back issues of *Recherches et Prévisions* shows that this response has been structured around two distinct practical themes:

– First, the automatic processing of entitlements thanks to information systems. This aspect induces both more efficient cost management and a much less personalised rapport with the recipients. Certain reports make considerable mention of the passiveness, removal from reality and new barriers introduced by this modernisation;

– Second, as a complement to the first theme, the institution of a personalised relationship in order to provide assistance for a certain category of recipients. This orientation implies integrating the various functions exercised by the office's agents, hence the renewal of a multi-skilled staff. It has also helped fuel a new debate over the use of specialisation and the boundaries existing between a regulatory form of multiple service provision and a functional form.

Which images of the service user are involved in this dual orientation? The literature published by the CNAF highlights two typologies which indicate a distinct evolution in the nature of user representation within the CAF's framework.

In an article published in *Recherches et Prévisions* [5], Danièle Debordeaux notes that at the end of the 1970's, an initial typology was being applied, according to which all welfare recipients were categorised into four groups:

- families considered well adapted to an institutional framework;
- families with a need for technical assistance;
- families with a need for personalised assistance; and
- families ill-adapted to an institutional framework.

This typology quite obviously emphasised certain criteria, such as information, the motivation to claim one's entitlement rights, the assimilation of rules and the level of autonomy in the entitlement process, which could be examined from the standpoint of a hierarchical series of effects generated for the agents in contact with the public (*"front office" effects*).

In 1992, a study conducted by Nathalie Bardaille and Jean-Luc Outin enabled devising a new typology, based on interviews held with 200 beneficiaries [6]. This effort made it possible to distinguish:

- The "good citizen" recipients. This category would occupy the most favourable position in terms of managing their interaction with the CAF smoothly. Their relationship with the institution could be qualified as quasi-professional.

- The "subscriber" recipients. This category could be discerned by a rather blasé personal attitude within a heavily automated system for managing mass disbursement schemes. They tend to remain somewhat removed from the institution. Their relationship with the CAF could be qualified as distant, even invisible.

- The "user" recipients. This category is in frequent contact with their CAF office, due to their eligibility for many entitlement programs, a situation often related to an unstable or precarious family and/or professional status. Their relationship with the institution could be qualified as tenacious, due to the economic significance of these transfer payments, yet their understanding of how the system works necessitates a personalised effort.

- The "marginal" recipients. For this category, the CAF plays an external social role. Their relationship with the institution could be qualified as deficient; while often as dependent as the previous category, they tend to voice their claims more fervently than those seeking to comprehend the system.

Within this updated typology, the strict relationship between staff and "users" is no longer central to the service provision. This relationship is especially useful in mobilising the qualification criteria for entitlement programs, the institution's image, the level of comprehension and the degree of co-operation on the part of the "user" recipient category. A re-qualification has in fact been carried out. No longer considered from the perspective of families, they have (once again) become recipients. Moreover, the typology serves to arrange them within an updated hierarchy. Is this feature, as the author is intimating, merely the consequence of a change in service provision, which has become both automated and personalised? Such a hypothesis could be easily refuted, in particular by considering the transformations taking place within the fourth category. Those "families ill-adapted to an institutional framework" have gone on to become the "marginal recipients". How should this transformation be interpreted? The determination inherent in this expression is plainly no longer internal, but rather external, economic and social. The entitlements eligible to these "marginal recipients" have changed in composition; the CAF no longer hold a monopoly and instead has become, no doubt due to the "poverty shock" effect [7], a kind of "solidarity funding source" [8]. The conclusion can thereby be drawn that at this point, we have reached the limits of a modernisation designed with solely the internal organisation in mind, and that a shift, albeit only partial, in family policy within the context of social policy has clearly been initiated.

Another contribution examines the results from a survey carried out on users with so-called "administrative autonomy deficiencies" [9]. The headings listed throughout this document paint a telling picture of the representations shared by both the authors and the institution: "Can't the entitlement applications be streamlined?", "The complexity of the administrative texts makes it difficult to lay claim to one's rights", "Some recipients can no longer react", "Information on user's rights: A real necessity", "The impression of a CAF that plays favourites", "The difficulty of the CAF in being understood", "A problem of representation?", "The lines of communication sometimes get cut", "The role of advisor against a backdrop of obstacles", "Caught between administrative rationale and a slice of life", "The automation of correspondence places the service technician in a difficult position", "The personalised written response is the exception rather than the rule", "Take the recipient's overall situation into account", "The perpetual back-and-forth between CAF and recipient", and "Efforts and breakthroughs in facilitating the service relationship".

This image comes through very sharply whenever an internal assessment is performed. Philippe Steck, Director of entitlement programs at the CNAF, made the following observation at a recent seminar: "Despite all of the innovative, ambitious and revolutionary actions initiated by both the CNAF and the CAF, it goes without saying that the recipient families have, for the most part, remained program participants subjected to a rationale of deciphering between entitlements and non-entitlements" [10]. Other authors have also stressed that the growing level of complexity in the entitlement programs, along with a legislative and regulatory inflation, go hand in hand with a process of legalisation. In the event of a litigation to be settled, which is preferable to raising one's voice at the service desk, a transference to another scene would take place, with a build-up in the corresponding bureaucracy. Under such conditions, "user"-family concerns fade into the background and the focus gets shifted to the recipient-customer and his counterpart, the recipient-victim, if not to the marginal recipient and the subsidised beneficiary, which would spell a regression for the conception of solidarity.

3.   Can an Organisation Be Redefined by its Users?

Positioned somewhat further from this institutional drive, other research has examined the interactions taking place between "the highly-differentiated demands expressed by service users and the practical-oriented responses being provided them", along the lines of a topic developed at a seminar co-sponsored by the "Plan Urbain", RATP and DRI organizations in 1989 and 1990 [11]. In order to analyse the service relationships, some researchers have focused on more or less collective forms of learning, on reactions to language and material aspects, on the directory of user organisations' activities, on the joint production of intermediary representations and standards by both users and agents, on the legal shortcomings, etc.

In 1991, Jacques Gautrat and Jean-Louis Laville studied the modernisation program undertaken by the CAF office in the provincial city of Ariège from this perspective. They noted that the institution is, in reality, caught between two distinct trends: the advent of a service component to its productive activities, with the development of "service-oriented social functions"; and a field-oriented approach, as manifested by an emphasis on quality and greater involvement in redistribution-related activities. They analysed the techniques employed for collectively establishing new rules, the inequalities inherent in the level of participation from one employee category to the next, and the different representations this modernisation effort has engendered among the receiving agents, the social workers and the recipients themselves [12].

By evaluating the manner in which communication is organised with users, Anne Boisset and Michel Dartevelle focused on both user expectations and skill levels exhibited by telephone operators and reception desk staff at two CAF offices. A sample of telephone exchanges, along with an analysis of both initial reception conversations and more in-depth dialogues with agents, has enabled deriving an assessment of the quality-productivity combination and then proposing to the offices a set of practical means for improving the conditions of the agent-user interaction, in the aim of greater user autonomy [13].

For Vincent Dubois, the institution he was monitoring was in fact reconfigured by virtue of its use(rs). The reception desk represents the ideal spot for meeting agents used to face-to-face dealings with the public. The motivations and expectations of those addressing the reception desk have multiplied in both number and variety: need to be reassured, information exchange, psychological support, and, for some, a kind of "last resort to be heard". Under such conditions, the role of reception agents, as characterised by a basically non-institutional use of the reception desk, has been heavily affected, with personal attitudes taking on greater significance for initiatives being introduced on a case-by-case basis in the field. In this light, would it be fair to say that the user is not only the organisation's analyser, but its reformer as well? [14]

On the basis of "difficult" exchanges held between staff and users, a more collective type of study has also contributed to an assessment of building up the notion of service quality. The four researchers involved in this effort have insisted on the misalignments relative to each actor's set of references. On the one hand, user requests tend to lack technical understanding while emphasising personal or familial references; yet on the other hand, the relevant legislation and standardised software applications tend to present a narrow framework for the corresponding legal or institutional expression. In their conclusion, the authors recommended a much more systemic perspective [15].

Lastly, and in the same vein, Philippe Corcuff has analysed the interactions taking place at the reception desk in two CAF offices; his work is entitled: "Institutional order, smoothness and compassion". His aim has been to explore several types of inversions encountered in the typical asymmetry exhibited between agents and recipients. He first focused on users' "manoeuvring room" and then on what he termed the compassion mode displayed by the reception agents; he refers herein to those instances when agents feel a surge of responsibility towards the recipients' distress [16].

The counterpoint can be provided by Pierre Strobel, head of the CNAF's research department. In the conclusion he draws from a summary of the latest research work, which was published under the title "The user, the customer and the citizen: What are their respective roles in modernising the public service?", his objective is to specify the limits of a modernisation strategy heavily driven by user considerations. He starts by pointing out that "the upside-down organisational pyramid championed by the public-sector 'modernisers' which consists of better satisfying the user-customer, cannot be implemented without difficulty and even in some cases without obstacles". He goes on to recall that the function of administering always connotes dominating, despite the persistence of conflicts arising between service relationship and public authority expression, the persistence of the principle of bureaucratic legitimacy, and the difficulty of the compromise existing between regulatory constraints, bureaucratic principles and service relationships [17].

Why then, despite this body of work, have user-related references continued to proliferate? Wouldn't it be possible to consider that: "If the user is being implicated into all sorts of regulation, it's undoubtedly due to the fact that he has become necessary to the proposed service by justifying not only the concept of a unitary production basis, but also its subsequent legitimacy, as a means of compensating for the lack of clear policy perspectives?" [18].

4.   The Trials and Tribulations of Equal Representation

Can equal representation, one of the particularities of organisations entrusted with overseeing welfare transfer payments, provide a complementary response to the issue of quality in public action? Yet, just what kind of equal representation is being considered here? While the Social Security system has remained tagged by this reference, the interpretation has less to do with arithmetic than it has with politics. Equal representation today has come to be practically interchangeable with all forms of joint management, based on some notion of social democracy, whether with or without an elective framework.

Recent research has broached this issue of equal representation from an overall perspective. Gilles Pollet and Didier Renard, in particular, have highlighted the employer-sided origin of equal representation. In the management of supplementary pension plans, employers would in fact have sought to protect, by these means, the autonomy of the very institutions they had helped to create [19].

With respect to the CAF, rather than being swallowed up by the Social Security system, as outlined in the unification principle issued in 1945, historical research has indeed shown how these entities were able to impose on General De Gaulle a separate system, which was then consolidated in 1946. At that time, support for the CAF was not at all in short supply: a political party, called the Popular Republican Movement (Christian Democrats); a workers' union, the French Confederation of Christian Workers ("CFTC"); the National Union of

Family Associations ("UNAF"); and the entire Catholic family movement. Against such a favourable backdrop, the pro-family proponents, a group which cannot be easily categorised either with employers or with labour organisations even though some linkages do exist in both directions, were able to win a seat on the CAF Board of Directors. As a result, family action-sponsored elected representatives were voted in during the 1940's and particularly in 1947, when they held over a quarter of all seats. Others were named as members or experts, usually in recognition of some merit of distinction. For the most left-leaning organisations, such as the Popular Movement of Families, the impetus lied not only in defending the subsidy-recipient families, but also in winning seats for a maximum number of women, especially mothers [20], [21].

It wasn't until 1967 that the public authorities would impose equal representation; this move instituted an identical number of representatives from both employers and employees (with a total of 18 seats) and replaced the elective system by a trade union-backed nomination procedure. In keeping with this narrow conception of equal representation, the elected family representation would disappear per se, with the exception of a few representatives and alternates appointed by the UNAF and UDAF. At this time, the pro-family proponents were rejecting the notion of equal representation and were demanding a three-party CAF management scheme; their demands were not met. Despite their minority status between 1967 and 1982, they would be able to retain the presidency of 24 CAF offices and the vice-presidency of another 22 out of a total of 87. Officially, since 1982, equal representation is no longer the rule and the electoral process has once again replaced the practice of nominations. Consequently, a family college has begun reappearing on these CAF boards, provided that the elected representative himself is a recipient.

Throughout the experience of family welfare agencies, the question of whether or not the family representation constitutes something distinct from the employees' representation, with respect to employers, is indeed a valid one. Put otherwise, should equal representation, a generic institutional form ascribed to this type of joint management, be set up with two or three components? Regardless of the response, both the CNAF and CAF still enjoy very special relationships with the organised family movements within the UNAF and UDAF, as well as with the Catholic family movement. The UNAF, as the institutional representation of families, continues to advocate a dual political and ethical approach towards social protection, in contrast with the surrounding economic-driven context. Depending on the family movement, the representation of users on Boards of Directors must go beyond the voicing of complaints and discussing the mood at the reception desk. And the CFTC is still presiding over the CNAF. It therefore seems likely that a legitimate role will continue to be given to families, in their capacity not only as beneficiaries, but also as solidarity-nurturing entities for both welfare recipients and the needy (spouses and children) and as an organised and representative group. Herein most assuredly lies a source of legitimacy-building for the organisation, which does not necessarily want to see it go untapped.

5.   The Effectiveness of Representation Entities

An analysis of the changes in both the techniques and issues involved in an equal management scheme have provided other interesting insights. While these organisations very closely resemble public services that associate certain intermediary bodies with their administration, how then, over the course of meetings and work sessions, are management objectives actually set by the various interested parties? Is it necessary to accept the thesis whereby equal representation, whose pros and cons are by now well known, would be in the process of becoming a formalism or a rite?

A few exceptional research efforts have been aimed at assessing the effectiveness of this institutional mechanism. These efforts contribute to a better understanding of how equal representation actually functions on a Board of Directors. They have also sought to evaluate the types of legitimacy and discourse adopted by the various representatives seated around the table.

Laurent Duclos has focused on exploring how equal representation-related functions within one of the Paris Region's CAF offices [22], before going on to draw more general lessons in conjunction with Olivier Mériaux [23]. Luc-Henri Choquet, who has conducted an examination of the subsidies for single parents, also provides some indications on decision-making processes [24]. Both of these researchers seek to understand how these entities jointly produce an organisation that's dedicated to serving beneficiaries, while at the same time remaining so removed from them.

Laurent Duclos offers a definition of equal representation that he distinguishes from simple parity, as the institutional and legally-sanctioned accommodation of the interests of both labour and capital which extends the principle of equality between employers and employees, in spite of their economic inequalities.

Equal representation would thus encompass all organisations exhibiting the following characteristics: permanence; involvement in the functioning of institutions which have been assigned public interest missions by the State; recognition of a formal correlation for those organisations which have been granted a status and which meet legal requirements in terms of representation; and evidence of the principle of interdependence among the interests generated by this set-up. In the example of the CNAF/CAF, the equally-represented organisations, which fulfil these various criteria easily, are included in the institutions' public interest management. Acceptance of a political dialogue with the State is thus granted, from a sort of French-styled neo-corporate posture.

Within this approach, the issue of the family and pro-family proponents still remains unanswered. For Laurent Duclos, according to his presentation at a GAPP seminar [25], the State in effect elevated the family to the rank of public interest following the Second World War, a feature which explains the effort to incorporate a number of its actors, by means of institutionalising the differences in their interests. However, the family, engulfed in the notion of Social Security and then in that of family policy, would in reality only be one means of expression among others in handling the capital/labour relationship. He went on to add that the representation of the UNAF has always been a topic of controversy. This point raises an important debate.

With equal representation, the system would have thus produced a new actor, the organisation. From this point forward, according to the analysis, the type of skills held by administrators is to be dependent upon the office's accreditation, and the distinction in skill level is actually performed by multiplying the number of commissions. The consensus has certainly been reached to ensure the durability of this organisation's institutional presence. The mission of socialisation has disappeared; equal representation has waned and can only be found at the upper echelons, instead of at the grass roots where it began.

For Laurent Duclos, the system is not functioning appropriately because of its lack of resistance. It has become too smooth, too flexible, too expeditious. There is a shortfall of objects for rallying all parties (employers, trade unions and family political movements) around the task at hand. It is quite clear that the strength of equal representation was at the origin of inciting this interest in "sitting at the table". For Pierre Laroque, "equal representation makes no sense in that it fosters mediation at the local level which is supposed to be handled between the State and society. (Yet) this project apparently turned out to be somewhat of a failure for the Social Security". Can it still serve today for a sector-by-sector re-appropriation? Can the family sector be satisfied by a neutral and transparent operator for managing the portion of redistribution it has been assigned, and erratically at that, by the State apparatus? The author is obviously not able to answer these questions in the affirmative.

Conclusion

In light of the political, technical and relational complexity inherent in the CNAF/CAF system and in spite of the institution's obvious drive to introduce tangible environmental improvements and to move towards a certain quality in the service relationship, including the application of regular self-evaluations, users nonetheless do not constitute an operationally homogeneous group. Their initial social situation serves to differentiate them and sort them into a hierarchy; afterwards, their handling by the institution serves to differentiate and sort them yet again. Under such conditions, the question can be raised whether this formulation, in its intermediate and hybrid form positioned between the system enrolee and the customer, is still the most appropriate for basing the quality of public action. The answer is no, if a de facto equivalence is allowed to develop between user and customer; a yes answer would necessitate not overlooking the role of citizenry in the user issue [26].

Should this type of reasoning continue to be applied, the conditions required for the practical effectiveness of user-based regulation remain unanswered; in this respect, the experience of the CAF offices can prove to be most useful. How is it possible to avoid reducing public service users, whether by analysis or by actual practices, to the status of simple service recipients, i.e. separated and sent back to their narrow specific interests? This situation is revealed to some extent in the two typologies being employed by the CNAF. In contrast, how can users be expected to act in an ethical manner, with respect for fellow users, and even more by making every effort, beyond their set of individual and legitimate interests, to defend the collective interest and encourage solidarity in all aspects of social protection? How can the transition be made from self-utility to stronger user relationships [27]? Beyond mere administrative learning, the real problem to be raised is that of political learning.

Equal representation is certainly one of the most historical forms of collectively organising and regulating this joint production, especially in the CAF and CNAF institutions. Yet, it's a form which is on the decline. The basics to decision-making would seem to be outside the bounds of its "social magistrate", except at the fringes; the professionalism of representatives hardly incites an efficient social representation. Nonetheless, the example of the CAF remains rich in terms of a singular partnership, that of the family movement since the post-World War period and, through this movement, the associative and voluntary representation of so-called user or beneficiary families. Regardless of the political evaluation rendered of this situation in favour of families, the issue of the representation of certain fundamental social groupings, beside the individualised welfare recipients [28], is to be raised more generally. How then can the quality of public service be based otherwise? [29]

References

[1]   V. Bussat and M. Chauvière, Les intérêts familiaux à l'épreuve d'une comparaison France-Angleterre. Étude sur les enjeux d'une catégorie d'action publique, GAPP, rapport pour la CNAF, 1997, 185 pages.

[2]   A. Catrice-Lorey, La Sécurité sociale en France, institution anti-paritaire?, *La revue de l'IRES*, **24** (1997), printemps-été, 81-105.

[3]   M. Chauvière, Équité, mon beau souci ! Enjeux non économiques de la réforme des allocations familiales, *Sociétés et Représentations*, CREDHESS, 1999, 13 p., (forthcoming).

[4]   I. Joseph and G. Jeannot (eds.), Métiers du public, les compétences de l'agent et l'espace de l'usager, CNRS éditions, Paris, 1995.

[5]   D. Debordeaux, Les allocataires et leur caisse d'allocations familiales, *Recherches et Prévisions*, CNAF, **34** (1993) 1-8.

[6]   N. Bardaille and J.-L. Outin, Les allocataires et leurs caisses d'allocations familiales. L'accès aux prestations à l'épreuve des inégalités. SET, Université de Paris 1, rapport de recherche pour la CNAF, 1992, 146 p.; See also: Logique de besoins et logique d'usage. Caisse d'allocations familiales et typologie des allocataires, *Espace et familles*, CNAF, **29**, 133 p.

[7]   P. Strobel, Services publics et cohésion sociale, *Recherches et Prévisions*, CNAF, **42** (1995), décembre, xxx.

[8]   G. Martin, Les CAF et le RMI, *Recherches et Prévisions*, CNAF, **34** (1993), 9-16.

[9]   A. Caizzi, A. Quiroga and J.-F. Riondel, Une enquête sur les usagers des CAF dits "à faible autonomie administrative", *Recherches et Prévisions*, **50/51** (1997/98) 129-142.

[10]   Séminaire du GAPP (1997/98), Problématiser les intérêts familiaux?. In: M. Chauvière (ed.), unpublished.

[11]   I. Joseph, G. Jeannot, *op. cit.*

[12]   J. Gautrat, J.-L. Laville, Gros plan sur la modernisation du service public: le cas de la CAF de l'Ariège. CRIDA, rapport pour la CNAF, 1991, 96 pages. See also: *Espace et familles*, CNAF, **22**, Modernisation du service public. L'expérience de la caisse d'allocation familiale de l'Ariège, 111 p.

[13]   A. Boisset, M. Dartevelle, L'offre d'information en CAF de Lyon et de Creil. Organisation des communications avec les usagers et compétences des agents d'accueil au téléphone et en face à face. ARIESE, rapport pour la CNAF, 1995, 200 p. See also: *Espace et familles*, CNAF, **34**, Le dialogue entre agents et usagers. L'accueil téléphonique et dans les locaux des caisses d'allocations familiales, 147 p.

[14]   V. Dubois, Une institution redéfinie par ses usage(r)s?, *Recherches et Prévisions*, CNAF, **54** (1996) septembre, 5-13.

[15]   G. Vallery, M.-A. Bonnefoy, R. Eksi, J. Tedesco, Les échanges "difficiles" techniciens-allocataires ou comment se construit la qualité de service, *Recherches et Prévisions* septembre, CNAF, **54** (1996) 15-26.

[16]   Ph. Corcuff, Ordre institutionnel, fluidité situationnelle et compassion, *Recherches et Prévisions* 54 (1996), septembre, 27-35.

[17]   P. Strobel, L'usager, le client et le citoyen: quels rôles dans la modernisation du service public?, *Recherches et Prévisions*, CNAF, **32** (1993), juin, 31-44.

[18]   M. Chauvière, J.T. Godbout (eds.), Les usagers entre marché et citoyenneté. L'Harmattan, Paris, 1992.

[19]   G. Pollet, D. Renard, Le paritarisme et la protection sociale. Origines et enjeux d'une forme institutionnelle, *La revue de l'IRES*, **24** (1997), printemps-été, 61-80.

[20]   M. Chauvière, De la sphère familiale à la sphère publique. La construction sociale de l'usager par un mouvement familial durant les années quarante et ses contradictions. In: M. Chauvière, J.T. Godbout (eds.), Les usagers entre marché et citoyenneté. *Op. cit.*, pp. 93-120.

[21]   M. Chauvière, Du bon usage des usagers et des familles usagères. Essai de classement. In: GRMF, La solidarité en actes. Services collectifs et expression des usagers dans le Mouvement populaire des familles. 1940-1955, *Les cahiers du GRMF* **11** (1999), (forthcoming).

[22]   L. Duclos, Paritarisme des conseils d'administration des caisses d'allocations familiales. La médiation des instances de représentation dans la production des services publics, GIP Mutations industrielles, rapport de recherche pour la CNAF, 1996, 118 p.

[23]   L. Duclos and O. Mériaux, Pour une économie du paritarisme, *La revue de l'IRES* **24** (1997), printemps-été, 43-60.

[24]   L.-H. Choquet, Législature administrative et magistrature sociale. La politique familiale de prise en compte des cas de rupture familiale (1970-1995), ADRESSE, rapport pour la CNAF, 1996, 138 p.

[25]   Séminaire du GAPP, *op. cit.*

[26]   Chauvière, J.T. Godbout, *op. cit.*

[27]   M. Chauvière, Le champ familial. Des usagers aux rapports sociaux d'usage. In: Ph. Warin (ed.), Quelle modernisation des services publics? Les usagers au cœur des réformes. La Découverte, Paris, 1997, pp. 221-242.

[28]   G. Jeannot, Les usagers du service public. PUF, Que sais-je?, n° 3359, Paris, 1998.

[29]   Ph. Warin (ed.), Quelle modernisation des services publics? Les usagers au cœur des réformes. La Découverte, Paris, 1997.

Citizenship and Policy-Making in the Netherlands: the limits of an interactive approach

Monique Esselbrugge*

1.   Introduction

Decision-making about the need and necessity of infrastructure projects is subject to criticism in several European countries. The discussion is no longer only evolving around the question of which projects should be realised. The question of how these processes should be organised and managed is also part of the discussion. The problems related to decision-making about infrastructure issues are well-known. Firstly, most projects are very expensive and government is blamed for being incapable of working efficiently. Secondly, it takes a long time to make decisions about infrastructure investments. Finally, criticism focuses on the inability of (national) government to deal with groups of citizens in an adequate way [1]. Many infrastructure investments have been facing considerable resistance from groups of citizens, groups which have become far more professional. Governments find themselves struggling between the diverging preferences of society. Infrastructure policies not only have to meet the claims of 'homo mobilis' but also must ensure a safe and clean environment. To cope with these high demands of society, the Dutch national government is redesigning decision-making processes in a more open and interactive way. New actors are invited to participate, like private organisations, citizens-groups and individuals. For example, the process called "Verkenningsfase Ruimteprobleem Mainport Rotterdam (VERM)" (Exploration phase shortage of space mainport Rotterdam Habour) was developed in a more open and interactive way. Interactive decision-making can be seen as an innovation in the decision-making processes, like public-private partnerships and creative competition [2].

These innovations are examples of serious reforms of Dutch public administration, both at local and national level. The process-innovations are part of the concept or model known as "New Public Management" (NPM). The reform of the public administration is linked with a wider package designed to reshape and reduce the state, to reform of the public industrial sector, including liberalisation, deregulation, privatisation and tax reform [3]. The reforms started with the necessity to perform the public tasks with less money, which forced the public sector to move towards public management [4]. Nowadays it is concluded that we are dealing with "a new paradigm for public management, aiming at fostering a performance-oriented culture in a less centralised public sector" [5]. No longer was an inefficient working method the only motive for reforming public administration, but also the inability of (national) government to deal with groups of citizens in an adequate way.

In contrast with the still developing field of institutional analyses, which focuses on the institutions which characterise the Dutch administrative-system, this contribution is focusing on the "process" of decision-making. Especially, on the "innovations" in the process of

---
* Monique Esselbrugge, Department of Public Administration, Erasmus University, Rotterdam, the Netherlands

decision-making, called interactive decision-making, which are developed to deal with different group of citizens and their often conflicting demands.

In the Netherlands it is recognised that government is no longer the central governing authority in society. Rather than depending on traditional hierarchical forms of organisation, public managers are experimenting with flatter structures and more participatory ways of organising. Government, nowadays, has to deal with different categories of actors and therefore a more transparent style of decision-making is demanded. It is assumed that policy making of any significance should be the result of interactions between public and private partners. Policy- or decision-making becomes a process in which different preferences and several actors have to be inter-twined to reach an acceptable compromise. In this perspective New Public Management can be seen as interdependency management, like network or process management. This assumption can be found in the so-called "governance club" [6]. This Dutch approach points to a model of public management in which actors seek actively to manage interdependence by promoting networks capable of creating new ways of acting. The common thought is that more open, participatory and interactive methods of decision-making will be able to cope with a variety of actors and their often conflicting opinions, preferences and claims. However, these new ways of decision-making seem to generate some tensions.

This chapter will attempt to give an answer to these questions: Are the open, participatory and interactive decision-making processes able to deal with (groups of) citizens and their often conflicting preferences in an adequate way? And does this mean that the closed structure will become history, or does it maybe also represent an important value? When the latter is true, and in this contribution it is so stated, then a new topical subject in public administration emerges. Decision-making is open and closed simultaneously.

2.   Interactive decision-making

2.1. Process innovation

The world is moving at an ever increasing pace, and change and complexity are commonplace. Under these circumstances, public managers are coming to recognise that maintaining control is far less important than encouraging creativity and change [7]. For this reason, they are shifting their focus from "giving orders" to "promoting dialogue and innovation". In addition, in order to achieve their goals, actors in networks need to participate in interactions between actors which develop around issues in which they have an interest [8]. Process innovations like co-governance, negotiating government, interactive policy making or co-production, illustrate the increasing awareness in practice of this need for consulting and co-operation. More and more governmental bodies are convinced that complex public issues, like infrastructure, cannot be solved alone. The classical vision on government, where problems were seen as solvable and manageable by the public authorities, is over. Policy making will have to originate from interaction and negotiation with other involved actors, both on the local and national levels.

The alternative approach that public managers have chosen has been inspired by innovative private sector organisations. Osborne and Gaebler (1992) analysed the characteristics of management that made these organisations successful [9]. Examples of these characteristics are:

1. They empower citizens by pushing control out of the bureaucracy, into the community;
2. They measure the performance of their agencies, focusing not on the inputs but on the outcomes;
3. They decentralise authority, embracing participatory management.

These characteristics can be recognised in New Public Management approaches, which are more open, participatory and interactive.

The new open ways of decision-making in the public sector can be covered by the term "interactive policy". Interactive policy can be defined as: *"a process to form a common conception, towards a collective policy practice in a network of mutual dependent participants"* [10]. The three main concepts in this definition are: mutal dependent actors, common conception and a collective policy practice [11]:

A) Mutual dependent actors: interactive refers to decision-making as an interactive process between public and private partners. Therefore, the concept of interactive decision-making is inextricably bound up with a network society. After all, in a context were one single actor can decide alone, co-production does not seem very fruitful. In a network there are no actors who have power over the others. No single person has control over all the resources necessary to carry out his own goals or preferences. Each actor has a specific resource at his disposal, for example: expertise, support or money. All of these resources are essential in the decision-making process. This means that actors in a network are mutually dependent. However, this does not imply that actors are of equal merit. There are, of course, differences in power. Teisman (1995) speaks of asymmetrical relations [12].

B) Common conception: as stated, actors differ in opinions, claims, problem formulation(s) and ideas about possible solution(s). All actors have different views of reality. It is therefore of great importance that actors in a process of interactive decision-making reformulate their perspective and come to a common conceptualisation about the problem, possible solutions and the role that each participant should play in the process. It is of relevance that actors can freely and openly speak about their preferences and opinions, without prioritising them immediately. The process should institutionalise an open debate in which preferences and opinions can be considered. Furthermore, it is important that actors recognise something of their influence and contribution in the final outcome and are able to identify themselves with the outcome.

C) Collective policy practice: interactive policy-making assumes that in the end a (collectively chosen) project will be realised. The process of developing a common conception should be followed by a collective policy practice. This collective policy practice will be different after each interactive process. An agreement or a fully public-private partnership can be concluded. In any event, interactive decision-making should result in an enrichment for all the actors involved.

Actors are involved in an early stage with co-producing problem formulations and possible solutions. The new initiatives for policy making have their origins in deadlock situations. Government was not able to solve problems by itself, and was not able to come up with solutions. Nor was it able to gain enough support for its plans. Interactive policy making seems to be the answer to dealing with a variety of demands and challenges.

2.2. Citizen involvement

When we focus on the degree of citizen involvement, Kalk [13] distinguishes different levels of involvement on his ladder of administrative renewal. The lower you go on his ladder, the more citizen involvement there will be. In the first step, citizens are only suppliers of ideas to certain policy fields. In the second step, citizens are co-producers of policies. In co-operation with local or national authorities, citizens can develop plans which eventually will be executed. In the third step, Kalk distinguishes citizen involvement as the level where citizens are (also) responsible for the agenda on a specific policy subject. Together with governmental bodies they produce problem definitions and possible solutions, which in the end, have to be approved by the political bodies. Examples of innovations in the decision-making process at local level are: citizen panels, city talks, co-production and referenda. On a local level innovations in the decision-making process were developed because there was some concern about the existence of a so-called cleavage between local government and citizens [14].

At the national level the need for interactive decision-making is particularly felt within the Ministry of Transport, Public Works and Water Management. According to Bressers, O'Toole Jr. and Richardson (1994), there are four motives for implementing more interactive forms of decision making on a national level [15]. Firstly, the implementation of plans is problematic, because these plans require decisions of actors outside the department. Also, the need of an integral approach (mobility, safety and environment incorporated) is felt within the ministry. Due to this integral approach the transport sector becomes increasingly dependent on other actors. Thirdly, actors outside the sector take decisions, which have a great impact on the possibilities of the transport system. Finally, the Ministry of Transport, Public Works and Water Management has adopted the policy that decision making should be done in an interactive way.

Within the above-mentioned Ministry we can distinguish three approaches to interactive decision making: the chain approach, the open-planning approach and the Infralab method. All new initiatives share characteristics of a more open-planning style in which policy making is the result of interaction with different categories of actors. Most interactive planning experiments are done in the field of motorways and highways.

To give an idea on how the concept of interactive policy works in practice the infralab-approach will be described.

Infralab was established in 1993 by Rijkswaterstaat (RWS), the engineering unit of the Department of Transport, Public Works and Water Management. Infralab is a platform where, in interaction with citizens, new methods and new ideas are developed. This infralab-approach is now known as "interactive planning". In 1993 the infralab-experiment started with the "vague" belief that interactive processes could gain more support from society than with traditional (closed) decision-making systems. Also they thought that the process would proceed faster than previously and would lead to better decisions. RWS formulated three central principles. Firstly, the opinion of the end-user is the most important. Secondly, co-operation between government and citizens throughout the process is obligatory. Thirdly, they agreed on a time limit of one year. The substance of the working method is that individuals (end-users) are involved in an early phase of the policy-making process and that they can speak out from their own background and knowledge. Their input should have an impact on the outcome of the process. The method is separated in the three following stages: problem formulation (stemfase), quest for possible solutions (agorafase) and finally the designing of the chosen solution (project) by co-makers (actiefase). Co-makers refer to experts who have a role or task in developing, using or managing the chosen solution.

So, citizens can be vital co-producers of decisions or policies, both at the local and national levels. The government no longer acts as an agent presenting a finished product or project to the citizen, but governmental bodies and citizens together produce the desired transformation.

2.3. Tensions

It became clear that the rationality of central government was limited and that it could not control society itself. Therefore, the traditional, more closed, decision-making processes did not seem very suitable in a context in which there were more participants involved, with their own views of reality, and none with enough steering ability to determine the strategies of the others.

Characteristics of a more closed policy style are a single, defined problem-formulation, anchored in one-sided, formulated aims [16]. In a network society, such as the Netherlands, in the field of infrastructure policies, there is a growing need to steer on the basis of a common conception of a collective policy practise. This requires a more open policy style, which is based on the assumption of plurality. Steering or governing is seen as an interaction process between a diversity of actors, from governmental agencies to individual citizens. This is why the government decided on a more open, participatory and interactive way to organise decision making. Thus, openness is seen as a reaction to a closed approach. At the same time, is should be recognised that other actors, like private organisations, interests groups and individual citizens are also faced with considerable limitations, particularly in terms of resources and instruments at their disposal and within their cognitive competence. These more open and interactive ways have their limitations. This should be considered whenever a process of decision making is designed in an interactive way.

The tendency towards more openness in the decision-making process generates some tensions which can be explained in terms of an open and a closed approach. In this section four fields of tensions between an open and a closed approach will be distinguished.

Firstly, we can observe a tension in the field of actors. Openness in this field implies that all relevant actors will be involved in the process of decision making [17]. This is necessary because otherwise, when certain actors are excluded, they will try to block the process. Or more positively formulated, a variety of actors is preferable because these actors have certain resources at their disposal, as also a specific expertise necessary to formulate a solution.

However, by doing so the number of actors will increase. The involved actors all have their own ideas about the problem and possible solution(s). This will lead to a more complex process, which results in uncertainty about the outcome(s) of the process. It also seems that a closed approach represents an important value in this field.

Secondly, we can distinguish a tension in the field of perceptions which refers to the inclusion of a variety of opinions and interpretations. This is advisable from a democratic point of view, due to the fact that in a democratic society we should (re)consider all opinions and interpretations which are existing in society. Also, openness in the field of perceptions is desirable to reach a higher quality with respect to the content of the process [17,18]. However, continuous openness in this field also creates risks. It can lead to a confusion of languages, impractical ideas and a multitude of perceptions that can result in not seeing what really counts. Again, a closed approach seems to be preferable under certain conditions.

Thirdly, there is a tension in the field of information, which is a very important resource for the decision-making process. Openness in the field of information is needed to come to well-considered decisions. Actors have access to different kinds of information and most of this information should be considered in solving a problem adequately. The confrontation between these different kinds of information can increase the quality of the information used. However, openness can lead to an overload, or again to incomplete information and thus to non transparency. This means that the actors involved in the process cannot deal with the huge and diverse amount of information; they cannot distinguish relevant information from details of minor importance. Nevertheless, decisions have to be made. In such situations the process should focus on reducing the risks which are at stake by making decisions. This means a closed approach is necessary at some time during the process.

The last field of tension between openness and a closed approach can be found in the field of decision-making moments. This field is of a different order because you can find the other three fields of tension within one or more decision-making moments. This field refers to the coupling between the several decisions made during the process and between the final outcome of the process and the activities following. For example, the interactive moment in the process is linked with the formal political decision-making moment. In the Netherlands the outcome of an interactive process is still an informal document, as the formal decision is still taken by political bodies. Tensions between this interactive form of decision making and the formal procedures can easily appear. It seems necessary to give a clear description about how (part of) these decisions will be coupled, as also the (legal) status of the outcome of open, interactive processes.

These tensions illustrate that both openness and a closed approach are valuable in the decision-making process. Because continuous openness does have its risks: confusion of languages, slackening, impractical ideas, etc. The possibility exists that interactivity will only lead towards inertia. Interactive methods of decision making are enormously time consuming, especially when representatives need to run back and forth between their supporter groups and the interactive meetings. Anyway; "...*Now, when the number of participants is much larger, this sort of complete agreement can be to our disadvantage. It becomes much harder to reach agreement when more people are involved. Attempting to get hundreds of people to reach consensus is usually exhausting and often impossible*" [19]. Therefore, we should recognise that a closed approach within the process also has value. Considering, only a limited number of actors, preferences and means implies that a single, unambiguous, problem definition can be given.

3.   Theoretical framework

3.1. Open and closed approaches

Referring to the four fields of tensions between open and closed approaches, it can be imagined that a decision-making process is open and closed simultaneously. Because, it seems to be possible that a decision-making moment can be characterised, for example, by an open appraoch in the field of actors and a closed approach in the field of perceptions. This can be the case when all relevant actors are invited to participate, but during the process are only allowed to talk about a predetermined problem definition or solution / project. If a decision-making process is both open and closed simultaneously, then a new theme in public administration is generated: the question of open and closed approaches. What are the consequences of organising (process-architecture) and managing (process-management) decision making on the basis of the simultaneous inclusion of open and closed approaches in a decision-making process?

To get a better understanding about the concept of openness we need to reflect on the concept of a closed approach. Network theorists are using a wide variety of interpretations of the concept of a "closed approach". However, a number of questions are still left unanswered, for example: What causes a closed appraoch and how can it be recognised in a (traditional) decision-making process?

The closed approach exists in the four distinguished fields where tensions can occur. Those four fields are based on the following questions: who (actors), what (perceptions), how (information) and when (moments)? We can then speak about a closed approach when the decision-making process is restricted for actors who wants to participate, notably when: some perceptions are not debatable, not all relevant information is freely exchangeable, and the coupling of decision-moments is predetermined (see table 1). Therefore, open and closed appraoches are pluri-dimensional concepts.

Table 1: Typology of open and closed approaches

Field of tension	Open approach	Closed approach
Actors	The entry of actors into the process is free from restrictions	The entry of actors is restricted
Perceptions	All perceptions can be subject to debate and are considered during the process	Some perceptions are excluded for debate and some are not considered
Information	All relevant information for the process is exchangeable (available and accessible)	Some information is not exchangeable during the process
Moments	The linkage with adjacent decision making is allowed	The linkage with adjacent decision making is predetermined

The presumption is that open moments in the decision-making process are favourable to generating a variety of actors, themes, perceptions, expertise and information, etc. by which it then becomes possible to think more carefully and in-depth about the formulation of the problem(s) and the(ir) possible solution(s). On the other hand, the closed approach is more appropriate in providing a single problem formulation because the closed approach reduces the number of actors, the variety of perceptions and the amount of information [20]. This is necessary to start debate on possible solutions in the decision-making process. It is more a matter of considering when the open approach is dysfunctional and the closed approach is functional (and in reverse order). So, both the open approach, as well as the closed, represent important values in (interactive) decision-making processes. Before conceptualising as to when open/closed approaches are (dys)functional in the process of decision making, it is important to distinguish the different types and causes relative to the closed approach. An examination of the closed approach will cover both the theory and practice. First, an examination of a closed approach is presented in an empirical case; The process of decision making by the Delft - Schiedam National Highway.

Case: A4 Delft - Schiedam National Highway

The decision-making process of the A4 Delft – Schiedam National Highway, in the Netherlands, has a long history which started in the late 1950s. In those days, the first plans for a second connection between The Hague and Rotterdam were drawn up. Already in 1965, the Cabinet had decided to construct the highway, but even now the highway is still not built. In this process, it seems impossible for all of the actors to look in the same direction. This does not seem very surprising, because the highway would sever the "Midden Delfland" countryside and cuts into too the residential areas in the cities of Vlaardingen and Schiedam. Environmental values, mobility and liveability are playing a major role in the decision-making process. Until now, this (value-)pluriformity has ended in a long, chaotic process. It is important to see how processes like this are advanced and how they can be improved to meet the high demands of society in the 21ˢᵗ century.

The plans to construct the A4 Delft – Schiedam Highway were primarily motivated by the concern that the main ports of Rotterdam and Schiphol would no longer be easy to reach without a junction on the main road between The Hague and Rotterdam. According to "Rijkswaterstaat" extra asphalt was the solution, manifested in the A4 Delft – Schiedam National Highway. This perception of RWS did not have to be a problem. However, when RWS was confronted with other often conflicting perceptions, for example the environmental issues which became an issue in the middle of the 1970s, it became a problem. After a calm beginning to the decision-making process, a period of societal protest started. Public support seemed to have vanished and power was mobilised to obstruct the project. It was no longer responsible to have a one-sided focus on traffic, also environmental values had to be included. However, representatives of environmental values were excluded from the decision-making process. Therefore, the different points of view were radicalised. The environmentalists chose to take juridical action to oppose the building of the highway. In this way they were able to delay construction for several years. Many new actors became involved in the decision-making process, such as the local authorities, provincial-level authorities, private organisations and individuals. They all had their own perception of reality and therefore differed in their problem definition and in finding possible solutions. Another round of debates started, notably to do with the catchword 'inpassing', which meant that the road should fit into its surroundings, that investments in infrastructure should go hand in hand with efficient use of space and spatial quality. Within this perspective many new initiatives were launched to accommodate the diverging and often conflicting claims. Nevertheless, the RWS and its Ministry did not change their one-sided problem definition and stated, even today, that extra asphalt was the only solution to coping with the traffic problem on the main road between

The Hague and Rotterdam. Therefore, the A4 Delft – Schiedam National Highway should be built.

The sketch of the decision-making process presented above can teach us some valuable lessons in terms of the closed approach. Already in the beginning of the process the RWS, the initiator of the process, monopolised the problem definition, objective and solution. Indeed, these are the characteristics of traditional and closed decision-making processes [20]. From a traffic point of view, the RWS perceived the problem that the two main ports would no longer be accessible in future years. Their objective was to resolve this problem with a second highway between The Hague and Rotterdam: the A4 Delft – Schiedam highway. The RWS did not consider other possible preferences, claims and interests due to their frame of reference. When other points of view originate in society, such as an environmental perspective, the RWS was not able (unconscious) or unwilling (conscious) to reconsider their one-sided formulated problem definition or their chosen solution. It seemed to be a well-known strategy of the RWS because they excluded all environmental representatives. Because the representatives were excluded form the decision-making process, they had to choose other strategies to influence. They started a protest campaign and legal proceedings. This resulted in a radicalisation of viewpoints. In the debate concerning the "inpassing" of the A 4 Delft – Schiedam highway, we can also observe the closed approach. Although most participants were willing to communicate with each other, other alternatives were never a serious subject of debate. After all, the RWS was not willing to debate their problem definition and solution. The different closed approaches can explain the long duration and chaotic debate. In this process, the open and closed approaches, which both characterise the process-architecture, were not managed adequately and therefore the process ended in a stalemate.

3.2. A conceptualisation

In this section a theoretical examination of the closed approach will be explored. In the literature on networks, we can find several insights into the closed approach and policy networks (e.g. Rhodes, 1980; Jordan, 1990; Schaap and van Twist, 1997; De Bruijn and Ten Heuvelhof 1991, 1998). In keeping with Schaap and van Twist [21] we can distinguish the closed approach of separate actors and the closed approach involved in networking processes. In other words, there is an internal and external perspective to the conceptualisation of a closed approach. The Internal perspective relatives to the individual actor (within the actor) and the external perspective may be seen in policy-network process (within the process or network). It may be possible that an individual decides not to co-operate or to participate, because he or she does not want to commit him/herself to the outcome of the process (internal). It is also possible that the individual is willing to participate but is excluded form the process because the actors already involved want to keep such a complex process manageable (external).

Closedness can be the result of a conscious strategy or of an unconsciously applied rule. For instance, in the field of actors the exclusion of actors can be caused by not knowing the jargon. Regarding the benefit- and-necessity discussions by decision-making processes of major infrastructural projects you see the exclusion of local people due to the jargon pragmatic civil servants use in terms of noise standards and risk contours. This results in *a unconsciously extern closedness in the field of actors* caused by the culture of the policy network or process. A conscious strategy from a internal perspective is present when actors use their power. For instance, the actor is not prepared to provide another actor with resources and therefore refuses to interact. Within this example you can discover the intertwining of different closed approaches: *the conscious internal closed approach in the field of information* (resource) causes *the conscious internal closed approach in the field of actors.* An example of the latter is, for example, when the actor finds the transaction costs too high and therefore excludes himself from the process; he is not willing to interact. To summarise briefly (table 2), it may be stated that the closed approach may be caused by:

Table 2

Perspective	Dimension	Fields of tensions		
		Actors	**Perceptions**	**Information**
Internal	Conscious	Rational choice by the actor	Unwillingness to perceive	Unwillingness to exchange / power-oriented
	Unconscious	Standard operating procedures	Inability to perceive	Inability to exchange
External	Conscious	Entry of actors are made formally, verifiably	Points of discussion are predetermined	Exchange-Ability is formally arranged
	Unconscious	Cultural frameworks within which networks are constructed	Group-think processes	Information is perceived as being unimportant

To give one more example we focus on *the internal conscious strategy to exclude some problem-definitions or possible solutions* form the discussion during the process. Sometimes actors are unwilling to perceive certain points of view. This is the case when actors declare a particular problem-formulation to be out of order. Phrases such as: "we're not discussing that now", or: "you can't consider every angle" are symptomatic of this [21]. The closed approach is present because participants are fixed on one view or perspective of the problem or possible solutions and are unwilling to debate other views.

This conceptualisation of the closed approach can be used to analyse complex decision-making processes. Types of closed approaches can occur within the network or be used by the actor on three different fields and in different decision-moments, both conscious and unconscious. After analysing the processes of decision-making, it becomes possible to reflect on the question: How should such kinds of processes be organised and managed adequately? It seems to be intelligent when evaluating decision-making processes, to analyse which type of open or closed approaches occur during the process. Do all actors have the possibility of entering the process? Are all ideas and perceptions of problems and solutions debatable? Is the information needed exchangeable? Are decision-moments intertwined?

4.   Process evaluating criteria

Within public administration there is still a lack of emphasis on the question of how processes within networks can be organised and managed, especially the so-called interactive processes. It has been stated that such kinds of complex decision-making is simultaneously open and closed. In this contribution the position is taken that both the closed and open approach can be functional and dysfunctional inf the decision-making process. The closed approach is functional for the decision-making process when the variety of actors, perceptions and/or information is reduced, whereby it becomes possible to select one unambiguous problem-definition or a solution. In contrast, an open approach is functional when the variety of actors, perceptions and information is increased, whereby more options are generated and inter-twining aims become possible. The preconditions on which we can decide if an open or closed approach is functional is still in an exploratory phase. The line of reasoning is the following: both the open and closed approaches should be part of the process-architecture and management: an adequate mix of open and closed approachesness will lead towards a reduction in the time required and will lead to qualitatively better solutions (project-propositions).

The tensions in the process of decision-making (mentioned above) in a context of interdependencies should be managed adequately. Management is adequate when the process works well, according to three evaluation criteria:

1. Variety: the idea behind this criteria is that the process should make it possible for all involved actors to participate in the process, freely debating their formulated problem and possible solutions without prioritising them immediately. Furthermore the process should also generate a variety of information needed to come to a decision. A variety of actors, perceptions and information is desirable from a democratic point of view and because is will increase the number of options.

2. Content criteria: this evaluation criteria refers to the criteria of variety in the sense that variety should be recognised in the final outcomes. The more participants recognise their points of view in the outcome(s), the more satisfied they become; satisfied in the sense that participants consider the process and outcome of the process satisfactory in their own perception. Teisman (1992) suggests this ex post criterion: the extent to which game participants consider the interaction and the results satisfactory [12]. This criterion focuses not only on the process but also on the actors' own perspectives of reality. This evaluation criteria does justice to the dynamic character of interactive processes involving a variety of actors with different and often conflicting and changing preferences, means and demands. Participants will include in their judgement the transaction costs for joint action compared with the fulfilment of their individual goals and demands.

3. Process criteria: this criteria refers to functional open and closed approaches relative to the fields of actors, perceptions, information and moments. This means that the process should facilitate open or closed approaches whenever needed in the process.

5.   Questions for further research

The definition of public policy as the result of an interactive process between many actors, of whom only a few are government bodies, has gradually become widely accepted in policy science [22]. This also was accepted by the Dutch government which started to reform public management as from the late 1960s. Only in the early 1990s did Dutch public administration, both at the local and national levels, start experiments to innovate in the decision-making process. Co-production, interactive policy-making and public-private partnerships are expressions of these innovations in the process. The innovations are commonly expected to produce both more openness and better outcomes qualitatively. This is necessary because, governments are dealing with societies whose problems are complex, diverse and turbulent. Therefore flexible responses are required. However, there are some tensions that seem to be inherent to these kind of interactive processes. These tensions can be expressed by using such descriptors as "open" and "closed" approaches. It is stated in this contribution that open and closed approaches exist simultaneously in decision-making processes. This means a new topic in public administration has been generated, notably: the question of open and closed approaches.

To cope with tensions in more open, participatory and interactive decision-making processes there are still some questions that need to be answered. These questions are:

- when is the open approach preferable to the closed approach in the process and visa versa?;
- how can open or closed approaches be organised/facilitated by process-architecture or management?

Finding the (dynamic) balance between open and closed approaches seems to be of greatest importance in a networking society. The closed approach in decision-making processes is as valuable as the open approach.

Of course, this will have major implications on the relationship between citizens and governmental bodies. Citizens will no longer be considered only as troublesome opponents, but also as sources of creativity. Citizens should participate in decision-making processes, simply because they are interested in that particular theme, or because they have interesting ideas about the possibilities of increasing the quality of a project. At the same time, the citizens can give their opinion on several projects at crucial decision-making moments. So, decision-making needs to deal with many actors who represent partly conflicting interests in a society where space and environmental quality have become scare commodities. The decision-making *process* and how it can be improved to meet the different, high and conflicting demands of society in the 21st century is the main topic for further research in the field of public administration.

References

[1]   G.R. Teisman, What changes for transport in the next century?, paper presented at the 14th International Symposium on Theory and Practice in Transport Economics, Innbruck, 1997.

[2]   Raad voor Verkeer en Vervoer, Ambities bundelen. Lakerveld, Den Haag, 1998.

[3]   V. Wright, The Paradoxes of Administrative Reform. In: W. Kickert (ed.), Public Management and Administrative Reform in Western Europe. Elgar, Cheltenham, 1997, p.8.

[4]   W. Kickert, Public Management in the United States and Europe. In: W. Kickert (ed.), *op. cit.*, p.17.

[5]   OECD, 1995.

[6]   W. Kickert, E.-H. Klijn, J. Koppenjan, Managing Complex Networks. Sage publications, London, 1997.

[7]   R.B. Denhardt, The Pursuit of Significance. Wadsworth, California, 1993, p. 3.

[8]   G.T. Allison, The Essence of Decision: Explaining the Cuban Missile Crises. Little, Boston, 1971.

[9]   D.E. Osborne, T. Gaebler, Reinventing Government: How the Entrepreneurial Spirit is Transforming the Public Sector. Addison-Wesley, New-York, 1992.

[10]   B.A.C. Meesters, Open keuken; zoektocht naar methoden voor interactive procesaanpak, in opdracht van Rijkswaterstaat Infraplan, 1997.

[11]   G.-J. Den Haag Benou, Balancerend besturen: over co-productie in twee Brabantse steden, term paper, Tilburg, 1996, pp. 14-15.

[12]   G.R. Teisman, Complexe besluitvorming: een pluricentrisch perspectief op besluitvorming over ruimtelijke investeringen. VUGA Uitgeverij, Den Haag, 1992-95.
[13]   E. Kalk, Te veel bestuurders en te weinig volksvertegenwoordigers; Over de noodzaak van politieke vernieuwing. In: De inspraak voorbij; ervaringen van burgers en lokale bestuurders met nieuwe vormen van overleg. Lex Veldboer, IPP, Amsterdam, 1996, pp. 137-149.
[14]   R. Gilsing, R., Lokale bestuurlijke vernieuwing in Nederland, *Acta Politica*, **1** (1994) 3-33.
[15]   J.Th.A. Bressers, L.T. O' Toole jr. and J. Richardson, Networks as Models of Analysis: Water Policy in a Comparative Perspective, *Environmental politics*, **3** (1994) 1-23.
[16]   V.J.J.M. Bekkers *et al.*, Sturingsconcepties en Instrumenten in het milieubeleid: Op zoek naar vormen van co-produktie, publikatiereeks Milieustrategie, Tilburg, nr. 2, 1996.
[17]   J.A. De bruijn, E.F. ten Heuvelhof, R.J. in't Veld, Procesmanagement, Schoonhoven, Academic services, 1998.
[18]   G.R. Teisman, Sturen via creatieve concurrentie, oration, Nijmegen, 1997.
[19]   M. Douglas and A. Wildavsky, Risk and Culture: an Essay on the Selection of Technical Dangers. University of California Press, Berkeley, 1992. p. 146.
[20]   G.R. Teisman, Sturen via creatieve concurrentie, oration, Nijmegen, 1997, p. 15.
[21]   L. Schaap and M.J.W. van Twist. The Dynamics of Closedness in Networks. In: W. Kickert et al. (eds.), Managing Complex Networks. Sage publications, London, 1997, pp. 62-78.
[22]   E.H. Klijn, J.F.M. Koppenjan, C.J.A.M. Termeer, Policy and Governance in Complex Networks, working paper no. 12, Rotterdam, 1994.

Unions of Civil Servants and the Quality of Governance in France

Jeanne Siwek-Pouydesseau *

In France, unions of civil servants date right back to the beginning of this century, despite being banned. In the beginning, state officials were autonomous, before joining the *Confédération Générale du Travail (CGT)* in 1927. Between the two wars, the unions of post office workers and of local council and health service officials belonged either to the reformist CGT, with socialist leanings, or to the unitarian CGTU, with "revolutionary" leanings since 1922.

The civil service side of the *Confédération Française des Travailleurs Chrétiens (CFTC)*, which was created in the wake the First World War, developed mainly following the Liberation, and ended up by being split, in 1964, between the small remaining CFTC and the secular *Confédération Démocratique du Travail (CFDT)*, which expanded considerably.

The CGT's reunification between 1936 and 1947 was beset by many trials and tribulations and finally broke up in 1948. After this, in the main the unions of civil servants divided into the current CGT, which continued the former "unitarian" tendency, and the *CGT-Force Ouvrière (FO)* which more or less continued the former "reformist" tendency. The teachers remained autonomous in a single organisation, the *Fédération de l'Education Nationale (FEN)*, which, in 1992, ended up by being split between the remaining FEN and the *Fédération Syndicale Unitaire (FSU)* which, as its name would indicate, is attached more to the "unitarian" tradition. Since then, the FEN has linked up with other autonomous "reformist" unions of civil servants, such as policemen, or belonging to the public and private sectors, some of which recently left *Force Ouvrière* to form the *Union Nationale des Syndicats Autonomes (UNSA)*.

Finally, various dissenting trade unions joined forces in the not-yet-officially-recognised *Groupe des Dix*, which essentially includes the *Syndicat Unifié des Impôts (SNUI)* and minority trade unions with more or less leftist tendencies from the CFDT, under the label *Solidaires, Unitaires, Démocratiques (SUD)* [1].

* Jeanne Siwek-Pouydesseau, Directeur de recherche au CNRS, France

The chart of trade unionism and its evolution in France is therefore particularly fragmented:

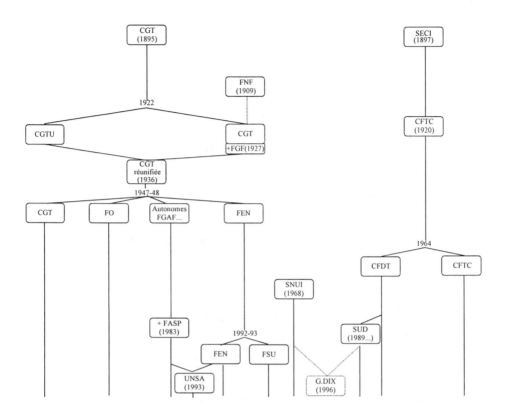

To attempt to simplify, at the risk of caricaturing the situation, I make the distinction between a dissenting faction, which currently includes the CGT, FO, FSU and the *Groupe des Dix*, and a reformist faction, which includes the CFDT, UNSA, CFTC and CGC, with the latter two not very well represented in the civil service. Some would challenge this dichotomy or the way it has been labelled, but it does correspond to forms of action and objective attitudes over many years and is still a relatively "robust" model over the long term. In fact, we are talking more about ideal models, factions around which the trade union organisations structure themselves, although the configurations can change over time. For instance, *Force Ouvrière* has moved from one faction to the other and the CGT is now shifting again. To complicate the situation still further, advocates of both tendencies can coexist within a single confederation until further realignments occur in the future.

The reformist/dissenter dichotomy makes it possible, without too much difficulty, to categorise the reactions of the unions of civil servants to the administrative reforms which have taken place since the eighties, but it is of no use at all for identifying their attitudes towards policies in general and towards citizen/users in particular. On the latter point, there is a more marked divergence between trade unions which see themselves as "forces of proposal and action" and those which seek to confine themselves to defending professional interests only.

1.   Unions of civil servants acting as wage-earning citizens and the quality of governance

The unions of civil servants have traditionally been considered as defenders of the citizen/employees of public authorities, who are not only the executors but also the persons responsible for the smooth running of public services. In their view, the duties of civil servants were to participate, every bit as much as to obey orders from their hierarchical superiors. Hence the concept of elected joint labour/management representation in consultative bodies, which was not effectively recognised until the general service conditions were established in 1946. The civil service higher council, the *Conseil supérieur de la Fonction publique* and the joint technical committees were given special responsibility for dealing with problems of organisation, and hence of good management, but their real influence remained weak up until the eighties. In fact, the public authorities considered that only they themselves were truly competent in these matters and the trade unions were interested mainly in professional guarantees.

For civil servants generally, the core element of the service guarantees was refusal of patronage, essentially political patronage, and job stability. All of the arguments have tended to legitimate the neutrality and efficacy of governance by referring to Weberian logic. However, it is primarily an internal logic, and the interest of users has often been used as a pretext for justifying the peculiar nature of the public service, which would itself require quite specific guarantees for its officials to make up for the obligations imposed upon them. For the trade union organisations, the quality of governance depends in great measure on the morale of civil servants and on their motivations, since it is the trade unions which, acting as mediators, pass on demands from the grass roots to the hierarchy and the public authorities. Relations with the management and consultation on all matters concerning not only the career structure, but also the organisation of services within the framework of administrative commissions, technical committees and advisory boards, are therefore considered to be factors of good management. Although these joint bodies play only a consultative role, since 1968 various forms of contractual relations have developed with the trade union organisations. Framework agreements have been concluded since 1989 on a number of issues, such as staff training, mobility, procedures for individual assessment, working conditions, job instability and cessation leave. These agreements generally cover a fixed period and are then re-negotiated periodically in line with the evaluations made by "monitoring committees" comprised of the signatory parties. Amendments are also discussed either at ministerial level or locally. This practice was also adopted for reviewing the job classifications in the 1990 Durafour Protocol, which was valid for seven years, as well as in an agreement on health, safety and preventive medicine in the three public service departments. Depending on the circumstances, simple consultation of staff representatives therefore evolves towards a wider consultation much like the contractual negotiations established in private sector collective bargaining agreements.

This system of relations operates with trade union organisations that often take different attitudes: some step up the pressure, whilst others sign the agreements. Public sector strikes are, as everyone knows, one of the peculiarities of labour relations in France. Their impact on the quality of governance has led to numerous, notably legal, developments which we shall not go into here. When the demands are not taken into account through the usual procedures, then trade unions seek, through conflict, to establish a new balance of power in order at least to reach a compromise. Appeals to public opinion are adopting an ever-greater role, thanks to the media, and corporations which find themselves in a sector strategic to the economy therefore seek to maximise their advantages. Let us point out only that this method of operation does help to achieve a certain equilibrium: the ability of employees to express their opinions through work stoppages acts as a sort of safety valve, the effects of which can admittedly be damaging in the short term. However, in the longer term, it is more helpful in integrating them into their working environment, over which they feel able to exert an influence, than in excluding them from it by making them feel totally powerless.

The main principles underpinning the modernisation of the public services have barely altered for over a decade, even though the terms vary according to shifts in the political landscape. This calling into question of the way public services operate has been criticised by the trade union organisations as an abandonment of the principles based on the interest of citizen/users but, most of all, it has been seen as destabilising the traditional service guarantees. In the face of these reforms, the unions of civil servants have, on the whole, been particularly adept at denouncing any departures from, or perverse effects of, the measures proposed by various governments. Since the sixties, they have been very quick to decipher the future developments in liberal ideologies and their reactions have all centred on defending the service conditions for civil servants, as guarantor of public service neutrality. However, their attitudes vary according to whether they are affiliated with either the dissenting or the reformist faction.

All of the so-called dissenting organisations have criticised the distinction between regulator and operator, which threatened to culminate in the creation of agencies whose staff would end up being governed by private law. Likewise, they have rejected the notion of minimum universal service, as well as the logic behind the Maastricht agreements. In particular, they have denounced all of the government's autumn 1995 measures for reforming pensions and social security. In their view, the State reform planned in 1996 would lead to job and career instability. All of these trade unions emphasise the independence of civil servants from political influences, and consider most of the criteria for staff assessment to be, to a greater or lesser degree, "politically correct". Thus it was that the CGT Posts and Telecommunications Federation recently wrote that the quality approach is a refined and pernicious management method which could become "an instrument for self over-exploitation". In their view, the anonymous competitive examinations and a career structure based on "objective" criteria, rather than on the subjectivism of hierarchical assessments, must be maintained in order to obviate the risk of individualising jobs and salaries. They consider the notions of occupation or skill to be dangerous. These organisations therefore oppose assessment on merit, mobility and multi-skilling, which call into question the service guarantees and the traditional role of the joint consultative bodies. They also reject the "de-concentrated" inter-ministerial form of management ["de-concentration" meaning the transfer of decision-making powers to local representatives of the central authorities] which would lead to enforced mobility. All of these criticisms of so-called liberal leanings which could lead to the "privatisation" of management, are advanced in the interests of a quality French-style public service, specific to a particular culture which was forged during the decades of republican "struggles".

For the reformist organisations, too, maintaining the principles of service conditions for civil servants still underpins the entire debate. Indeed, the general interest mission would call for employees to be recruited and trained for the purpose, subject to a series of inordinate common law rights and obligations. Job stability and career guarantees would assure the neutrality of the public service and motivate staff, which is needed, moreover, to successfully implement the administrative reforms. However, these organisations deem public service reform to be essential and have also come out in favour of the Maastricht agreements. They have, on the whole, shown themselves to be quite favourable to the reforms undertaken by Michel Rocard in 1989 and Alain Juppé in 1996, as well as by Lionel Jospin in 1998. They stress both the range of needs which have to be satisfied and the necessity of modernising governance. They accept the de-concentration measures, provided that the approach is negotiated with officials and their representatives. Like the dissenting organisations, they feel that the reduction and reorganisation of working time must form part of the fight against unemployment, with priority being given to defending public service jobs and combating job instability.

The public authorities' room for manoeuvre is, as we see, rather limited, since the dissenting trade unions are just as well represented as the reformists, with whom it is possible to conclude agreements. Moreover, the dissenters are quick to brandish the threat of strike action and their reactions cannot be disregarded. One might wonder whether it would not be better to move from a management/labour confrontation to a tripartite system in which citizen/users are able to express their opinions directly, rather than through mass media.

2.   Trade unions and citizens/users

We shall not tackle the issue of user participation in the quality of the public services generally, which has already been dealt with at some length. This is the issue which is most frequently raised, either from the angle of political or legal principles, or from the angle of the specific services each with its own specific problems [2]. Instead we shall position ourselves at the level of the civil service and administrative reform ministry, the *Ministère de la Fonction publique et de la Réforme administrative*.

When reformist trade unions rethought the issue of social organisation in the wake of the First World War, they integrated the participation of the citizens into the management of the services, in the form of a tripartite arrangement between public authorities, staff representatives and users. In fact, user representation has always been difficult to define. After the Liberation, user participation in nationalised corporations was planned, although it had only a minor influence, since it was very difficult to find users outside of the client enterprises who were really representative. However, bureaucratic, government and corporatist deviations led many people to forget this dimension, leading to a joint labour/management system that was closed in on itself. User representation came to be seen as competing with staff representation, with the possible risk of developing conflicting rationales.

Today, the attitudes of civil servants unions towards user participation in running public administrations are diverse. The CGT, CFDT, UNSA and FSU all declare themselves favourable to participation, whilst *Force Ouvrière* declares its fierce hostility to it. Below we recall their main arguments, before looking at solutions which could be envisaged at both local and national levels.

Adopting a "republican, radical and secular" stance, *Force Ouvrière* deems that Parliament alone is authorised to represent citizen/users. In its view, the principle of citizens' equality before the law implies the rejection of pressure groups to defend specific interests, as in tripartite management committees comprised of representatives of the administration, staff and users, for example. The FO has often likened this citizen representation to that of "tax-dodgers", a concept which is particularly developed in the Finance services. To further the involvement of private individuals in public service management "naturally calls into question not only the secular nature, but also the entitlement of each citizen, in a democracy, to benefit from the laws of his country... The citizen/users or clients of the public service will now be required to be apprised of the content of service projects in order to assess their rights" [3]. However, according to the FO, history shows that the development of autonomous intermediary bodies can lead to the establishment of corporate structures, with all the dangers that this entails.

The dissenting and anarchist-trade unionist tendencies of *Force Ouvrière* were strengthened during the seventies, as a reaction against the CFDT's evolution towards self-management. A distinction was then made between the social sphere, where trade unions were required, on the one hand, to participate in collective bargaining agreements, joint bodies and the contractual policy concerning pay and, on the other hand, the economic and political sphere in which it wished only to be informed and consulted. Running the administration came within this sphere, and the language that was used crystallised the conflicting arguments. Whilst the FO spoke of a counterbalance in the country's economic and social policy, the CFDT referred to trade unions as a counterproposal. *Force Ouvrière* leaders have often repeated that, for them, there was no question of helping to improve the public service quality, which they consider to be entirely the responsibility of the public authorities. FO does not consider itself to represent the interests of citizens or users; it "is not a proposer of either a project for society or of an ideal method for organising the State", and has no ambition to co-manage it.

By contrast, according to the CGT, users are central to the issue. Their specific rights must be recognised in the new bodies to be created at local level, notably in the *département* commissions for modernising the public services, in which users and staff must be acknowledged as players in their own right. For this, trade unions must draw up concrete proposals, and citizens must be allowed to effectively express their needs, and to be apprised of and control the use of the public resources that are mobilised. Finally, convergence must be sought between the general interest of users and staff demands. In particular, responding to the new needs of citizens should make it possible to increase the volume of public sector jobs, because having dealings with certified employees with strong service guarantees also acts as a guarantee for users [4]. The UGFF-CGT therefore sees itself as a force of proposal and action for a real confrontation and a proper democratic debate "with joint action being taken by users and civil service employees" [5].

Likewise, the *Union Nationale des Syndicats Autonomes* affirms the necessity to involve the general public in the democratisation of local life, stating that users, as well as staff, must play a direct part in evaluating public services. Several years ago, the *Fédération Générale Autonome des Fonctionnaires*, part of the UNSA, undertook to raise civil servants' awareness of user needs, in a campaign entitled "Service Plus". More recently, the UNSA mobilised its efforts to support a European Public Service Charter, clearly affirming its citizenship of Europe. Finally, it called for users to be given a role in deciding on and evaluating services, through the creation of advisory committees, or participation in management bodies, following the National Education model [6].

The CFDT approves as self-evident the experiments to integrate user expectations into the running of public services. Its Post and Telecommunications Federation even uses the term "customer", which most other civil service organisations scorn. It was involved in a "pragmatic, contractual and participatory" approach to set up new counters in post offices and judged the customer survey to be positive, but does not seem to have envisaged consulting user representatives as such. However, like the other trade union confederations, the CFDT possesses a consumer association, the ASSECO, which may have contributed. Clearly, all of the staff trade unions, even the most open-minded among them, are hardly going to be inclined to accept any institutional representation other than their own.

Consulting individual users through opinion polls or surveys is one thing, but consulting the organisations representing users is quite another. However, the minister for the civil service, State reform and decentralisation was indeed referring to the latter in his policy paper of November 5, 1997, for organising the "de-concentrated" administrations. The Prime Minister's circular of June 3, 1998 [7] relating to the preparation of multiannual programmes for modernising the administrations, by contrast, was more vaguely confined to an "analysis of the needs of users of the administration" and "to the quality procedures embarked upon in each administration, stressing the function of listening to and serving users". In one issue of *Revue Française d'Administration Publique*, devoted to labour relations in the public sector, a very influential senior official thought it would be interesting to see users' representatives among the qualified figures represented on the *Conseil supérieur de la Fonction publique* [8].

After a few legal difficulties, institutional user representation is due to be set up within the framework of the commission for modernising the public services, separate from the *Conseil supérieur de la Fonction publique*. Indeed, the ratio of user representatives to State representatives was unacceptable and distorted the bipartite labour/management composition of the *Conseil*. A simple decree is due to provide for the appointment of six "qualified figures", locally-elected representatives and user representatives. A tripartite formula, requested in particular by the CGT and the FSU, would mean amending the law of January 11, 1984 concerning the general service conditions of civil servants. It would perhaps be simpler to provide for user consultation bodies separate from staff bodies, especially since senior officials, as well as grass-roots trade union officials, would very much need to listen to points of view that differ from their own. The collaboration of user and staff representatives in the evaluation procedures should also be envisaged.

Another possible approach might be to involve consumer associations. At present there are nineteen consumer and user associations which have been approved by the ministry for consumer affairs. A number of them are interested in public or private services and would certainly be prepared to work in defence of the interests of public service users, given some encouragement [9]. Some of these associations already participate in the boards of directors of industrial and commercial public services, such as the French electricity board (*EDF*), the French Post Office and *France Télécom*. Committees of public service users have also been called for at national and European levels [10]. Their large number should not delude anybody, since, locally, their establishment is much more limited, and it would be quite easy to identify those which could be considered as representative. At national level, not all share the same specialisation and their representativeness could be assessed in accordance with their field of competence. Furthermore, one public corporation, the French national consumer council - the *Institut National de la Consommation* (INC) - is supposed to co-ordinate all of these organisations and could, after being reformed, be consulted at national level on issues concerning public service users. We do not underestimate the numerous problems which this would pose, especially in relations between the ministries of consumer affairs and State reform, but they do not appear to be insurmountable.

Appealing to third parties in the confrontation between the public authorities and their staff has always been the subject of reservations on both sides. During the seventies and eighties, the public authorities' consideration of user expectations, apart from the obvious reasons of efficacy and legitimisation, was aimed at providing a counterbalance to trade union power. User problems were "looked into", but without going so far as to provide for their autonomous representation, which was liable to complicate the workings of the consultation bodies. During the eighties and nineties, the trade unions themselves also frequently appealed to user "needs" in order to demand more resources, more staff and more service guarantees. For the most part, they did not reject the principle of consulting individual consumers but were, in fact, reluctant or opposed to, their collective and institutional representation, which would mean competition for them. Finally, nobody really tried to surmount the difficulties inherent in user representation, and one of the main obstacles continues to be trade union hostility. Although, in National Education, parent representation was established many years ago, with the organisation of elections, this was because teacher trade union officials were widely represented.

Conclusion

The French model of labour relations in public administrations presents some unusual features which to other countries no doubt seem strange. The wide variety of trade union organisations prevents the public authorities from adopting a single approach to their trade union interlocutors and requires them to adapt their strategies to a variety of different positions. In actual fact, improving the quality of services and of governance is not the most important or direct issue in these relations, which take place at the central level of the civil service ministry. The confrontations arise chiefly over pay, job classification or job numbers. However, invoking citizen/user expectations is still a strong argument for the two partners which, when confronting one another in the joint bodies, seek to avoid a confrontation by appealing to third parties. Although the representation of clearly-identified and predictable users, such as locally-elected representatives or company managers, does not pose any problem, the representation of individual users is a more redoubtable challenge, both for the public authorities, which are supposed to represent the general interest, and for the staff trade unions, which wish to remain the only force opposing the establishment, considering themselves to be the legitimate representatives of "the masses" in dealings with the state authorities.

It would be interesting to make comparisons with the experiences of other European countries, outside of the industrial and commercial public services where the issue is better understood.

References

[1]   J. Siwek-Pouydesseau, Le syndicalisme des fonctionnaires jusqu'à la Guerre froide. Presses Universitaires de Lille, Lille, 1989; Idem, Les syndicats de fonctionnaires depuis 1948. PUF, Paris, 1989; Idem, Les syndicats des grands services publics et l'Europe. L'Harmattan, Paris, 1993; Idem, Les syndicats de fonctionnaires. *Revue Française d'Administration Publique*, **80** (1996) 609-620.

[2]   M. Sapin, La place et le rôle des usagers dans les services publics. Rapport au premier ministre, 1982; IFSA. L'évolution des rapports entre l'administration et les usagers. La Documentation Française, 1991; B. Delaunay, L'amélioration des rapports entre l'administration et les administrés. Contribution à l'étude des réformes administratives entreprises depuis 1945. LGDJ, Paris, 1993; P. Warin (ed.), Quelle modernisation des services publics? Les usagers au coeur des réformes. La Découverte, Paris, 1997; Administration: droits et attentes des citoyens. Colloque IFSA. La Documentation Française, Paris, 1998.

[3]   *La Nouvelle Tribune*, FGF-FO, 2ème trimestre 1997, p. 41; *Revue Française d'Administration Publique*, Oct.-Dec. (1996) 695-699.

[4]   *Fonction Publique*, UGFF-CGT, Dec. 1997-Jan./Feb. 1998, p. 11.

[5]   *Fonction Publique*, UGFF-CGT, August 1996, p. 17.

[6]   J.P. Gualezzi, Les conditions de la réussite de la réforme de l'Etat et de la modernisation de l'administration, *Revue Française d'Administration Publique*, October-December (1996) 705-712.

[7]   *Journal Officiel*, June 9, 1998.

[8]   J. Roché, Les enjeux de la concertation institutionnelle, *Revue Française d'Administration Publique*, October-December (1996) 621-629.

[9]   A list of these associations, with their contact details, is published in each issue of the journal *Soixante Millions de Consommateurs* (French national consumer council - *INC*).

[10]   P. Emaer, Aspirations et exigences des utilisateurs. In: P. Bauby and J.C. Boual (eds.), Les services publics au défi de l'Europe. Les Editions Ouvrières, Paris, 1993, pp. 49-58.

Citizens and the Quality of Public Action: Seeking a New Form of Management. Public Participation and Contracting Practices in France

Nicole de Montricher*

Introduction

For some twenty years, activities related to administrative reform have been intensifying throughout the developed world. Among the host of initiatives which have been undertaken and independent of the implicit hypotheses underlying the approach towards modernisation, three distinct recurring orientations can nonetheless be identified: the first of these consists of considering how to re-establish the authority of political leaders in implementing the collective decisions that serve to protect their self-interests; the second pertains to efficient resource management; and the third involves the quality of public services provided in terms of satisfying citizens' needs and demands [1].

In order to achieve these objectives, the methods employed vary from one country to the next, yet a noticeable trend does appear in favour of negotiation as the form of management which is capable of mitigating the disadvantages associated with monopoly and hierarchy, while not overlooking the inherent public interest goal, which today still represents the cornerstone of the legitimacy of all public action. This feature has been recalled from time to time in official documents, beginning with the reform's initiating text on the State's role in France - the Rocard circular dated February 23, 1989. Within such a framework, two tools for intervention are considered to be particularly pertinent: participation and contracting. These procedures prove to be of particular interest by virtue of their long-standing use in the public sector as a means for shaping relationships with the private sector in the aim of either delegating a service's operations or ensuring the feedback of information from the public at large. In short, these tools serve as the standard techniques for organising various forms of partnerships.

Nonetheless, the considerable importance ascribed to context-specific features in the launching of public action is well known. For this reason, it seemed worthwhile to question what both participation and contracting had become, as instruments of intervention, within the scope of the State's modernisation policy. The conditions under which this policy has been implemented in France should first of all be specified. The setting here is one of a unitary country in which all reform-related decisions are taken by the central powers, as opposed to the situation in the United States or Germany. It's also a country in which the administration has entrusted government agencies to lead the reform themselves, as opposed to what has been occurring in the United Kingdom. And lastly, it's a country in which the number of public-sector employees has remained stable over the recent past and in which a portion of the public sector supports modernisation efforts, especially at the operations level and within technical divisions [2]. Reform has thus been driven from the premise that change could be

* Nicole de Montricher, Chargé de recherche au CNRS, GAPP - ENS, France

carried out within the conventional structures and with the existing public-sector workforce. The instrument of change thereby lies in the relevance of the means applied to mobilising agents.

Before presenting the current conditions pertaining to both public participation and contracting, it would be most useful to recall the previous situation. At the end of the Second World War, a handful of public-sector companies were founded on the model of a participatory public decision-making process; they were set up with a Board of Directors which combined representatives from the State, user groups and company personnel. It can also be recalled that the principle of participation lies at the very heart of France's Gaullist philosophy, according to which participation serves to provide the central powers with information unavailable inside its own administrations. Participation, in this form, could be defined very generally as the organisation of a mutually-inclusive informational exchange between administrative authorities and service users. Along these lines, the example of the "CODER" (the nation's regional economic development commissions), which were created in 1964, is most illustrious. These commissions were presided over by the regions' Prefects and invited private-sector concerns to sit side-by-side with the local elected officials, so as to provide input regarding the strategic orientations of local economic planning. However, it is a well known fact that stimulating participation in public action requires offering the actors some kind of incentive, without which their interest would wane. The failure of the "CODER" commissions can be explained precisely by this phenomenon: the private companies felt that the procedure demanded an effort on their part which was not at all rewarded inasmuch as no change was getting introduced into the content of the decision-making process and, moreover, the companies saw no financial return from their efforts [3]. In contrast, the same does not apply to the participation of representative associations when their customer base is small and easily identifiable, such as the case with associations for the disabled. In these instances, associations are represented within the centralised government agencies where they can often influence decision-making. Lastly, another scenario is illustrated by the Ministry of Agriculture which had, for a considerable period of time, been predominantly influenced by the country's most powerful farmers' union.

Generally speaking, the goal of public participation is to establish the objectives of the public action to be undertaken in conjunction with the target group. The difficulty herein lies in finding an equilibrium between the administration's manipulation and its co-opting by the customers.

Like participation, contracting has presented a variety of aspects; however, it can be defined on the whole as a relative negotiation for the implementation of a public action by a target group. Besides the classical route of subcontracting in setting up public services, contracting also enters into consideration in the development of a common project. The administration is thus faced with proposing the types of public intervention and then with financing programs according to how well they fulfil the prescribed objective. In this respect, the example of the regional financing contracts which tied the Ministry of the Interior to a jurisdictional entity responsible for encompassing all of the region's municipalities is worthy of recognition. Lastly, from a different perspective, the Ministry of Environment had, as of 1971, opted for an action strategy in co-ordination with polluting industries through contracting relationships rather than through a unilateral regulatory-enforcement type of intervention.

Even though the procedural definitions have, in theory, been clearly laid out (since the contract implies an equilibrium in the assignment of responsibilities whereas the notion of participation merely presupposes the exchange of information), a high lack of precision was nonetheless observed in practice as regards the actual contract mechanisms. Contracts have often functioned like subsidies, while the level of participation was eroding once the actors' interests were no longer being taken into consideration. This phenomenon helps explain how these two procedures can be assimilated.

If it were acknowledged that the State's modernisation effort can be summarily characterised both by the drive to reinstate the authority of central government agencies over public action and by the quality standards imposed on public services, the focus would then turn to determining how best to achieve these objectives [4]. It is long-standing knowledge that an organisation's structures impact its capacity to undertake action. Nonetheless, this statement has sparked much debate and attention within the private sector; only recently has it been applied to the public sector, a sector in which the basic tenet has now become that an oversized organisation leads to inefficiency and wastefulness. In this vein, the change in France has been most spectacular in light of this country's heavy experience with political, administrative, economic and social centralisation. A movement was initiated at the beginning of the 1980's to decentralise the State's hold on power; once the conditions shaping the power structure at the local and regional levels had been transformed, this movement induced an attempt to adapt central government agencies to the revised context by means of breaking down structures into smaller units. A multitude of political actors thereby came to the fore over this period, e.g. the rise in the departmental and regional councils' power, and administrative actors such as external field divisions or agencies. In light of this skyrocketing number of actors, along with their diverse interests and rationale, co-operation has become vital to the generation of public action and difficult to carry out due to the new co-operation mechanisms which must be introduced to replace the former co-ordination-oriented structures. Such is the objective of the participation and contracting procedures which seem to be well adapted to the new situation owing to their capacity to structure the negotiation between competing interests in the establishment of common objectives.

The major innovation over the recent past pertains to the massive use of these tools within the administration; however, reliance on such instruments has also been spreading beyond the confines of the administration as a way to organise the enactment of public policy in a number of fields requiring the mobilisation of private-sector actors. In many respects, these procedures could be considered as "uncertainty reducers" in that they tend, in theory, to enhance the transparency of the action and increase its stability.

In order to determine how these instruments are being utilised at the present time, I chose the major orientations of the modernisation efforts as indicators of the state of permanence or change. We will thus be projecting the impact of these instruments on the central government's authority to shape the scope of the action, then their impact on efficiency in resource management and, finally, their impact on the adaptation of customised services. At each of these three stages, I'll focus on studying the interactions taking place between the tool and the action so as to display the extent to which these tools modify the nature of public action.

1.   The impact of contracting practices and participation on the authority of central government administrations

The first series of reasons leading to the adoption of participation and contracting procedures is of a political-administrative nature in that from the central administration's standpoint, the key lies in ensuring that, despite a certain leeway left by its local-level representative, the public action's implementation will comply with the administration's announced objectives. This raises the classical issue of the link existing between policy-making and service operations. I have selected two dimensions to present this issue: the central power's capacity to define strategic orientations, and the acknowledgement of this capacity by the other actors.

The central power's capacity to define strategic orientations lies at the very heart of the administration's structural reforms. It explicitly constitutes the "raison d'être" of these "centres of responsibility" which were created by the February 23, 1989 circular. The empowering legislation stipulates that these centres' directors must integrate both national-level policy and locality-specific features in order to optimise the way in which requests by users, individuals and local authorities are being met. From a technical standpoint, setting up responsibility centres proves to be relatively complex in that contractual agreements are necessary both between the centre and its affiliated central government agency and between this agency and the Budget and Civil Service Ministries. The administrative decomposition of the geographical jurisdiction was in no way modified; it turns out that the vast majority of these responsibility centres are former field divisions of the Ministries, tied contractually for three-year periods to achieve a set of specifically identified goals. On occasion, these documents are complemented by contracts with yearly objectives, e.g. within the Ministry of Public Works. In such cases, the contract resembles a list of actions that the signatory agrees to carry out during the upcoming year. This document is laid out in a descending hierarchical sequence between the director and department heads, and then between department heads and unit heads [5].

To lend some meaning to these contracts, the central administration must start by establishing a national policy. The difficulty experienced by Ministerial divisions in setting general orientations is well known not only because public policy determines social change in terms which are quite often ambiguous, but also because of competition among these divisions. Moreover, they are only rarely able to make use of the means of information necessary for objectively assessing the projects proposed by their field units. More generally, what gets qualified as a "contract" is not really an agreement that contains a set of reciprocal service specifications, but rather an understanding related to the same view of priority actions; this format often overlooks the issue of the operations director's latitude in granting waivers to the contract's rules. The contract, in this instance, is hence especially helpful in ensuring the bottom-up flow of information within the administration. In this vein, it could be postulated that if the administration were to successfully process the quantity of data amassed until now, it should be able to foster a public interest that's less abstract than in the past. Such an assessment is justified by considering that from this point forward, input into the public policy-making process will no longer be monopolised by central government civil servants, whose jobs revolve around this task, but instead will be shared with heads of operating units, who are better able to provide practical information regarding citizens' needs. In the long run, difficulties in governability can nonetheless be anticipated, inasmuch as the departments' missions are no longer to be separated from their respective environments, but rather to be deeply rooted therein, a feature which will potentially complicate any policy change.

From the standpoint of implementing public policy, the experience with joint financing contracts is most worthwhile in that the contract has been designed as an instrument of co-ordination between national-level and local-level development; it should be kept in mind that no national financing plan has been adopted since 1993 and that the region is now considered as the pertinent jurisdiction with respect to local development matters. The principle consists of having the Prefect of the Regional government and the President of the Regional Council negotiate a five-year agreement whose objective is to align the Ministries' various projects with the needs being expressed at the regional level, which in terms of local development comprises the user. The first such experience took place for the signing of the 1994-98 agreements. In reality, neither of the two signatories possessed the resources necessary for reconciling these interests at their appropriate level. Hence, the contractual tool on its own was not able to incite the co-operation of the State and a region's local authorities. Furthermore, what makes this example truly noteworthy is not the inadequacy of the contractual instrument, but rather the lack of understanding of its use conditions and especially the fact that an unprepared negotiation opens the door to power brokering. This is exactly what happened in 1994. Each time the regional Presidents considered themselves in a strong enough political position, either they requested and obtained national standard waivers from the central administration or they imposed such waivers upon the Prefect. In order to instil meaning into the contractual procedure, it would need to be conducted subsequent to a lengthy participatory session during which the actors would build their own co-ordination instruments so as to gradually reconcile the competing interests. It should be added that some regions have found the cost of participation excessive in terms of both meeting time and document-production time, in comparison with the limited advantages to be gained.

These examples reveal that in France the negotiation of contracts between the central administration and its local representatives with respect to the interpretation and adaptation of centrally-issued directives is a new practice which has not yet been associated with an appropriate methodology. However, it can be observed that the obligation to negotiate does induce contradictory consequences which are exhibited in two ways. Firstly, this obligation leads the operations centres to engage in strategy-building sessions which could ultimately engender the decomposition of administrative structures. Secondly and conversely, this obligation incites greater transparency in performing actions that should increase the authority of the central agencies over their departments' activity, while improving their knowledge of the real needs being expressed in the field.

2.   The impact of contracting and participation on the efficiency of resource management

The second series of reasons behind the choice of these negotiation procedures is managerial in nature in that a managerial framework enables guaranteeing the compliance of efficiency-related standards. Modernisation most often gets portrayed by generalising the budget, along with a performance obligation for department managers. It has been found that placing emphasis on performance exerts a direct influence on the goal of public interest since this sort of constraint obliges setting relatively precise objectives which are tied to an organisational identity perceived as the purpose of an organisation that's based on its inherent cumulative skills. Resource management efficiency can thus be defined as the capacity to produce more with the same amount of resources. This would imply that the rationale employed is shaped around three points: setting the goal in relation to experience and strengths; optimising the use of the available human and financial resources; and making use of a method that enables evaluating the outcome of the particular action.

The identity-oriented approach turns out to be the basic focus of the "public service overhaul" policy outlined in the 1989 circular which stipulates that each centre must engage in collective strategy-building as regards the perception of the public service project as a determination of the values, ambitions, strategy, objectives and key actions for improvement on the part of all staff members. This project must be developed by incorporating the environment, the partners and the users. It is generally held that the incentive of building an organisation's identity lies in its power to unite, which is aimed at encouraging the workforce's mobilisation. Nonetheless, a strong organisational identity also leads to a narrowing of both objectives and customer groups, which then gets manifested by a specialisation of activities. The question of whether this method is well suited to the provision of public services can legitimately be raised inasmuch as the method's compatibility with the implementation of company objectives stems from the companies' autonomy in their decision-making process. The same does not necessarily hold for the public sector in which the political institutions set goals by virtue of negotiated compromises with the electorate, a situation which means having to serve different publics by proposing a wider range of services.

This feature helps explain why the field agencies of certain Ministries have experienced difficulty in determining their identity, as is the case for the Ministry in charge of Social Affairs. Yet, this feature also explains why certain centres have cut back a portion of their activity. This is how, for example, a department head was able to decide to no longer offer any free legal advice to smaller municipalities because he deemed that this activity was too costly. By the same token, the principle of public service accessibility has been jeopardised while not a single political leader has raised the issue.

Lying at the heart of this identity-building approach is also the notion that ministerial action must emanate directly from the expertise of those agents in contact with the service's users, as quality service provision does necessitate specialised skills. This notion represents a radical change in administrative design, which gives rise to the increase in power held by both professionals and their professions, in comparison with the generalist training required of the traditional civil service career path. This change lies first of all in the recognition that a professional owes loyalty to his profession before his organisation, which leads to assessing the administration's specificity by considering it as just another employer. Change is also due to the public service's loss of specificity as a result of these conditions. The user is thereby faced with a choice from among a variety of products offered by either public-sector or private-sector organisations. In the area of public works, each of the country's territorial departments possesses its own network of Public Works Offices, yet may also rely upon the State's expertise or even commission private consultants. This implies that from now on, public services will be placed within a context of competition that will increasingly impose greater efficiency in order to survive.

In conjunction with the policy of modernisation, the efficiency standard serves to thoroughly transform the conditions under which the service is provided, as a result of the increasing influence of the service's "managers" who reason with an economic rationale, thereby marginalising those actors who prove incapable of expressing themselves in terms of the standards framing such a rationale. This would apply in particular to technicians, the very symbol of public sector expertise. It should be added that in many instances, the preoccupation of posting satisfactory results has led to deviating away from reasonable management in favour of economic efficiency since the latter is based on a set of parameters which are easily and directly quantifiable. In contrast, no indicator capable of clearly establishing the social impact of the action has yet to be accepted by all actors. As expressed by the representative of a central government office, "efficiency is difficult to evaluate". It can thus be observed that reliance on contracting obliges better cost control of public services, while the hierarchy of values gets altered by the administration without any involvement on the part of an elected body.

From a technical standpoint, generalising budgets provides a management flexibility that allows operating departments to intervene more autonomously than according to the former model. However, the smooth running of the procedure obviously presupposes that the field manager possesses the necessary resources, in terms of both equipment and manpower. Herein lies one of the negotiating points and explains why the Budget and Civil Service Ministries are parties to the agreement. Has the contracting method served to improve resource management? From a certain perspective, the answer is yes, since the performance obligation has indeed led the operating departments to implement modern management tools along the lines of "control charts" which, so these departments claim, has constituted a highly valuable innovation. In contrast, since the State has held onto its privileges, the extent of its commitments can still be revised. In this manner, budget constraints have heavily impacted the initial experiences in that program financing arrived too late or, moreover, it had been cut back considerably, thereby upsetting the contract's obligations balance. Lastly, it should be noted that human resources appear everywhere as a determinant in the success of service quality improvement efforts; however, in this respect, contracting proves incompatible with the rules of public service provision and with the uncertainties of job cutbacks.

In the end, has this change in resource management actually impacted the quality of service? It is difficult to answer this question given the current state of information relative to the reform's introduction. However, one could assume that contracting would encourage devising an evaluation approach on the basis of a set of qualitative indicators, in addition to the quantitative indicators, provided they can be built. In this case, an assessment of the activity of a home care unit, for example, could be no longer based on the strict number of hours of service produced, but rather on the improved condition of the elderly patients being cared for. Nonetheless, the issue of departmental cutbacks in certain activity areas, as part of their "identity-definition" phase, does remain unresolved.

3.   The impact of contracting and participation on the adaptation of public services to meet citizens' requests

The final series of reasons justifying the choice of these contracting and participation procedures is political in nature in that the focus herein lies in reshaping a Board of Directors-based organisation. This new format will be aimed at ensuring a representation of citizens' specific and practical concerns, be they as residents of a particular area, as parents to schoolchildren, as economic actors, etc. It is clear that this task does not suggest organising a separation between the administration and its environment, but rather mobilising the user by including him in the process of defining a desirable level of service and, consequently, in the determination of quality indicators. Under these conditions, the objective has been to obtain relevant context-related information and to act upon the most appropriate variables. In more general terms, enhancing the influence of administration-oriented advisory mechanisms, stemming from private sources, can be observed as competition to the expertise wielded by central government civil servants [6]. Nonetheless, it is widely known that major methodological safeguards must be introduced in order to achieve this objective. Such safeguards pertain not only to the way these aspirations are manifested, but also to the actors' expert capacities and to the trade-off protocol employed.

The initial use of these procedures can be observed in the development of opinion polling operations, which may encompass very distinct objectives. Let's select two for our purposes herein. Firstly, polling is aimed at better identifying users' behaviour, their assessments and their expectations with respect to the services being provided. Practically all administrations have, in this manner, solicited their users in order to ascertain their opinions on the service's receptiveness to the public. Secondly, polling may be used entirely differently by an administration seeking to make the public more aware of its specific scope of activity. Such is the case with the Ministry of Environment.

From another vantage point, "impact study" types of procedures enable citizens to express *their opinions* regarding a project which would exert a sizeable influence on their lifestyle. However, such measures could only be used to transform the relationships existing between the administration and citizens if the citizens themselves were able to amass enough knowledge to evaluate and qualify situations and if their involvement were requested far enough in advance in order for their point of view to be taken into consideration. This practice was instituted by a December 1992 circular which exposed such improvement projects to interested parties prior to the definitive decision-making stage. Generally speaking, the construction of administrative action in conjunction with users is being witnessed to a greater extent, with the corollary to this form of intervention being that the groups which actually exert some influence over the contents of the action happen to be the most well-established and those affiliated with the appropriate political movement. In this manner, the link with the users leads to a gradual specialisation of organisations, along the lines of the private sector's customer-segmentation model, coupled with the risk of seeing the disappearance of support structures for the weakest groups. It must be noted at this point that this situation may be temporary due to a poor handling of the participation procedures. Pierre Lascoumes did in fact cite the singular, yet reproducible, case of the "EPIDOR" project for the ecological protection of France's Dordogne River Basin, according to which the methodology employed enabled avoiding these obstacles and then advancing in both a progressive and collective fashion throughout the design of a common project [7].

Participation is also used to incite co-operation among the set of actors assigned the implementation of a public policy. Such is the case, for example, with the transfer of professional training-related actions for young people into the hands of the region. The central thrust of the 1993 legislation which outlined this type of training was the choice of the region as the appropriate administrative level for this action; the Regional Council is the most aptly-positioned entity for selecting the conditions of application throughout its jurisdiction. Yet, since this political body would not be able to impose its authority on the central government's field agencies, co-operation has been laid out in the law as the mobilisation of all actors for the development of a regional plan that upholds a certain number of principles, chief among these being due consideration paid to "population groups in difficulty". It should first be pointed out that neither the students nor their parents have been integrated into this procedure which combines local elected officials, both national- and local-level civil servants, and representatives from the professional world. This example clearly highlights the uncertainty surrounding the notion of the user as well as the tangible issues associated with the selection of those certified to participate. From another standpoint, observation has revealed that the enactment of the 1993 law presents some very distinct characteristics from one region to the next, with respect not only to the local economic context, but also to the ideological options of political leaders, to the mobilisation-oriented expertise, etc. In short, this example demonstrates that if participation were to be emphasised, the notion of "quality of service" would then become exponentially related to the citizen's location as well as to the selected user categories. Consequently, national-level co-ordination would prove difficult, despite the existence of the general set of guidelines stipulated in the law. Under such conditions, the key issue is to determine how this representation of practical collective concerns actually corresponds with a political representation, whose inherent upheaval is a well-known phenomenon.

Conclusion

Contracting and participation procedures have become heavily used by public authorities in their efforts to increase the number and intensity of interactions both within the administration and between the administration and society. By the same token, could it be stated that these procedures have also contributed to improving the quality of services being provided to the citizen?

Without establishing the precise causal link, a few remarks can nonetheless be forwarded. Firstly, with respect to the structures in place, the use of these instruments has become, above all else, a means of communication within a primarily unstable relational system. Should they be applied in conjunction with a well-known and well-run methodology, especially prior to the decision-making stage, these tools could provide a crucial contribution to innovation in the area of defining political problems and adapting rules at the time of policy enactment, in particular by making it possible to overcome sectorial and corporate divisions. However, this objective can only be reached if society organises itself around some solid intermediate structures.

Secondly, the value of these procedures lies in their insistence on a decision-making mode that initially instigates a strategic review of the action and encourages transparency during the operating modes. Yet, these procedures only prove to be worthwhile if they stimulate research which leads to advancing the state of knowledge relative to the building of qualitative indicators.

Thirdly and lastly, the mobilisation of the citizens themselves depends upon the quality of the amenities proposed by public services. The democratisation of public authority operations necessitates citizen co-operation, which can only be nurtured in conjunction with the upgrading of the population's educational level. The ultimate goal herein is either for the social and political issues to get voiced by a real organ that's capable of constituting a counterbalancing power or for the quality of service to become rooted in an actively-expressed behaviour on the part of citizens mobilised around the notion of social utility.

References

[1]   P. Aucoin, Restructuration du gouvernement à des fins de gestion et de prestation des services publics. In: B.G. Peters, D. Savoie (eds.), Réformer le secteur public, où en sommes-nous?. Centre canadien de gestion, Les presses de l'Université Laval, 1998, p. 238.
[2]   L. Rouban, Les cadres supérieurs de la fonction publique et la politique de modernisation administrative. DGAFP/Plan, La Documentation française, Paris, 1994.
[3]   P. Grémion, Le pouvoir périphérique. Seuil, Paris, 1976, p. 74.
[4]   A.A. Altshuler and R.D. Behn, The dilemmas of innovation in American government. In: A.A. Altshuler and R.D. Behn (eds.), Innovation in American government. The Brookings Institution Press, Washington D.C., 1997, p. 3.
[5]   G. Barouch and H. Chavas, Où va la modernisation?. L'Harmattan, Paris, 1993, p. 232.
[6]   J. Pierre, Consultation publique et participation des citoyens: les dilemmes de la fonction conseil. In: B.G. Peters and et D. Savoie, *op. cit.*, p. 103.
[7]   P. Lascoumes, L'éco-pouvoir. La Découverte, Paris, 1994, p. 294.

The Safeguarding of Public Service Users in Italy and the "Carta dei Servizi Pubblici"

Stefano Battini *

1.   Traditional means of safeguarding public service users

Up until relatively recently, public services in Italy have been, directly or indirectly, provided by the State (or other local authority). In some cases, public services were provided by a State organisation or public authority. Other scenarios saw public services provided by officially private, but substantially public, companies, such as joint stock companies with a public majority (or sufficiently powerful as to ensure control of the company) shareholder, or the provision of public services by private companies bound to the State through some form of public administration constraint - administrative concessions - and thus entirely at the mercy of the all-pervasive supremacy of the concessionaire.

In all these cases, public services were provided by organisations expected to safeguard the general interest, whose management choices could therefore have been easily oriented and directed from within by the controlling political power.

In fact, these public service management practices perfectly corresponded to a supplier-user relationship model which still followed the traditional State-citizen relationship format developed in Italy between the end of the last and the beginning of this century: users were made to submit to the supplier (i.e. the State) in return for protection.

This submissive relationship found theoretical justification in the two parties' differing interests: public and general those of the supplier, private and specific those of the user. And in fact this was the basic reason why the relationship totally or partially escaped the control of common law and was readily submitted to the provisions of administrative law which is known to be structured around the principles of inequality of the parties and unilateral definition of the relationship.

On the other hand, protection, justified at theoretical level on the basis of the idea that the service supplier is responsible for safeguarding the general interest, the interests of the community to which the user also belongs, was mainly demonstrated through the provision of services at a cost guaranteed to be accessible to all individual users, the State (i.e. the service supplier) sustaining a large part of the costs incurred.

The most systematic contribution to the organisation of public services, previously regulated by private law, into the framework of the newly approved administrative law was made by Santi Romano [1] at the beginning of the century. He recognised that "even when public administration service content is materially identical to the content of privately administered

* Stefano Battini, Researcher, Università degli studi di Urbino, Facoltà di economia e commercio, Istituto di studi aziendali, Italy

services, the fact that the body concerned is different alters its legal nature quite considerably"; "Secondly – he observed - in most cases, private law does not govern an entire institute but rather is based, and not insignificantly, on public law which obviously leaves its mark". As a consequence, the legal relationship between private parties and the postal service "do not have a real and proper contractual nature". The idea of the contract "is irrelevant" as the will of the private party "constitutes only a legal condition that the first (the public party) will act in the way determined by legal regulations which can never be altered" and because "the private party pays a tax according to the definition attributed to this word by public law". In the same way, admission to a public institute of education also has no contractual value, and is "included in the category of authorisations or administrative concessions".

Naturally this model, of which only a very basic outline is given here, differed greatly according to the type of service provided.

In some sectors, such as education and health, the aforementioned elements were particularly well defined. On one hand, the principle of submission of individual concerns in favour of the general interest was so widely spread as to totally exclude the implementation of private law regarding the relationship between service supplier and user: unilateral admission by the service supplier who unilaterally defined the conditions of supply with the user being relegated to a position of passive beneficiary. On the other hand, the protection element ensured that the cost of service was almost entirely sustained by the general collective.

Other sectors, such as transport, energy, post, telecommunications etc., saw the same model applied in a more lenient form. On one hand, the acknowledged submission of the user with regards to the service supplier did not hinder the private and contractual status of the legal relationship between the parties but merely imposed the need for derogation to common law, through privilege clauses such as the limitation of the public service supplier's responsibility. On the other hand, even through costs to the user were kept at an accessible level, despite the fact that charges were set at authority level, the user was nevertheless expected to individually sustain a certain, not necessarily particularly low, percentage of the cost of the service supplied.

2.   The crisis faced by the traditional model

This model became progressively more and more crisis-ridden and now seems to be completely obsolete.

In fact, this development can be traced by first examining the changes in service management and then analysing the consequential alteration in the relationship between the service supplier and user.

As is to be naturally expected, the first and foremost changes involved those sectors in which the traditional model had experienced the most trouble in taking root i.e. the public utilities sector.

In fact, the simultaneous influence of various factors, including technological progress and the process of European integration, has given rise to changes [2] recently defined as telluric [3].

Firstly, many of the public companies involved in the supply of public utility services have been involved in privatisation policies with Law N° 474 of July 30, 1994 which provided for the transfer of shares in companies providing public services into private hands on the condition that suitable regulating authorities were founded for each sector, confirming the practice of entrusting public utility services to real and proper private companies: companies which are private not only in form but also in substance [4] [5].

Secondly, liberalisation procedures implemented by the European Community have tended to eliminate special or exclusive provisions previously granted to service suppliers by member states, thus forcing them to compete [6] [7] [8].

The consequence of the combination of these two developments - in many ways related to one another - has been a change in the service supplier's position. The service supplier is no longer a public administration duty bound to look after the public interest but rather a private party whose business is to make a profit.

As previously mentioned the changes in the social service sector are not so immediately obvious, yet, here too, recent reforms seem to point in the same direction. On one hand the service is provided by a network of public and private institutions (local health centres, educational institutes) who are continuously being granted more and more autonomy from the State and other local authorities. On the other hand, it has been shown that these organisations are attempting to introduce competition between themselves.

Obviously these changes influence the relationship between the service supplier and the user which now seems to have outgrown the traditional State-citizen model in order to come closer to the private sector producer-consumer model.

In fact, if rather than looking after the public interest, the service supplier acts in his own interest, the service supplier-user relationship can no longer be based on the theoretical principle of user submission and as a consequence the relationship is governed by common law with the subsequent elimination of the need for privilege clauses.

On the other hand, however, the same reasons which have led to a decline in user submission also lead to a reduction in the other element of the aforementioned model, i.e. protection.

Thus the user risks losing State protection or at least the kind of protection he was traditionally guaranteed.

3.   The search for new forms of safeguarding and the "Carta dei servizi pubblici".

This period of transition from one service supplier-user model to the other forms the background against which the experience of the "Carta dei servizi pubblici" must be analysed and assessed [9] [10].

This transition can be considered as an attempt to implement the substitution of traditional protection tools based on a conditioning - from the inside - of the service supplier's management choices with other mechanisms more in line with the new model currently in the process of confirmation.

Firstly, once public powers have renounced their hold over service management, these mechanisms can only consist in constraints - from the outside - imposed on the service supplier.

Secondly, the aim of these mechanisms is to make the formal equality already acquired in the service supplier-user relationship a substantial equality through the creation of suitable conditions and the allocation of suitable tools to allow users to exercise sufficient pressure on the service supplier in order that individuals or members of a smaller collective group can enjoy the same protection previously granted to the general collective.

Thus the bilateral State-user relationship, in which the State both supplies users with services and looks after their interests, is substituted by a tri-partitional relationship: the services are provided to users by private or largely autonomous service suppliers; the State - now an external authority - regulates this formally equal relationship in order to redress any substantial inequality existing between the parties.

There are basically two routes which can be followed.

The first begins with confirmation of the user's freedom to choose the contractor, service supplier, of his choice. However, although the "Carta dei servizi pubblici" recognises the principle of freedom of choice, it is not suitably powerful to ensure that the conditions necessary for the implementation of this right are provided. The general and special provisions aimed at guaranteeing a competitive market, such as the regulations regarding the reorganisation of the national health service and the educational system which provide for competition between individual organisations supplying services, are really indirect user protection measures. In fact, even though they do not directly interfere in the service supplier-user relationship, they do however have a decisive influence on legal measures concerning the service user's ability to autonomously protect his own rights.

The second option, which is not an alternative to the first one but certainly a more important one where the user's right to freedom of choice is not guaranteed, lies in forcing the service supplier to respect specific standards of service supply and quality with regards the user.

Since 1993 Italy has opted for this second possibility with the implementation of a national "Carta dei servizi pubblici" which has since been extended with the adherence of individual service suppliers to thousands of local level service charters.

Once public service suppliers have adhered to these charters, which constitutes a State regulated obligation, users enjoy a series of specific rights to service quality which can be largely grouped into two categories.

User rights to service supplier behaviour standards are confirmed meaning users are able to demand a suitable level of information dissemination and participation; this latter providing users with the possibility to express their opinion and judgement of the quality of the service supplied.

Thus, for example, should a user delay payment of a bill, the electric energy or gas service supplier concerned is duty bound to inform him before suspending the service indicating the means available to avoid suspension. Furthermore headmasters or presidents of educational institutes are obliged to receive parents and students, via telephone where appropriate or during parent-teacher meeting times duly announced through special notices; in addition, health centres are obliged to provide suitable offices which users can readily access via telephone or in person, open not less than twelve hours a day and able to provide basic information such as where to go, what time, and which documents to take.

As far as user participation is concerned, service suppliers are obliged to respect certain standards. For example, educational institutes must obtain parent and student opinions on the organisational, teaching and administrative standards provided by the service using questionnaires which allow users to grade their opinions and formulate proposals and suggestions, and electric energy and gas service suppliers must publish an annual report on service quality based on user opinions to be transmitted to the relative authorities and consumer associations.

As well as behavioural standards such as those illustrated above, the Charters have also introduced users rights to the fulfilment of service supplier efficiency and quality standards. For example, many electric energy and gas service suppliers including Enel are obliged to activate supply within a maximum deadline after stipulation of the supply contract, and have also defined the maximum duration of any accidental interruption of supply. The transport sector has encouraged many local companies to define the maximum time which can elapse between the passing of one means of transport and the next, or the maximum distance between one stop and the next. The education sector has obliged thousands of institutes to ensure that students are issued with certificates showing relative marks and assessments within five days of request.

Many aspects of the regulation of the "Carta dei servizi pubblici" with regards to both structure (regulation of the relationship between administration - or service supplier - and citizen in terms of user rights and service supplier obligations) and content (information, participation, efficiency and effectiveness) follow the model introduced by Law N° 241 of August 7, 1990 on administrative procedures, thus extending the area of implementation of public administration regulation authority to include service suppliers.

In fact, for example, by obliging administrations to conclude proceedings within a certain pre-established date, the law provides citizens with the right to a certain quality standard from bureaucratic services, which can only be measured through punctuality [11].

At the same time the "Carta dei servizi pubblici" obliges suppliers to define their minimum quality standards regarding various factors of their service, and requires that they be respected, thus providing the user with the right to a series of services which are considered not only as far as punctuality is concerned, but also with regard to another set of elements, which determine the quality of service perceived by the user. Furthermore, the definition of quality standards according to results achieved is merely a reflection -according to the citizen's subjective situation - of a more complex process of reorganisation of the entire administrative system around the principles of efficiency and effectiveness. In this framework, the results achieved and product supplied are subject to administrative controls (Law 20 of January 14, 1994) and responsibility for their standards lies with the directors and personnel of the administrative service (Law decree N° 29 of February 3, 1993).

4.   Criticisms: unilateral concession of Public Service Charters and the lack of judicial authority

Having very briefly described the background against which the "Carta dei servizi pubblici" is required to operate and illustrated the type of user protection it can provide, in conclusion this article will ask the reader to consider some reflections on various points of criticism and the main problems posed by the Charter.

Fundamentally divided into two areas, one concerns the definition of the content of the Charters and the other regards the control exercised over service suppliers' respect of their obligations.

As far as the first aspect is concerned, while it is true that the State has forced service suppliers to adhere to Charters, limiting their autonomy through policies such as the general terms of reference, it is also true that the user's role - be the user individual or part of a group - has been limited by the very definition of the Charter contents.

In fact, just as the last century saw national constitutions granted by sovereigns to their subjects, today the service supplier is finally willing to grant users the benefit of the "Carta dei servizi pubblici".

Actually, despite the fact that most of the aspects left over from the old unilateral service supplier-user relationship model have now been superseded, the content of the charters still provides the service supplier with an opportunity to continue certain abusive or elusive practices to the damage of the user.

One recurring elusive practice, for example, is the definition, for quality factors which need to be measured through specific standards (i.e. verified by each user), of overall standards, which the individual user is unable to recognise. For example, the Charter regarding the Italian post office, in which the post office sets the standard for delivery of correspondence at "within 48 hours in 85% of cases": the service supplier thus avoids acknowledging the user's right to the delivery of correspondence within a certain time merely creating a simple expectation in its place.

As far as the second aspect is concerned, the obligations imposed by the Charters have proved traditional legal regulations to be completely inappropriate as neither administrative nor ordinary judges are able to provide suitable legal instruments to ensure timely and effective user protection.

As far as both points of criticism are concerned, the founding of the various public utility service regulation authorities pursuant to Law N° 481 of November 14, 1995 seems to have introduced several effective control measures and as a consequence users of entrepreneurial service suppliers seem to be more protected than those using services supplied by social services.

On the one hand, the law has established that service quality standards cannot be unilaterally defined by service suppliers but rather must be drawn up by the regulating authority after consultation with service suppliers and user associations.

In particular, pursuant to Section 2.12, letter h, of the Law, the authority can integrate or amend service regulation procedures defining the general level of quality guaranteed to users for an overall group of services and the specific level of quality for individual services, having consulted the service supplier and user and consumer representatives. Furthermore the law (Section 2.12. letter g) provides that the authority shall have the power to determine cases of automatic user compensation in cases of failure to respect these standards.

On the other hand, the authorities regulating the level of protection of user rights provided by the Charters have large scale sanctioning powers - which can also be activated by individual or associated users - and are able to order conciliation and arbitration procedures in cases of service user-supplier disputes.

As far as the authority's sanctioning powers are concerned, both regarding controls carried out by the authority (pursuant to Section 2.12, letter g), the authority shall control the supply of services with the power to inspect, access and acquire any necessary documentation and useful data) and the assessment of individual or associated, user or consumer, claims, appeals and complaints regarding quality standards and tariffs (Section 2.12, letter m), the authority can: a) order the service supplier to alter the ways and means in which the service is supplied (Section 2.12, letter m); b) order the service supplier to ceasing behaviour which contravenes user rights (Section 2.20, letter d); c) order the service supplier to pay compensation in certain cases pursuant to Section 2.12, letter g (Section 2.20, letter d). Should the service supplier fail to observe the authority's provisions, penal administrative sanctions between a minimum of Lit. 50 million and a maximum of Lit. 300 billion can be issued. In cases of repeated non-observance, the authority can order the temporary suspension of the service supplier's activity or the suspension of the concession (Section 2.20 letter c) .

As far as the authority's powers regarding the settling of user-service supplier disputes are concerned, Section 2.24 of the law provides regulations for the definition of criteria, terms and conditions, ways and means for the carrying out of conciliation and arbitration procedures, in public discussion at the authority's offices, in cases of controversy arising between users and service suppliers. The authority can also adopt temporary provisions in order to guarantee the continuity of service supply or stop forms of abuse or incorrect supply by the service supplier (Section 2.20, letter e).

It is still too early to give an opinion on the effectiveness of the level of user protection offered by the regulating authorities, although in a few years' time the implementation Law N° 481/1995 can be weighed up and appropriate measure taken.

References

[1]   S. Romano, Principii di diritto amministrativo. Roma, 1901.
[2]   S. Cassese, La trasformazione dei servizi pubblici in Italia, *Economia pubblica*, (1996), 5 and following.
[3]   G. Amato, Autorità semi-indipendente ed autorità di garanzia, *Rivista trimestrale di diritto pubblico*, (1997), 645 and following.
[4]   M. Clarich, Privatizzazioni e trasformazioni in atto nell'amministrazione italiana, *Diritto amministrativo*, (1995), 519 and following.
[5]   S. Cassese, Le privatizzazioni: arretramento o riorganizzazione dello Stato?, *Rivista italiana di diritto pubblico comunitario*, (1996), 579 and following.
[6]   F. Cavazzuti and G. Moglia, Regolazione, controllo e privatizzazione nei servizi di pubblica utilità in Italia, *Economia Italiana*, (1994), 9 and following.
[7]   A. Arrigoni, Regolazione e gestione nelle public utilities: principio di separazione e libera concorrenza nell'applicazione dei principi constituzionali e comunitari, *Rivista trimestrale di diritto pubblico*, (1995), 87 and following.
[8]   P. Ranci, Concorrenza e servizi pubblici nella Costituzione. In: G. Della Cananea and G. Napolitano (eds.), Per una nuova Costituzione economica. Il Mulino, Bologna, 1998.
[9]   G. Vesperini and S. Battini, La Carta dei servizi pubblici. Erogazione delle prestazioni e diritti degli utenti. Maggioli, Rimini, 1997.
[10]   C. Lacava, L'attuazione della carta dei servizi pubblici, *Giornale di diritto amministrativo*, (1996), p. 873 and following.
[11]   M.Clarich, Termine del procedimento e potere amministrativo. Giappichelli, Torino, 1995.

Partnership Boards in Northern Ireland:
An Administrative Innovation in Active Citizenship or Another Quango?

Derek Birrell & Ann Marie Gray *

Introduction

The introduction of a number of EU funding programmes in recent years has been accompanied by new forms of administration aimed at sharing responsibility between traditional political elites and other sectors of society. This process has been influenced by the decentralised delivery of many EU programmes, which has generated new forms of organisations and inter-organisational relationships generically named "partnerships". The development of EU thinking on partnerships is evidenced in initiatives such as Poverty III which identified the need and value of partnership working to tackling multidimensional problems [1].

The establishment of complex inter-organisational structure of governance has become a common feature throughout Europe in the last decade. This process is marked by a decreasing government role in service provision and increasing involvement of alternative agencies. Conventional direct government action is replaced by more complex systems of policymaking and implementation involving new sets of participants and relationships. This process has engendered speculation about a move to new forms of active citizenship, participatory democracy, governance and subsidiarity. Ireland is among those countries where the model of local partnerships is strongest and Adshead and Quinn [2], in a study of development policy in the Republic of Ireland, describe the introduction of bottom-up strategies which increasingly seek to involve local actors and agencies in the policy process. There has been an emphasis on the creation of partnerships which have fostered innovation bringing together actors from the statutory, voluntary, private and public sectors. Adshead and Quinn see the Irish government's formal incorporation into the policy process of new actors and agencies as challenging the traditional structure of subnational government. Walsh *et al.* [3] identify partnerships in Ireland as a formal organisational framework for policy making and implementation which mobilises a coalition of commitment of a range of partners around multi-dimensional action programme to combat social exclusion.

Rhodes [4] has identified the possible emergence of a new form of governance involving self-organising networks where the state becomes a collection of inter-organisational networks made up of governmental and societal actors with no sovereign actor able to steer or negotiate. Smith [5] raises the scenario of policies determined at EU level and influenced by a myriad of networks which challenges traditional state control in Britain. Roberts and Hart [6] refer to the recent growth in domestic pressure for the development of partnership working, often of a cross-sectional nature, particularly through the launch of an increasing number of

---

* Professor Derek Birrell & Dr. Ann Marie Gray, School of Social and Community Sciences, University of Ulster, Northern Ireland

competitive programmes for local and regional regeneration. This is seen largely as a consequence of EU requirements. Marks [7] sees multi-level governance as prominent in the implementation stage in the European arena. He argues that partnership is implemented unevenly across the EU but just about everywhere it institutionalises some form of direct contact between the Commission and non-central government actors including, particularly, regional and local authorities, local action groups and local businesses and that such links break open the mould of the state. Other commentators have stressed the significance of the involvement of the private business sector in governance. For instance, Jacobs [8] argues that partnerships and the development of complex inter-organisational arrangements are a response to market conditions. Others relate the process to the emergence of community development strategies and community groups demanding grass-roots participation, a process particularly relevant in Northern Ireland although also relevant in Great Britain [9] [10]. In Great Britain and Ireland these processes are still mainly operative within the local government structure. Burns *et al.* [11], see radical decentralisation strategies developing within the local government arena coupled with support for community and voluntary sectors and Geddes [12] suggests that partnerships are widely accepted as a key component of local regeneration strategies.

This paper examines the nature of Partnership Boards set up to deliver an EU programme, the Special Support Programme for Peace and Reconciliation, which has a special sub-programme exclusive to Northern Ireland. This EU special support programme was additional to the Objective I structural funds and community initiatives such as Leader and Interreg and was a response to the unique opportunities and additional needs which sprang directly from the paramilitary cease-fires announced in Northern Ireland in 1994. The cessation of violence was seen as providing an opportunity to tackle deep-rooted social and economic problems. The programme was based on the recommendations of a specially constituted EU Commission task force. At the official launch of the Peace and Reconciliation Programme in December 1995 Commissioner Wulf-Mathies indicated that the Commission had chosen to funnel aid to local groups dealing with needs and opportunities at ground level. The expectations were that the combined efforts of those organisations and the beneficiaries would make a significant difference especially to people and areas which had suffered from conflict and exclusion and thus help to sustain peace and reconciliation (Northern Ireland Partnership Board Annual Report, 96/97). The programme was particularly noteworthy for the innovative delivery mechanism that was adopted.

1.   Partnership Boards

The new innovative administrative machinery involved the establishment of District Partnership Boards in all 26 District Councils, i.e., local government areas in Northern Ireland with responsibility for the allocation of the funds. Each Board consists of one-third membership of elected councillors from the local government sector, one-third representing the community and voluntary sector and one-third covering private business, trade unions and statutory agencies.

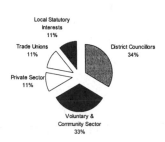

Local Statutory
Interests
11%

Trade Unions
11%

Private Sector
11%

District Councillors
34%

Voluntary &
Community Sector
33%

Each Board has between 18 and 30 members and consequently a total of 568 people from a wide range of interests are involved.

Some 33% of members are women. The procedure used was for each nominating body to submit nominees and each Partnership Board is to have a community, gender and geographical balance within its membership.

The Partnership Boards have to operate under guidelines. The strategic aim was to concentrate on those areas and people who had suffered the most in the conflict in Northern Ireland. The overall financial allocation was based on an index of population for each district weighted for deprivation and the District Partnerships had to allocate the funding across four priority themes of employment, urban and rural regeneration, social inclusion and productive investment/industrial development.

Significantly a further mechanism was established to oversee the delivery of the sub-programme. The Northern Ireland Partnership Board was set up as a regional inter-sectional partnership. This Board has quite extensive powers, which impact upon the independence of the Partnership Boards. It is under the direction of a Government Department, the Department of the Environment, which is responsible to the EU for the delivery of the programme. The Board structure consists of Directors, a secretariat and observers from Government and the European Commission. The primary functions of the Board are to ensure that each District Partnership is properly constituted, that each action plan meets the criteria laid down by the Peace and Reconciliation Programme of Northern Ireland Partnership Board to assess value for money, provide block funding and review progress [13].

The District Partnerships were set up as an institutional innovation, as an inter-sectoral partnership, which amounted to something different from the diverse posts, described by (Northern Ireland Partnership Board, 1998) as "free-standing and different drawing on the strengths of the different parties within a locality". The local government sector has for some twenty five years constituted the only local political forum in Northern Ireland and this sector brings the value of political representation and accountability plus a local administration structure to support the partnerships. Local Government in many parts of Northern Ireland have also developed close links with local community groups through other government programmes, e.g., on community relations. The representation of voluntary and community groups is a key element in harnessing the energies of the sector towards local regeneration and reconciliation. This representation brings local knowledge and user participation which in turn strengthens the credibility and role of community development groups. Since the 1970s there has been a thriving community sector in Northern Ireland. Many community development initiatives have been directed at local economic development, anti-poverty programmes, urban and rural regeneration and building community confidence and self-esteem. Another feature of community development in Northern Ireland has been the significant role which many women have played in initiating and sustaining community action. Private sector representation brings management expertise, entrepreneurial skills and access to resources. The formation of the Partnership Board did not happen naturally so it is a manufactured administrative form. The structure may bring together unlikely sets of groups and individuals [14] and for many it is their first opportunity to work with other sectors.

2.   The Benefits of a New Form of Governance

Speaking of the partnership innovation in 1998 following the award of continuing and additional funding under the next tranche of the EU peace programme the Northern Ireland Secretary· of State, Mo Mowlan, stated "partnerships represent far more a new form of governance corresponding to, but different from, formal politics, a kind of non-political politics" [15]. A number of value-orientated claims have been made for the outcomes of this innovation.

2.1.   Participative Citizenship

Sweeney (1997) argues that through a new participating process partnerships have exposed the inadequacies of traditional political structures and are breaking down the old barriers between public and private and between representative democracy and participative democracy. Partnerships can be seen as a practical form of politics enabling people from all walks of life to work together in the interests of all the community. In a sense they can be said to enhance and extend democracy by allowing a representative range of groups to participate through their nominees on an important area of decision-making and service developing for the community [16].

2.2.   Innovation and Flexibility

It is argued that some excellent and innovative strategies have been produced which have clearly demonstrated the Partnerships' imagination and desire to make a difference, opening up new civil issues, seeing new possibilities and leading to new and creative solutions to different problems [17]. The approach of the diverse community and voluntary sector in particular has infused the other sectors with a more open and community based approach to move forward. This issue has been considered in relation to urban regeneration partnerships. McArthur [18] suggests that more effective policy can emerge through a 'process transformation' which, he argues, can be at work within partnerships. This transformation involves each participant looking to change the attitude and working practice of the others so, the potential is there for the voluntary and community sector partners to influence the other sectors - although this does depend on power and influence being equally distributed among the partners. Empowered to employ consultants and consult with user and community groups the Partnerships have opportunities to develop new strategies to tackle long-standing problems.

2.3.   Infusion of Expertise

The Partnership Boards have facilitated the involvement of a wide pool of expertise from the different sectors, which assisted in a more accurate identification of areas of greatest need.

Partnership Boards can channel a wide range and balance of expertise at problem issues. It can be argued that they have mobilised individuals and organisations and encouraged them to play a role in reconciliation and regeneration in local communities. The degree of community participation can also provide a continuous read-out of how economic and social policies are working locally. Ideally Partnership Boards are seen as orchestrating different approaches to produce a well-formed long-term sustainable vision [19].

2.4.   *Inclusiveness and Consensus Building*

A major expectation from Partnership Boards is that they would have the potential for consensus building around issues and cultivate understanding and assist in the search for reconciliation. This has been described as "the momentum for peace by encouraging politicians, the commercial, trade-union, public and voluntary sectors within a geographical areas to come together and agree on a common peace building vision" [20].

Part of the process was the promotion of inclusiveness by building new relationships and trust where before there was division and acute polarisation between the communities. An evaluation of the contribution of the voluntary sector noted that all sector representatives were enthusiastic about partnership as a method of participatory inclusion [21]. It has also been suggested that partnerships have served to strengthen and deepen civil society in Northern Ireland [22]. The importance of community participation lies not only in what it can achieve in terms of practical outcomes for disadvantaged groups, but also in the process of involving members of those communities in working for change. This can then impact on the capacity of individuals to become more active citizens. Lister [23] argues that, while a conventional understanding of political citizenship limits it to the sphere of formal politics and could discount community activism, this is a very narrow definition which fails to take into account of the importance of civil society (as underlined by Putnam, [24]) for economic development and effective government. Such claims can be expressed more practically in that Partnerships are a practical form of consensus politics in enabling people from different interests to work together in the interests of all the community. An added advantage is that partnerships can harness the involvement of people previously disenchanted by the unappealing nature of electoral politics in Northern Ireland.

2.5.   *Localism and Effectiveness*

Partnership Boards have a strong local identity associated with place and people. The focus on the locality means that local needs can be more easily addressed and services delivered more effectively. Thus this approach encompasses the principle of subsidiary in decentralisation to the lowest possible community level and represents a reversal of Government centralism. Such a bottom-up approach if pursued can encourage local community participation and ownership.

3.   **Partnership Boards: A form of quango?**

Can Partnership Boards be considered an innovative form of administration or "just another quango" - an administrative form which has come under increasing criticism in the United Kingdom?

Quangos or Non-Departmental Public Bodies (NDPBs) are defined by Payne and Skelcher [25] as bodies created as a result of government action, and which have no direct electoral accountability. Their functions can be:

a.   commissioning, purchasing, delivering certain public services;
b.   adjudicating over individual decisions made by public services;
c.   advising public policy makers.

In the UK much political and academic attention has focused on the widespread and increasing use of such bodies and on the extent of their responsibilities and functions. Weir [26] talks of "the explosion of unelected and largely invisible activity" while Lamb (1995) raises concerns about "the threats to democratic governance posed by non-elected executive agencies". A comprehensive review of quangos by Weir in 1995 and Weir and Hall [27] (for Democratic Audit) exposed their growth and argued that they lack "the essential democratic underpinnings of scrutiny, openness and accountability".

The nature and growth of quangos in the UK has changed throughout the 1980s and 1990s in line with changes in public administration. Some commentators (e.g.: Kooiman, [28]) argue that we live in a "centreless" society where the task of government has been to encourage a variety of arrangements whereby responsibility for governing will be passed to several actors, including quangos and Next Step Agencies. This hiving off of responsibility has resulted in an erosion of ministerial and political accountability which undermines the whole political system and which has enabled politicians to scapegoat responsibility for policy failure or inactivity. Through the use of patronage an elite has been created which is assuming responsibility for a large part of governance.

4.   The Use of Quangos in Place of Local Government in Northern Ireland

Northern Ireland has a long history of administration by quango dating back to the 1880s. However, in the context of political reform in the 1970s they were given direct responsibilities from local government. Until now they have operated in a situation where Direct Rule Government from London has meant there has been no regionally elected body to which they have been held to account. In the field of public administration they have been largely responsible for implementing and delivering policy decided at the parliament in London with little regard to the appropriateness of it to Northern Ireland. In such a context the concerns about the use of quangos raised above take on an added significance. Knox [29] has referred to Northern Ireland as a "worst case scenario" in which quangos continue to evolve on the back of an administrative system dogged by problems of electoral accountability.

4.1.   Major concerns about the use of quangos in Northern Ireland

A study of quangos in Northern Ireland [30] has pointed to a range of difficulties emanating from their extensive use. These could be grouped into broad categories of:

a.   Representation;
b.   Transparency and Openness;

c.   Accountability.

a.   Representation

While appointment to quangos are approved by the Secretary of State for Northern Ireland, it is the Northern Ireland Civil Service Departments which have responsibility for the nomination and appointments process. Despite the fact that quangos have played such a central role in the governance of Northern Ireland, until recently little was known about their composition or about systems of nomination and appointment. A number of studies [31] [32] point to deficiencies in the system of appointment which result in quango membership being restricted to a narrow range of people who were not representative of the general population and to problems relating to the unaccountable nature of many quangos.

According to government statistics [33] 33% of quangos members are women. This figure represents a significant improvement on the mid 1980s figure of 16% but has some way to go to reach the government target of 40%. Women are also much less likely to hold paid positions or be appointed to senior positions on quangos. However, this level of representation does compare well to electoral politics in the province - Northern Ireland has no female MPs in the Westminster Parliament; in the recent elections to the new Northern Ireland Assembly only 14 of the 108 members are women and only 18% of local government councillors are women.

A survey of quango members carried out in 1997/98 [34] stresses the substantial under-representation of young people highlighting the small number of members under the age of 45. It also shows that in a number of other respects membership is not representative. For e.g. the vast majority of quango members (72%) are educated to higher education level, compared to 6.5% of the general population. None of the members who responded to the survey were "unemployed". Membership is largely drawn from the business and professional community, with a relatively small proportion of people being drawn from the voluntary and community sectors.

One of the barriers to broader representation has been the resistance of those with responsibility for appointments to the introduction of 'new blood' i.e.: people with no previous experience of serving on quangos. The result of this is often that the same people are likely to move from quango to quango.

Local councillors have legal right to representation on a small number of boards. This was an attempt to incorporate a degree of local representation but there have been accusations of political bias in the selection of councillors with critics pointing to the over representation of the cross-community Alliance Party and the under representation of the more extreme Loyalist and Republican parties.

b.   Transparency and openness

The lack of transparency and openness has made it difficult for the public to hold quangos to account. The membership and work of quangos in Northern Ireland has traditionally been clouded in secrecy with little information being made available. This has made it difficult for citizens to access this form of governance; they have thus been largely excluded from a whole range of service providers and decision-making systems that have a direct impact on their day-to-day lives.

c.   *Accountability*

There has been a stark absence of mechanisms for accountability. Until now the ability of local politicians to influence the governance of Northern Ireland has been very limited. Ministers have a constituency base in England and no direct accountability to the citizens of Northern Ireland. Debates about accountability have often focused on the more limited concept of financial accountability and an emphasis on easily calculable fiscal objectives rather than on issues such as public access and accountability.

The whole system of accountability and standards in public life has been the subject of debate and policy change in the United Kingdom. In 1995 the Nolan Committee on Standards in Public Life recommended a number of changes to the system of public appointments. As a result of these, all appointments to executive quangos (as opposed to advisory bodies) should be subject to greater openness and scrutiny. This includes the public advertising of posts, the drawing up of "job" specifications and selection of quango members by a panel comprising an independent element. All executive appointments are now monitored, regulated and approved by an Independent Commissioner for Public Appointments.

Although this new system is still in its early stages it would seem that little substantial improvement has taken place. The more "open" system of recruitment has not resulted in a significant increase in the proportion of under represented groups. The most recent report of the Commissioner for Public Appointments for Northern Ireland [35], notes that the increase in the number of women rose by only one per cent in more than a year. Concerns have been expressed about the often rigid specifications set down for appointments and the fact that these may deter women from putting themselves forward and questions have been raised about the "independence" of selection panels.

4.2.   *Partnership Boards - Quangos by Another Name?*

The Northern Ireland Partnership Boards do share a number of the properties generally associated with quangos. They have no direct electoral accountability, in fact they are in the first instance answerable to another quango, the Northern Ireland Partnership Board. This board, as are most of Northern Ireland's quangos, is itself accountable to a government department in this case the Department of the Environment for Northern Ireland. The autonomy and independence of partnership boards is also limited by the fact that their policy guidelines and the allocations of funds are controlled by central government. The question for this paper is whether the District Partnership Boards offer improved attempts to incorporate some kind of more representative and participative governance which encourages active citizenship? Do they present a model of administration which could usefully be extended to encompass areas currently administered by quangos? Or could they be more accurately described as a localised form of quango? The following issues are relevant to the discussion.

Lack of independence from government

At present partnerships are not autonomous of government. There is a continuing line of accountability to government and major decisions and project are subject to central government approval. This means that partnership boards are not sufficiently independent for them to be considered a new form of governance. Their relationship to central government is one of dependence.

In terms of their relationship with government the partnership boards share the characteristics of the majority of quangos. Appointment to partnership boards are ultimately sanctioned by government and Hughes *et al.* [36] have pointed to the confusion which exists around nomination processes and to the difficulty experienced by partnership boards in obtaining/maintaining membership balance especially with regard to young people, women and voluntary and community sector representatives. Policy guidelines are set down by government, government has control over allocations of funds and the district partnerships are formally accountable to a government department. Their area of responsibility in service provision is limited by a community development approach to particular areas of social need, the total financial budget allocated for projects is not large and the areas of service provision are prescribed with little scope for discretion. It also appears that even within the partnership structure government representatives may tend to have the dominant influence.

Added value of partnership boards

Some of the key anticipated added values from partnership boards are no different from those associated with specialist quangos. This is particularly true in relation to expertise, sepecialism, impartiality, knowledge, innovation and flexibility. However, partnership boards have the potential to combat marginalisation and social exclusion (as shown by Walsh, Craig and McCafferty [37]) - but this assumes wide-ranging representation. As mentioned above both quangos and partnership boards have experienced difficulties achieving this. There is the opportunity for "bottom-up" participation to be enhanced through broader public involvement e.g.: Each partnership should have a strategy for informing and involving the citizens in their locality by holding public meetings and workshops with community groups. However, Hughes *et al.* [38] in their evaluation of sub-programme VI suggest that this may amount to little more than token consultation. The Northern Ireland Partnership Board [39] has acknowledged that there has been some difficulty in achieving genuine user-group participation in the projects supported. In particular, concern has been expressed about the inability of partnerships to date to involve what has been termed the "inactive poor" and the most marginalised. There is a danger of such new structures, as identified by Burton and Duncan [40] creating new elites which falls short of a participatory and democratic model of decision-making. Walsh *et al.* [41] argue that experience in the South of Ireland has shown that while local partnerships can broaden the policy-making circle to include previously excluded groups this may be achieved only on an individual basis or through the co-operation of weaker partners. Thus, community representatives in local partnerships may become part of a new policy-making elite that is accountable to the wider community and on which they have very little input.

Partnership boards have encouraged an element of subsidiarity through the localised structure for the planning, administration and delivery of projects. Conceptually partnership boards are not clearly distinguishable from a form of quango as to herald an innovative form of governance, but they do have some potential to increase active citizenship through empowering previously excluded groups and individuals to take decisions which could lead to enhanced social and economic conditions and improved community relations. Local partnerships have the potential to result in shared decision-making. Indeed, as Walsh *et al.* [42] (p.234) note: "...they are designed as arenas for negotiation between sectors that are normally opposed to another one. In turn, this model if developed, might be adaptable to the operation of mainstream quangos - especially in areas of health, social care and economic development. Particular advantage could stem from the transfer of ideas and practices from the voluntary and community sector to the other partners."

References

[1]   V. Belher, Partnership and the Fight Against Exclusion. The Lessons of Poverty 3 programme EelG, Lille, 1994.
[2]   M. Adshead and B. Quinn, 'The mover from government to governance: Irish development policy's paradigm shift', *Policy and Politics*, 26, **2** (1998) 209-226.
[3]   J. Walsh, J. Craig, and D. McCafferty, Local Partnerships for Social Inclusion. Oaktree Press, Dublin, 1998.
[4]   R.A.W. Rhodes, 'The New Governance: Governing Without Government, *Political Studies*, 44, **4** (1996) 652-67.
[5]   M.J. Smith, Reconceptualising the British State. Theoretical and Empirical Challenges to Central Government, *Public Administration*, 76, **1** (1998) 45-72.
[6]   P. Roberts and T. Hart, Regional Strategy and Partnership in European Programmes. Joseph Rowntree Foundation, York, 1996.
[7]   G. Marks, Decision making in Cohesion Policy, Describing and Explaining Variation. In: L. Hooghe (ed.), Cohesion Policy and European Integration. Building Multi-Level Governance, *Journal of Common Market Studies*, 34, **3** (1996) 342-78.
[8]   B. Jacobs, Networks, Partnerships and EU Regional Economic Development Initiatives in the West Midlands, *Policy and Politics*, 25, **1** (1997) 39-50.
[9]   C. Miller and Y. Ahmad, Community Development at the Crossroads - A Way Forward, *Policy and Politics*, 25, **3** (1997) 269-84.
[10]   G. Craig and M. Mayo, Community Empowerment. Zed Books, London, 1995.
[11]   D. Burns, R. Hambleton and P. Hoggarth, The Politics of Decentralisation, Revitalising Local Democracy. Macmillan, London, 1994.
[12]   M. Geddes, Partnership Against Poverty and Exclusion?. Policy Press, Bristol, 1997.
[13]   NIIS (Northern Ireland Information Service), Press release, March 23, 1998. Northern Ireland Partnership Board (1997), Annual Report 1996-7, Belfast.
[14]   NICVA (Northern Ireland Council for Voluntary Action), Making Partnerships Work, NICVA, Belfast, 1996.
[15]   NIIS, 1998, *Ibid.*
[16]   C. Knox, The Democratic Deficit in Northern Ireland. University of Ulster, Belfast, 1996.
[17]   NICVA, 1996, *Ibid.*
[18]   A. McArthur, Community Partnership - A Formula for Neighbourhood Regeneration in the 1990s?, *Community Development Journal*, 28, **4** (1993) 305-15.
[19]   NICVA, 1996, Ibid.
[20]   NICVA, 1996, *Ibid.*
[21]   NICVA, 1997.
[22]   NIIS, 1998, *Ibid.*
[23]   R. Lister, Citizen in Action: Citizenship and Community Development in a Northern Ireland Context, *Community Development Journal*, 33, **1** (1998) 226-235.

[24] R.D. Putnam, The Properous Community: Social Capital and Public Life, *The American Prospect*, **13** (1993) 35-42.

[25] T. Payne and S. Skelcher, Explaining Less Accountability: the Growth of Quangos, *Public Administration*, 75, (1997) Summer.

[26] S. Weir, Quangos - Questions of Democratic Accountability, *Parliamentary Affairs* 48, 2 (1995).

[27] S. Weir and W. Hall, The Untouchables: Power and Accountability in the Quango State, The Scarman Trust, London, 1996.

[28] J. Kooiman, Modern Governance. Sage publications, London, 1993.

[29] C. Knox, *op. cit.*

[30] A.M. Gray, D. Heenan, and W. Cousins, An Examination of the System of Public Appointments in Northern Ireland. University of Ulster, Belfast, 1998.

[31] A.M. Gray and D. Heenan, The Significance of Public Bodies in Northern Ireland and their Representation of Women, *Administration,* 43, 1 (1995) 57-75.

[32] C. Bradley, Keeping a Secret, *Fortnight*, **335** (1995), January, 25-26.

[33] Cabinet Office, 1997.

[34] A.M. Gray, D. Heenan, and W. Cousins, *op. cit.*

[35] Office Commissioners Public Appointments (OCPA), Commissioner for Public Appointments for Northern Ireland, Third Report 1997-1998, OCPA, London, 1998.

[36] J. Hughes, C. Knox, M. Murray, Qualitative Evaluation of Sub Programme 6, District Partnerships, European Union Support Programme for Peace and Reconciliation in Northern Ireland and the border counties of Ireland, University of Ulster., Belfast, 1998.

[37] J. Walsh, J. Craig, and D. McCafferty, *op. cit.*

[38] J. Hughes *et al.*, *op. cit.*

[39] R. Spencer, Conference address, *Partnership News*, Belfast, 1997.

[40] P. Burton and S. Duncan, Democracy, accountability in British politics: new agendas in British governance, *Policy and Politics*, 24, 1 (1996) 5-16.

[41] J. Walsh, J. Craig, and D. McCafferty, *op. cit.*

[42] J. Walsh, J. Craig, and D. McCafferty, *op. cit.*

New Public Management and its Critics.
Alternative Roads to Flexible Service Delivery to Citizens?

Carsten Greve & Peter Kragh Jespersen [*]

1.   Introduction [1]

The New Public Management (NPM) movement has swept across countries world-wide in the 1980's and 1990's [1] and most visibly been implemented in New Zealand, Australia, USA and Britain, but also in many European countries, including Scandinavia [2].

As a concept, NPM is certainly broad and inaccurate and most authors define it by listing a number of elements such as: Desegregating bureaucracies into state owned enterprises or executive agencies, making contracts, separating purchasing and provision of services, introducing market-like mechanisms, decentralisation of management authority, performance schemes, performance related pay and quality measurement [3].

Some would mention even more elements including ethical questions [4], but we prefer a more restricted list not including all kinds of administrative reforms in order to maintain a coherent concept.

The core of NPM is the combination of market mechanisms and private sector management ideas and techniques in the public sector and so NPM speaks both of institutional reform (by introducing market mechanisms) and administrative reform (by improving management) [1,4]. The focus seems to have shifted from corporatisation, systematic introduction of market-type mechanisms and decentralisation of management competence to include systematic quality measurement, evaluation and user involvement as well as ethic conduct guidance [5].

The purpose of this article is *not* to review current NPM developments but to explore the criticism aimed at NPM. There have been few attempts so far to identify main lines of criticisms [6]. We will review the criticisms both from the empirical and theoretical side and in this way we seek to fill a gap in the literature of NPM. We will then consider alternative roads to flexible service delivery to citizens. We will illustrate our arguments with examples from Denmark. Since Denmark has a history of decentralised local government and citizens' involvement Danish experiences might serve as inspiration for other countries.

[*] Professor Carsten Greve, Institute of Political Science, University of Copenhagen & Professor Peter Kragh Jespersen, Department of Economics, Politics and Public Administration, University of Aalborg, Denmark
[1] We are grateful for comments on this chapter from our colleagues in Aalborg and Copenhagen.

2.   Five Main Points of Critique

2.1.   *Lack of Working Economic Incentives*

The development of markets and market-like competition has been a key part of NPM strategies. Reforms vary from the creation of internal markets (e.g. freedom of choice among suppliers, separation of purchasers and providers and internal contracts) to various forms of greater involvement of private firms through contracting out and privatisation. According to public choice and principal-agent theory it is important to create institutional arrangements with build-in incentives for actors at different levels. Government should be organised to minimise opportunism and transaction-costs between self-interested parties. The theoretical argument is that separate entities with clear organisational goals, greater focus on results, performance control and individualisation of wages and other rewards will create a system of incentives for management and front-line personnel to be more efficient and cost-conscious.

Two kinds of critiques can be raised in relation to this line of argument. First the incentives must be strong and lasting in order to produce substantial change in organisational routines and behaviour. Here the empirical evidence from countries such as New Zealand and Australia where such principles have dominated shows that it has been very difficult to make the principles work. One reason is the disadvantages of a more competitive public service culture. It might increase the efficiency of each single organisation but it must be weighed against negative factors such as duplication of functions, higher transactions costs and inter-agency conflict. Another point is the unintended effects of harsh economic expenditure policy accompanying competition. It is difficult at the organisational level to maintain fixed cost-output relations under conditions of diminishing budgets and for the individual the incentives are hard to recognise if wages cannot be raised, career opportunities are hard to find and workload is raised. The total effects of such difficulties are undermining incentive mechanisms.

While the first point of critique is based on empirical evidence the other has to do with lack of consistency in the NPM strategy itself. There is clear conflict between elements aiming at strengthening the market and elements aiming at the transformation of governmental organisations in the direction of more flexible, innovative and flat hierarchies. Such modern organisation demands engaged, well-educated labour and management using typical "soft" Human Relations Management techniques. The competitive order depersonalises the provision of services by viewing labour as just any other resource. By contrast, the transformational order attempts to make public organisations more personal by asking for enthusiasm and commitment and by linking personal and organisational values. Public choice and principal-agent theory will criticise the "soft" NPM techniques in the transformational order for not considering the incentive structures enough and the receipt will be more competition, detailed contracts and clearer incentives at all levels. The problem is that this kind of medicine probably will reinforce the negative unintended consequences mentioned above.

2.2.   *Implementation Failures in Administrative Reforms*

A critique concerning Implementation failure can be found both in official reports (e.g. [7] on New Zealand, [8] on Sweden and [2]) and in theoretical analyses (e.g. [9], [10], [11]).

The empirical evidence shows that decentralisation of budget responsibility and competence are implemented without great difficulties in most countries and that general management ideas and practices have gained in relation to traditional administrative and professional leadership. But when it comes to quality improvements, innovation, responsiveness and flexibility results are disputed and ambiguous and there is virtually no solid documentation concerning the outcomes of the administrative reforms in the NPM strategy. [3]

Nevertheless some general trends can be found in the literature. First the tendency of decoupled administrative reforms. Within the new institutionalism in organisational sociology the concept of decoupling is used in order to explain why administrative reform so often failure [12, 13, 14]. The argument is that administrative reforms often reflect different and contradictory institutional requirements and that organisations in order to survive must respond to demands for administrative reform while at the same time protecting their operational core against sudden and contradictory changes.

Many NPM reforms suggest a public administration heading towards better government, more rational, effective and innovative. And it is virtually impossible to be against e.g. modernisation, quality improvement and flexible organisation.

So, the organisations of public administration are expected to react in a suitable way to modernisation programmes and one very common way of doing this is to decouple administrative reforms. On the surface they do implement all modern principles but the organisational daily routine remains practically unchanged. This has been labelled a state of organisational hypocrisy [12]. Decoupling can exist between organisational levels, (e.g. central and local government) between subjects and in time.

Secondly, implementation theory has shown the importance of attitudes and qualifications of professionals in front-line jobs. Most NPM reforms are top-down reforms but eventually those reforms will meet the micro-politics of professional service provision [15] and this meeting determines what actually happens with administrative reforms. The traditional regime in most service organisations could be labelled as a bureau-professional regime because it reflects both the traditional bureaucratic administration and the strong position of the professionals. The process of NPM reforms has not resulted in simple adoption of the new managerial regime but in complex and uneven patterns of institutional change.

This is hardly surprising because modern policy theory tells us [16, 17] that the influence of the street level bureaucracy and the professionals on the results of administrative reforms should not be ignored if real transformation is wanted. In the area of service provision this is very important because the extensive people processing of social welfare requires professional skills and competencies combined with personal engagement. Still most NPM reforms are implemented as typical top-down programs aiming at increasing efficiency, controlling the output of professionals and centralising the budgetary control. This strategy conflicts with traditional professional values and professional discretion but it has not yet changed the traditional bureau-professional regime. Clarke and Newman concludes that managerialism is not yet hegemonic but certainly the dominant force in the field of social welfare [18, p. 77]. Most common according to Newman and Clarke is a kind of subordination where traditional professional judgement is framed by managerialism through budgetary management. The professional assessment encounters budgetary implications at an earlier stage, so that professional judgement takes place alongside the resourcing of professional actions. In this way professional workers are perhaps slowly incorporated into the new structures of NPM but this is not the case until now.

2.3.   *Public Values Under Threat*

This point concerns the fate of traditional values like equity, due process and general public interest under the new managerial regime. The traditional bureaucratic administration does not correspond well with the new managerial regime where rules are just one kind of mean among others. In the language of NPM bureaucratic rule is certainly ineffective, not responsive and often irrational. But while it may be true that bureaucracy does not ensure effectiveness it is capable of securing equity and due process maybe better than most NPM reforms. This is the critique from public administration theorists like Rainey [19]. They argue that the distinctive characteristics of public organisations complicate public management.

NPM reforms tend to deny this and replace the traditional ethical values of equity and due process with the constant economic rationalisation of all activities. Nothing is wrong with economic rationalisation but something important about the public sector is missed. It is also important to ask if NPM does mean "more democratic", "more just" and "more human" and to ask not only if the public sector produces services in effective ways but also if it produces the right services and if it responds to the right needs [20, 21, 22].

This critique is rather profound because it questions the fundamental theses in NPM that the public sector can and should be managed in the same way as private companies and that the principles of rationalisation are uniform and not for discussion.

According to this critique it should be possible to find indications of values threatened in the NPM reforms. The first indication can be found in the problems of maintaining the division between policy and operational management. It has been one of the dogmatic principles that political representatives should not consider operational matters but the dominant public perception seems to be that these matters are the responsibility of government with the result that they are repoliticised and the result is shift between "hands-off and hands-on management" [23]. In spite of these instabilities the dominant tendency has been to depoliticise political decision making and this process has raised the criticism of a "democratic deficit". It has been raised as a problem that the shift of public services to more autonomous form exclude or minimise democratic forms of accountability.

If public management is able to match the complexity of social and political problems in the 1990s good management may hold its legitimacy but some problems seems to be inherent in the institutional arrangements of NPM.

The first problem is rooted in the shifting balance between centralised control and the dispersal of power to local government and a wide range of service providing organisations, some of them private. Governments are seeking to control rather unstable organisations in which problems and issues repeatedly denies to be depoliticised. The result seems to be endless short term survival policy interventions with no coherence between them. This might be called "Crisis Mismanagement" [24].

The problem seems to be that public administration during the years with NPM inspired operational management has lost its ability to deliberate policies and advice elected representatives about coherent reforms.

The second problem is due to competing provider organisations. The competitive mechanism might produce cost-efficient services but it has other effects and one of them is that management strive to control costs by excluding difficult clients, patient and citizens, by limiting the range of services and by shifting the responsibility for difficult "cases" to other department as it e.g. has happened in disputes about the responsibility for elderly people between hospitals and local government in Denmark. This kind of "Boundary Management" is an important technique for the new public manager. What is involved here is a question of legitimate demands on public services. Traditional public values operates with (equal) rights of the individual. If individuals are excluded from public services because they fit badly into the "core business" of the new cost efficient and output oriented provider organisations it will raise questions of legitimacy. How is it possible to legitimise this kind of exclusion and badly coherent public services in the long run? The problem for NPM is that it has no answer.

2.4. Lack of Citizen Involvement

NPM is certainly very concerned about the citizen as a consumer. It is part of the standard vocabulary to talk about consumer orientation and responsiveness to consumers. At the same time the concepts of citizen, citizens rights and citizen participation are almost non-existent in NPM debates. It raises the question of the adequacy of the consumer concept in relation to public services and the problem of citizen participation.

In the traditional welfare state the client role was dominating. The citizen received services offered by the welfare institutions, and were expected to behave in a passive way with no direct influence. With the NPM era the role changed to a user role where limited influence is allowed and in some cases even encouraged as in the Danish legislation about user dominated governing boards in schools, kindergartens and high schools. This could be labelled a kind of privatised user-democracy because this kind of democracy is limited to certain areas and particular interests.

But is the consumer role adequate for understanding the relation between citizens and public organisations? The ordinary consumer role will exist where a consumer pays for commodities at a market. But in the area of public service production the citizen pays nothing or little for public services, he receives services which are not commodities but have direct user-value for him and even if market like conditions are established one of the defining elements of the market is missing, that is the providers right to define if a service should exist or not. In the public sector this right belongs to political representatives not to the direct provider and the consumer.

It is however fully possible for management to think of public services as commodities and to act as if they were, but it changes the character of public services in a fundamental way because it removes the normative foundation which is intimately connected with fundamental principles of equal rights, fair process and redistribution of wealth governed by elected politicians. Those principles cannot be maintained if market conditions prevail and the citizen is reduced to consumer.

If citizens are not satisfied with the form and content of public services they will react not alone as consumers by using NPM established exit mechanisms but also as citizens using ordinary political channels. The "lack of citizens involvement" critique of NPM is that NPM institutional arrangements tend to close political channels of influence for citizens.

Even the politicians lack influence in relation to quality, lack of co-ordination and accessibility problems with particular services because of the NPM established division of policy and operational functions. Only at certain points in time is it possible to influence the daily operations by changing contracts and institutional arrangements and it is certainly not satisfactory for politicians facing critical citizens to argue that maybe the problem can be solved in the next election period in connection with the renewal of contracts.

Maybe it is possible to combine user influence with citizen involvement but certainly NPM reformers have been very reluctant in this area. Theoretical and practical models have actually been developed e.g. by Ranson and Stewart [22] (Britain) and Eriksen [20] (Norway) and in Denmark user dominated governing boards have been established but without any formal relation to the ordinary citizen.

The challenge is whether it is possible to find forms where public service organisation can combine user orientation and responsiveness with democratic accountability to politicians and citizens.

2.5.   No World-wide NPM Does Actually Exist

Christopher Hood and others have argued that instead of a world-wide uniform NPM trend it should be recognised that what we can observe is a pragmatic country-specific adoption of different elements from the NPM strategy [25]. This is hardly surprising because every administrative reform partly is a response to the specific problems of a certain country and has to be implemented in a specific political and administrative structure reflecting the historical development in that country. Many evaluations of NPM reforms in specific countries shows that in fact there is a lot of pragmatism and specific institutional patterns [7, 11, 26, 27 and 28].

In a review of NPM in the Scandinavian countries, Klausen and Ståhlberg [28] conclude that even within those countries it is not possible to find a common trend of NPM in a strict sense. It is, however, possible to speak of a Nordic variety of NPM in a wider sense because all countries have introduced standard NPM concepts and program at the state level but when it comes to local government differences are much stronger. This reflects the strong position of local government in the Scandinavian countries. Local government does not simply implement central NPM policies. They build on their own experiences, they invent new ideas, introduce new relations between politicians, local managers, user representatives and voluntary organisations and they find new ways of controlling service providers and they do in many different ways.

Naschold [29] has e.g. observed that in local government Norway, Sweden and Finland have used performance control more than in Denmark where user boards and the involvement of voluntary organisations have been more widespread than in the other countries.

On the other side it can be argued that there is in fact a common core in NPM especially in the theoretical foundation in classical liberal economic theory and public choice theory [1] and that some ideas e.g. the idea of Total Quality Management travels world-wide and takes the character of institutional superstandards that no modern administrative organisation can escape [30, 31]. The two strands do not necessarily contradict each other. World-wide ideas and reform perspectives can exist but they are interpreted and transformed in each country to suit the existing institutional structure and perceived problems.

Summing up, we have discussed five different critiques of NPM in this section. Other critiques could have been elaborated upon; de-professionalisation, the scant acknowledgement of inter-organisational networks, and NPM as part of a new right ideology. We have judged that the five critiques above are the most common in the literature. Three of the critiques can be dealt with within an NPM framework; 'lack of incentives', "implementation failure" an "no world-wide NPM exists". Two of the critiques are aimed at NPM from an external point of view, and thus, they are more profound; "public values under threat' and 'lack of citizens involvement".

3. Danish Experience with NPM

In this section, we present the main trends in Danish NPM at both central and local government level. The purpose is to get some empirical reference for our discussion on the five points of critiques and the Danish development is generally considered to be a part of the NPM wave, making it a suitable vehicle for discussion.

Four separate trends in the 1990's will structure our discussion: letting go through corporations and contract agencies, pragmatic tool-orientation, control, and citizen involvement.

3.1. Letting Go. Corporations and Contract Agencies

In the early 1990's, the Social Democratic government set out to continue the modernisation programme of the public sector which its predecessors, the various Conservative governments of the 1980's had started. In 1993 a report entitled "A New Look of the Public Sector" was issued [32]. Most NPM elements were present in the 1993 report. In local governments, reports to inspire debate were issued as well. The general report was soon followed by two more concrete initiatives of letting go: Corporatisation of public enterprises and internal contracting.

Corporatisation and privatisation have been on top of the government's agenda since 1993 where a report on state owned enterprises was issued [33]. The rationale behind corporatisation has been to "encapsulate politics"; Separate policy making from management. Parliament passed legislation enabling companies to follow commercial objectives. The state owned shares in 1997 in 46 companies plus *Post Denmark* which is an independent public enterprise. The government has controlling influence in 16 of the 46 companies [34] including important infrastructure companies such as *Copenhagen Airport, Danish Oil and Natural Gas, Combus and Scandlines*. Privatisation has occurred in some companies, most notably in *Tele Denmark* where the state sold all its shares to the American telecommunications company *Ameritech* but the general trend has been to create new corporations outside direct political control.

Internal contracts has been another important trend. In central government there are 56 agencies on contract with their department in 1998 compared to only 20 in 1993, and 25 more contract agencies are expected in 1999 [35]. Contract agencies sign contracts stating their aim and aspirations, much in the same way as the British Next Steps agencies. However a recent review showed that many key performance targets were not included in the contracts [36].

In local government, the contracting trend is also increasing. Budget chiefs in local governments expected contracting to flourish in 1997 [37]. Contracting is widespread in areas such as cleaning and supply services but in the 1990s contracting is used also in core fields such as hospitals and care for elderly people but not without problems.

To take hospitals as an example of contractualisation, some counties have used them in order to develop competition between hospitals. But the lack of incentives for the individual hospital and clinic is evident. There is no described system of sanctions connected with the internal contracts in case of non-fulfilment and money for out county patients treated does not automatically follow the patient to the treating clinic.

Contracting out is another debated policy issued. The government has endorsed contracting out in a number of reports, and the aspiration is voiced in local governments which are responsible for delivering public service to citizens. Despite the efforts contracting out, has only had a limited impact on the Danish public sector until now [38]. The attention to contracting out has been concentrated on a few spectacular cases in local government where service companies have tried to gain entry to a Danish welfare market.

Both corporatisation and contracting were evaluated in a Ministry of Finance publication on new forms of governance in the public sector [39]. Corporatisation showed mixed results. For example, one company went into liquidation and another showed impressive profits. Contracting has been judged a partial success, and the contract idea is widened to more areas of the public sector. Contracting is considered an important management tool in the future [40].

3.2. Pragmatic Tool Orientation

Shying away from starting more institutional reforms attention was in the beginning of the 90's directed towards internal efficiency through decentralised management reforms and pragmatic tools.

The most ambitious attempt to let public organisations construct their own modernisation effort was made when the Ministry of Finance published a "Toolbox for Welfare" [41]. The toolbox consisted of 13 reports with advice on e.g. writing managers' contracts, creating better employee conditions, management by objectives strategies and how to utilise consultancy in the best possible manner. Much emphasis was put on quality. The success of this campaign is not known and the Ministry of Finance has done little to document its success or failure. It was meant as an inspiration for public organisations and some organisations took up the challenge. In recent years the Ministry of Finance's strategy has been a model of inspiration and knowledge distribution where the initiative to modernisation is decentralised to individual departments [42]. In local government various forms of Management by objectives and the use of service declarations are widespread [43].

3.3.   Control & Evaluation

Having set endorsed state owned companies and contract agencies and encouraged public organisations to modernise themselves, the government and local councils have recently felt that it was time to take control again. A whole series of control devices currently fills the administrative landscape. Contrary to earlier bureaucratic control which relied on rule-making for the whole of the public sector, control is directed towards the output of single organisations in the 1990's.

A visible feature of the control trend is the use of the "controller" function in both state and local government. The control trend took off with a working group in the Ministry of Finance reporting in 1996 on "Internal control and follow-up on results" [44]. The idea was to see if management information systems and control measures could handle the increased autonomy of many public organisations that had been contractualised or gained competence through decentralisation. One new tool is the "enterprise account". By 1998 150 public organisations are required to publish material on what objectives that have achieved and how they have achieved them [45].

In 1997 local governments were required to make declarations of all their services. The service declarations should make citizens better able to judge the quality and amount of services they receive from local governments. The initiative was evaluated in 1998 [46]. Service declarations enable control from citizens as consumers and make central government control of local governments easier. Central control has also been facilitated by introducing administrative audit and extending the control by The Ombudsman to local government. The overall effect of these various control mechanisms can bee a shift away from a traditional bureau-professional regime in public services to a kind of regime strongly influenced by managerialism where traditional professional judgement and power positions are framed by budgetary management and new control mechanisms.

Control measures have also been tightened towards state owned companies. There are requirements for sending in both annual reports and six monthly statements to the Ministry of Business and Industry, for publishing information on new strategic initiatives (such as take-over bids), and the role of the Parliamentary Auditor has been clarified as to what kind of information he can retrieve from the companies. Summing up, control is emphasised again in the late 1990's.

3.4.   Citizens' Involvement

Of more interest than the purely managerial reform attempts are the inclinations towards making citizens more active in policy making and decision. Mostly, NPM is concerned with citizens as consumers. But users of public services are drawn into the administration of services through elected boards in welfare service institutions. In this way a new kind of democratic rule is established in local government. In Denmark it is called user democracy and it combines the roles of user and citizen.

In some policy areas like health care, citizens' involvement as users is notably difficult. But for other services such as schools, citizens' involvement has a history in Danish democracy. User involvement takes places at the regional and local level.

Most user boards are established by law since the beginning of the 1990s. User boards are found in schools, high schools kindergartens and elderly care. User boards give some influence to parents, but only on "strategic matters", and not operational matters. Research has shown that members of user boards also want influence on operational matters and general policy questions [47]. Without combining the aggregate democratic aspects with the integrative democratic aspects, the user boards cannot be absorbed in democratic governance properly [48].

Second, citizens in Denmark as users can take over some services themselves. In Denmark the legislation permits users of public services to organise service delivery typically in the form of. self-owned institutions with economic agreements with local government combined with some kind of direct fees. This happens with kindergartens and schools especially. In this way users are not drawn the wider public policy making, and their influence is confined to the particular service they want to see provided.

Third, voluntary social organisations are used more in Danish public service delivery in the 1990's. A new law on Social Service from 1998 presupposes that local governments work together with voluntary organisation in delivering public services. Voluntary organisations have been long-standing partners in delivering public service in Denmark but now their role is formalised and more citizens are in this way involved in service production.

Summing up various form of citizens involvement are developed in Denmark partly as a part of the NPM consumer orientation but also reflecting long institutionalised traditions for citizen involvement in public service production hardly compatible with NPM.

4.   Towards a Public Management that Works

In this paper, we have discussed five points of critique against NPM and assessed the critiques against the backcloth of the Danish experience with administrative reform in the 1990's. We have made three points clear.

First, we have shown that it is possible that lack of incentives, implementation failure and the absence of a world wide NPM could be dealt with within NPM framework itself. All three critiques could be adopted by governments around the globe: More incentives must be build into NPM programmes. Learning must take place from previous implementation failures. The specific variation in NPM elements for each country must be recognised by the OECD. NPM could be then be refined and widened.

Second the threat of public values and lack of citizens involvement critiques are more profound, and we see no indications that it is possible to deal with them within the NPM strategy. Instead they amplify the need for other strategies to be developed.

Third, it is possible that NPM reforms are more effective in some areas than in others. In the areas of people-processing services such as education, social services and health care we find more problems than in supply services and infrastructure. The reason could be that interaction of professionals and citizens requires considerably autonomy for front-line personnel, that separation of policy and operational managing is more difficult to maintain in such areas and that citizens react much more if public people-processing services are organised and delivered in a way that threaten traditional public values. NPM strategies has a tendency to control professional more tightly but has not been able to establish new ways of engaging the professionals and engagement is essential in people-processing services.

In conclusion, NPM is not a satisfactory general strategy for reforms in the public sector and is not a precise theoretical concept. NPM stands for market-based and managerial solutions to problems in public services neglects but tend to ignore other relevant aspects. Therefore, we have to look for other approaches.

Instead of NPM, we want to end this article by describing an approach to public service delivery based on the Danish experience with democratic governance. The alternative road is inspired by existing citizens' reform initiatives in Denmark. One principle, citizens' involvement, suggests itself as crucial in that discussion.

Citizens' involvement has a particular strong basis in Denmark, but is also present in other Scandinavian countries. For example, the Swedish researcher Stig Montin [49] ends a review of NPM in Sweden by noticing that participatory democratic and communitarian models are on the brink of a comeback in local governments. A citizen's perspective would concentrate on making citizens actively involved also in new discussions and reinterpretations of traditional public values, draw on citizens knowledge in preparing services, judging the quality of services by citizens panels and informing citizens by way of service declarations.

Some citizens are already very active if we are to believe the prospect of the "everyday maker" [50], a type of citizen who is not afraid to take initiatives and be responsible, but who do not process their political engagement through the established channels of political parties or social movements. More importantly, perhaps, most public service delivery in Denmark is based on local governments serving local people so a transformation to a "citizens' management" perspective is perhaps not such a big transformation.

By following a citizen involvement policy approach, the control trend reported above, could be relaxed as public service delivery would take place in interaction between citizens representatives of various professions and local governments. It is however not without problems to involve citizens more in public service delivery.

Besides the well-known problem of balancing control and autonomy, at least three issues seem problematic.

The first problem is users versus citizens. If users of a single organisation do not represent citizens at large, the involvement of users in administering and providing public service can be problematic. NPM wanted public management to look after citizens as users, and did not really care about other types of citizens involvement. A citizen involvement policy will require new roles for elected politicians, professionals and there is no guarantee that the involvement of citizens as users result in solutions optimal for the public at large. The question is how the interests of more passive citizens can be secured.

The second problem is the possible combination of active users and entrepreneurial bureaucrats. What will happen if new public managers and professionals of autonomous agencies form alliances with active "everyday makers" who fight their own individual cause? The two entrepreneurial forces may result in innovative, but expensive schemes in some areas which could worry the citizen as taxpayer and harm other areas . Such a combination of entrepreneurial public managers and active users can bypass both politicians and citizens at large who are, after all, the original inhabitants of representative democracy.

Nevertheless, we think that after a long period of NPM inspired strategies the time has come to formulate new and more comprehensive concepts of public management. We find that a citizen involvement policy including discussions and reorientations of central public values must be part of such a new concept.

References

[1]   D. F. Kettl, The Global Revolution in Public Management: Driving Themes, Missing Links, *Journal of Policy Analysis and Management*, 16, 3 (1997) 446-462.

[2]   OECD, Governance in Transition. Public Management Reforms in OECD Countries. OECD, Paris, 1995.

[3]   Ch. Pollitt, Justifications by Works of by Faith? Evaluating the New Public Management, *Evaluation*, 1, 2 (1995) 133-154.

[4]   P.M. Christiansen, "Styring mellem mål og resultater: Mellem hierarki og institutionelle reformer" i Økonomistyrelsen: Resultatstyring i praksis. Økonomistyrelsen København, 1997.

[5]   OECD, Improving Ethical Conduct in the Public Service. OECD, Paris, 1998.

[6]   P. Dunleavy and Ch. Hood, From Old Public Administration to New Public Management, *Public Money and Management*, (1994) 9-16.

[7]   A. Schick, The Spirit of Reform: Managing the New Zealand State Sector in a Time of Change. Report, Wellington, State Services Commission, 1996.

[8] Statens Offentliga Utredningar 1997 nr 57. I Medborgarnas Tjänst. En samlad Förvaltningspolitik för Staten, Stockholm, 1997.

[9] K.A. Eliassen and J. Kooiman, Managing Public Organizations. Sage, London, 1993.

[10] J. P. Olsen and B. G. Peters (eds.), Lessons From Experience: Experimental Learning in Administrative Reforms in Eight Democracies. Scandinavian University Press, Stockholm, 1996.

[11] Rune Premfors: Reshaping the Democratic State: Swedish Experiences in a Comparative Perspective. Stockholm SCORE center rapportserie 1996, No. 4, 1996.

[12] N. Brunsson, The Organization of Hypocrisy. Talk Decisions and Actions in Organizations. Wiley, Chichester, 1989.

[13] N. Brunsson and J. P. Olsen, The Reforming Organization. Routledge, London, 1993.

[14] K. A. Røvik, Moderne Organisasjoner. Fakbokforlaget, Oslo, 1998.

[15] M. Reed, Managing Quality and Organizational Politics. TQM as governmental technology. In: I. Kirkpatrick and M. Martinez Lucio (eds.), The Politics of Quality in the Public Sector. Routledge, London, 1995.

[16] W. Parsons, Public Policy. Elgar, London, 1995.

[17] M. Hill, The Policy Process in the Modern State. Prentice Hall, Hemel Hempstead, 1997.

[18] J. Clarke and J. Newman, The Managerial State. Sage, London, 1997.

[19] H. G. Rainey, Understanding and Managing Public Organizations. Jossey-Bass, San Francisco, 1997.

[20] E. O. Eriksen, Den offentlige Dimensjon. Tano, Oslo 1993.

[21] St. Ranson and J. Stewart: "Management in the Public Domain". *Public Money and Management*, spring/summer (1988).

[22] St. Ranson and J. Stewart, Management for the Public Domain, Enabling the Learning Society. Macmillan Press, Basingstoke, 1994.

[23] S. Harrison, D. Hunter, J. Marnoch and Ch. Pollitt, Just Managing: Power and Culture in the National Health Service. Macmillan, Basingstoke, 1992.

[24] A. C. Hay, Re-stating Social and Political Change. Open University Press, Buckingham, 1996.

[25] Ch. Hood: Exploring Variations in Public Management Reform of the 1980s. In: H. Bekke, Perry and Toonen (eds.), Civil Service Systems in Comparative Perspective. Indiana University Press, Bloomington, 1996.

[26] S. Montin and N. Elander, Citizenship, Consumerism and Local Government in Sweden. *Scandinavian Political Studies*, 18, 1 (1994) 25-51.

[27] J. Grønnegård Christensen and T. Pallesen, Coping with Leviathan: The Mixed Record for Danish Public Sector Reform. Institute of Political Science. Aarhus University, 1997.

[28] K. Klaudi Klausen and K. Ståhlberg (eds.), New Public Management i Norden. Odense Universitetsforlag, Odense 1998.

[29] F. Naschold, The Modernization of the Public Sector in Europe: A Comparative Perspective on the Scandinavian Experience. Helsinki, Ministry of Labour, Labour Policy Studies no 93, Helsinki, 1995.

[30] K. A. Røvik, Moderna Organisasjoner. Fakbokförlaget Oslo, 1998.

[31] K. Sahlin-Andersson, Standardizing in International Organizations. A study of OECD's Public Management Commitee, Paper SCORE center, Stockholm, 1997.

[32] Finansministeriet, Nyt syn på den offentlige sektor. Schultz, Copenhagen, 1997.

[33] Finansministeriet, Erfaringer med statslige aktieselskaber. Schultz, Copenhagen, 1993.

[34] Finansministeriet, Orientering til Finansudvalget om udviklingen i de statslige aktiebesiddelser samt den selvstændige virksomhed Post Danmark. *Aktstykke 270*, Folketingsåret, 1997-98.

[35] Økonomistyrelsen, Mål og resultatstyring kræver ledelse. *Nyt fra Økonomistyrelsen*, 3, 1 March (1998).

[36] Statsrevisorerne, de af Folketinget valgte 1998: Beretning om kontraktstyring. København, 1998.

[37] C. Greve, Målstyring, kontraktstyring og udlicitering i den offentlige sektor. *Økonomistyring & Informatik*, 13, 2 (1997/98) 109-131.

[38] C. Greve (ed.), Privatisering, selskabsdannelser og udlicitering - et politologisk perspektiv på udviklingen i Danmark. Forlaget Systime, Aarhus, 1997.

[39] Finansministeriet, Budgetredegørelse 96. Tillæg: Nye styringsformer i den offentlige sektor, Schultz, Copenhagen, 1996.

[40] Finansministeriet, Administrationspolitisk status. Schultz, Copenhagen, 1997.

[41] Finansministeriet, Værktøj til velfærd. Schultz, Copenhagen, 1995.

[42] N.Å. Andersen, Selvskabt forvaltning, Nyt fra Samfundsvidenskaberne. Copenhagen, 1995.

[43] N. Ejersbo (ed.), Politikere, ledere og professionelle i kommunerne. Effekter af strukturændringer. Odense Universitets Forlag, Odense, 1997.

[44]   Finansministeriet, Intern kontrol og resultatopfølgning. Schultz, Copenhagen, 1996.

[45]   Økonomistyrelsen, Økonomistyrelsens hjemmeside for virksomhedsregnskaber (www.oes.dk).

[46]   Indenrigsministeriet, Servicedeklarationer - en rapport om serviceinformation til borgerne. Schultz, Copenhagen, 1998.

[47]   N.N. Kristensen, Skolebestyrelser og demokratisk deltagelse. Jurist og Økonomforbundets Forlag. Copenhagen, 1998.

[48]   Eva Sørensen, New forms of Democratic Empowerment: Introducing User Influence in the Primary School system in Denmark". København, Working Paper no. 4, 1997, The Democracy Project.

[49]   S. Montin, New Public Management på svenska. *Politica*, 29, **3** (1998) 262-278.

[50]   H. Bang and E. Sørensen, Fra græsrødder til hverdagsmagere. København 1997, Working Paper No. 3, The Democracy Project, Copenhagen.

Between Autonomy and Subordination: Bureaucratic Legitimacy and Administrative Change in Germany

Klaus H. Goetz [*]

1. Between Autonomy and Democracy: The German Formula of Bureaucratic Legitimacy

Assumptions about the legitimacy of public administration underlie much of the contemporary discussion about administrative reform, "modernisation" and the New Public Management. Yet these assumptions are rarely made explicit. Traditionally the debate over administrative legitimacy has revolved around the question of how - normatively and empirically - democracy and bureaucracy can be reconciled. Two main answers have been given to this question. One line of argument stresses the need for the effective subordination of public bureaucracy to the structural and procedural norms of a democratic polity. The democratic principle requires that public bureaucracy be steered and controlled by individuals and institutions that enjoy a direct democratic legitimisation through popular elections. In this conception bureaucratic legitimacy is derived (or mediated) rather than intrinsic, and one of the main challenges facing democratic governments is to tame bureaucratic power. Another perspective highlights the legitimising effects of functional autonomy. Public bureaucracy is understood as a distinct, internally differentiated and specialised social system that operates according to specific rationality criteria. Sociological accounts of public bureaucracy stress that the developmental logic of modernisation implies autonomisation and self-regulation as preconditions for the effective operation of public bureaucracies. At the institutional level, the autonomy of the civil service is grounded in its claim to act as the guardian of the public good against particularistic interests; at the individual level, the professionalism of career civil servants ensures impartial, objective and regular administration.

In the Federal Republic, a dual conception of bureaucratic legitimacy prevails that balances democratic accountability with the positive recognition of bureaucratic autonomy [1]. Democratic accountability is secured through far-reaching steering, guidance and control rights of democratically legitimated persons and institutions, notably the political executive and parliament, vis-à-vis the bureaucracy. In the German constitutional order democracy as representation is complemented by the notions of the constitutional state under the rule of law, subsidiarity, inclusivity and transparency. Accordingly, democratic public administration is also fully subject to the Constitution and to the substantive and procedural requirements of the *Rechtsstaat*. Moreover, decentralisation and deconcentration, for example in the form of federalism; opportunities for popular participation in administrative decision-making; and stringent conditions on the openness of administrative activity and citizens' rights of information are further essential means of ensuring a democratic administration.

The restrictions on the autonomy of public administration have, until recently, typically been discussed in terms of democratic arrangements within the nation-state. The problem of

[*] Dr. Klaus H. Goetz, Lecturer, London School of Economics and Political Science, United Kingdom

democratic public administration was considered within the framework of national sovereignty. Thus, the constitutional *Rechtsstaat* was understood as sovereign state in which the Constitution represented the highest and most fundamental norm overriding all other legal norms and parliamentary, executive and judicial acts and decisions. Subordination to law meant above all subordination to laws passed by national and Laender parliaments. Decentralisation and deconcentration were structural, procedural and substantive principles to guide the development of the national administrative system; and participation and accessibility were developed through national, regional and, in particular, local mechanisms of inclusive and transparent administrative policy-making.

Democracy is to be balanced by functional autonomy. The latter is normatively grounded in the distinction between the public good and the interest of the political executive. As guarantors of the public good, the civil service is expected to act to some degree as a counterweight to the changeable and volatile political executive. In one of its early judgements the Federal Constitutional Court clearly emphasised this role. Thus it noted that the Constitution regards the "civil service as an institution, which (...) should secure a stable administration and thereby constitute a balancing factor (*ausgleichenden Faktor*) vis-à-vis the political forces that shape the life of the state" [2]. A degree of autonomy from the transitory wishes of political decision-makers is, therefore, necessary, if the civil service is to make its distinctive contribution to the constitutional order. Public bureaucracy enjoys a legitimacy that is grounded in its specific orientation towards the public good, its bureaucratic character and the professionalism of its personnel. German bureaucratic theory, in particular from legal perspective, has therefore repeatedly warned against a public bureaucracy that is comprehensively subordinated to external direction, including by parliament.

The tensions between autonomy and democracy as legitimising principles have often been described. For much of the post-war period, they were accommodated through a particular configuration of administrative arrangements which, in the following, is called the traditional model of public bureaucracy. However, as is argued below, the public bureaucracy model is subject to fundamental challenges, notably post-modernisation and Europeanisation. The latter challenge its specific mission, organisational character and professionalism, on the one hand, and its embeddedness in the nation-state, on the other. In the context of post-national and post-modern statehood, both the normative validity of the dual legitimatory bases of bureaucratic authority and the practical efficacy of traditional arrangements that legitimise the exercise of bureaucratic authority are called into doubt.

Outline I: Public Bureaucracy in Germany: The Traditional Model

1.   Basic Conditions

a) modernity
b) nation-state

2.   *Key Internal Features of the Administrative System (inter alia)*

a) sovereignty (*Hoheitlichkeit*)
b) rule of law
c) territoriality
d) functional-institutional differentiation and specialisation
e) professional career civil service
f) bureaucratic rationality

3.   *Forces of Integration*

a) public law
b) political homogeneity
c) highly developed mechanisms of inter-institutional co-operation and co-ordination
d) unifying administrative culture

4.   *Constitutive Administrative Environment*

a) liberal-democratic political system anchored in the nation-state
b) social market economy
c) pluralist society with effective intermediary associations

5.   *Legitimatory Patterns*

a) orientation towards the common good, specific bureaucratic rationality (e.g., impartiality, objectivity, regularity) and professionalism as normative bases for functional-institutional autonomy of public bureaucracy
b) subordination to substantive, structural and procedural principles of democracy, in particular through steering and control by democratically legitimated individuals and institutions; subsidiarity, popular participation; transparency and information

2.   The Traditional Model of Public Bureaucracy

The *basic conditions* of the traditional model of German public administration are well known. Modernity represented a constitutive element of bureaucratic administration. Viewed from the perspective of sociological modernisation theory, modernisation and the emergence of bureaucracy as a function and organisation can be understood as a process of co-evolution. Modernity was a historical precondition for the development of public bureaucracy as a social system. As part of the process of social modernisation, which involved differentiation, specialisation and rationalisation, public bureaucracy increasingly acquired the character of a distinct value sphere, with its own organisational principles and a distinct bureaucratic rationality.

The logic of modernisation not only fostered the emergence of public administration as a social system; it also characterised its internal development. Accordingly social science accounts of public administration regularly stress the importance of differentiation and specialisation - hierarchical, functional, territorial, institutional, procedural, instrumental and personnel - as defining characteristics of public bureaucracy. Finally, modernity also constituted a basic condition of the ecology of public administration. In sum traditional public bureaucracy has emerged within the context, and as a consequence, of modernisation; its internal development has been shaped by the modernisation paradigm; and its constitutive environment has been modern.

In the modernisation discourse within political science the emergence of nation-states and democratisation tend to be regarded as important defining features of modernity. The importance of a territorially and functionally limited democratic statehood for public administration is obvious. This statehood assigns to public administration a sphere of action that is spatially clearly defined; at the same time, it has important implications for the structures, procedures, instruments and substance of administrative action. In other words: liberal democracy in the nation-state requires a particular type of public administration and shapes the relationships between administration and politics, the economy and civil society. As Comparative Public Administration shows there remain substantive differences in the administrative systems of Western democracies [3]. Yet the academic debate on administrative development in the post-Communist states of Central and Eastern Europe has served to underline the fundamental differences between democratic and non-democratic public administration and the commonalties in the administrative traditions of the continental West European democracies [4].

The key *internal features* of public bureaucracy that developed within the framework of the liberal-democratic nation-state include, in particular, (i) the sovereignty (*Hoheitlichkeit*) of administrative action; (ii) the subordination of administration under the rule of law; (iii) the importance of territory and (iv) functional-institutional differentiation and specialisation as central principles of administrative organisation; (v) the professionalisation of bureaucratic personnel; and (vi) the dominance of a specific bureaucratic rationality.

The high degree of internal differentiation requires strong *integrative forces* if differentiation is not to lead to fragmentation and disintegration. Four types of integrative factors have proved of special significance in this respect. Perhaps the most important has been public law, notably constitutional and administrative law. Public law not only marks the boundary between the state and the private sector. Constitutional and administrative law also provides a comprehensive and binding set of common norms to all parts of public administration. It shapes administrative organisation, but, in particular, administrative procedures and the forms and instruments of administrative action. Public law, thus, contains public bureaucracy with an overarching normative framework.

A second important integrative factor has been the high degree of political homogeneity that has characterised the "Bonn Republic" and the "politics of centrality" to which it has given rise [5]. A centripetal party system and a low degree of ideological confrontation in party-political competition have facilitated a consensus- and continuity oriented politics of the "middle way" [6]. The remarkable stability of the political framework favoured continuity and routinisation in administrative action. Political homogeneity also assisted inter-administrative communication and negotiation, because it lessened the impact of party politicisation in parts of the administrative system. Party-political boundaries did not develop into insurmountable obstacles of inter-institutional co-operation and co-ordination. The cross-party co-operation amongst the German Länder in the system of executive federalism illustrates this point.

Highly developed mechanism of inter-institutional co-ordination and co-operation are, accordingly, a third decisive integrative force within the traditional administrative system. Deconcentration and decentralisation in the form of horizontal and vertical functional-institutional differentiation require specific co-ordinative arrangements, if the necessary degree of inter-institutional co-operation is to be achieved. For example, commentators on the German federal system have for many years emphasised the decisive importance of formal and informal structures and procedures of intergovernmental collaboration as a precondition for the functioning of Germany's system of "co-operative federalism" [7]. By contrast inter-institutional relations within the different tiers of the administrative system have received much less academic attention. We know little about the co-operation between the Federal ministerial administration and non-ministerial Federal field services. Even the classic topic of inter-ministerial co-ordination has remained empirically largely unexplored since the important studies of Mayntz and Scharpf dating from the early 1970s. Nonetheless, the practical importance of the rich repertoire of nation-based co-ordinative and co-operative arrangements seems beyond dispute. The frequent characterisation of the Federal Republic as a 'co-ordination' democracy' is, therefore, justified.

A stable legal and political framework and co-operative administrative structures and procedures are important conditions for the development of a common administrative culture. The administrative culture of the "old" Federal Republic exhibited considerable regional and sectoral variations. Nonetheless the importance of shared value orientations, associated with an orientation towards the common good, is well attested.

A further constitutive element of the public bureaucracy is the pattern of its relationships to its *environment*. Such relational criteria are of special significance in comparative categorisations of administrative systems. In this respect the relations between public administration, on the one hand, and politics, the economy and society, on the other, are of special importance [8]. For the Federal Republic, these constitutive environments can briefly be characterised as: a liberal-democratic political system anchored in the nation-state; a social market economy; and a pluralist society with strong intermediary organisations. They formed the constitutive environment of the administrative system since the early 1950s, and they shaped not only administrative organisation and procedures, but also the substance, form and instruments of administrative action. For example, the characterisation of Germany as a "social state" was a decisive impetus behind the massive extension of welfare administration, while the guiding principle of the social market economy shaped the tasks of economic administration. Strong intermediary institutions served to lighten the load of public administration, since they could often be used for public service production and delivery, but they also restricted administrative autonomy.

3.   Challenges to Public Bureaucracy: Post-modernisation and Europeanisation

There are many indications to suggest that the traditional model of public bureaucracy as outlined in the previous section is subject to a far-reaching process of change that calls into question the identity and stability of public bureaucracy and undermines the traditional balance between functional autonomy and democratic subordination. These changes cannot be traced to a single transformative force; but changes in the basic conditions of public administration are of special importance. They can briefly be characterised with reference to the notions of post-modernisation and Europeanisation.

The concept of post-modernity and, by implication, of post-modernisation is certainly ambiguous and has, up to now, defied a commonly accepted definition. If post-modernity is understood as a historical-empirical phenomenon – rather than an epistemology – [9], it describes in the first instance the historical conclusion of the age of modernity. The latter's axial developmental principles are either reversed or, in less radical analyses, modified to an extent that suggests a historical discontinuity. Whereas modernisation stands for progressive functional-institutional differentiation, specialisation, and rationalisation, post-modernisation is associated with dedifferentiation, de-specialisation, and the growing porosity, if not breakdown of systemic boundaries and the inter-penetration of value spheres.

Many, if not most, of the gradual changes in the internal features of public administration can be understood as the result of modernisation [10]. For example, the pluralisation of the organisational forms of public administration can be explained fairly straightforwardly in the categories of sociological modernisation theory. At the same time, however, the systemic boundaries of public administration are subject to a process of rapid erosion. The "dialectics of differentiation" formulated by Crook, Pakulski and Waters [11] help explain the seeming contradiction between progressive modernisation and concomitant de-differentiation. According to these authors, under the conditions of post-modernity the principles of differentiation and specialisation give way to hyper-differentiation and hyper-specialisation. This further intensification of the modernisation logic implies that, at the macro level, systemic boundaries and systemic rationalities lose their distinctive quality. Applied to public administration the "dialectics" can be formulated as follows: growing differentiation and specialisation remain of central importance for institutional, organisational and functional developments. But what appears as modernisation at the micro-level leads to de-differentiation and de-limitation at a systemic level. The specific internal characteristics of public bureaucracy become less pronounced, the boundaries to the administrative environments less distinct, bureaucratic rationality is supplemented, and increasingly supplanted, by entrepreneurial rationality and the rationality of the market.

The process of Europeanisation can also be understood as a form of "delimitation". The almost inflationary use of this notion in the social sciences in recent years attests to its suggestive qualities, but has not contributed to substantive clarification. Insofar as Europeanisation is used about the political-administrative systems of the EU member-states, it would appear to carry at least three different meanings:

(i)   Europeanisation describes the strengthening of supranational political decision-makers at the expense of national powers. From this perspective, Europeanisation is associated, in particular, with the loss of national sovereignty and the gradual hollowing out of the statehood of the member states.

(ii)   Europeanisation describes the gradual approximation or convergence of the governmental and administrative systems of the member states. The adaptive imperatives arising from the economic and political integration processes lead to a gradual EU-wide convergence of national institutional arrangements.

(iii) Europeanisation describes the emergence of a "fusioned federal state" [12] as the latest stage in the development of European statehood. National constitutional traditions are subject to major adaptive pressures as a result of the process of progressive fusion; but there are no *a priori* reasons to assume that national adaptations necessarily lead to EU-wide convergence.

The understanding of Europeanisation adopted in this paper accords with the third definition that assumes a progressive opening of national statehood and its supranational and international inter-penetration. This development does not mean that all elements of national statehood are challenged by European integration. On the contrary, integration is often compatible with national traditions and, in some cases, might serve to reinforce them. For example, the study of intergovernmental relations in Germany shows that Europeanisation has not been equivalent to a profound reshaping of the national system of Federal-Länder relations. Rather, adaptations within the intergovernmental system have tended to intensity institutional properties that initially evolved with little or no reference to the European integration process [13].

Unlike in other EU member states the European integration process in the Federal Republic did not confront a stable and historically validated institutional order. The political and institutional consolidation of the West German state and the political and institutional consolidation of the European integration project were mutually dependent. The democratic stabilisation of the Federal Republic relied on its firm anchoring within the European framework. The Federal Republic was, therefore, from the outset a "penetrated polity" [14].

Accordingly the Europeanisation of German statehood is not a recent phenomenon [15]. However since the mid-1980s the dynamics of European integration have profoundly altered the relations between the member states and the EU institutions. Five developments are of particular significance: (i) the continuous sectoral extension of supranational powers; (ii) the more intensive use of EU rights of command, prohibition and control; (iii) the progressive extension of EU promotional policies; (iv) the growing role of the EU as a co-ordinator of national policies; and (v) the emergence of the EU as an actor in the international system.

There is much to support the domestic Europeanisation thesis; but at least for public administration, empirical research on the phenomenon is still thin on the ground. There are, for example, some more recent studies on the Europeanisation of public law in general and administrative law in particular (see below), studies on the impact of European integration on intergovernmental relations, and also some policy-oriented studies [16]. Systematic and historically grounded analyses are, however, not yet available. The Europeanisation of public administration is, thus, for the moment, a plausible hypothesis rather than a carefully documented and conceptually and theoretically well-understood reality.

Outline II: Public Administration in Germany under the Influence of Post-modernisation and Europeanisation

1.   Basic Conditions

a) post-modernisation
b) Europeanisation

2.   Key International Features of the Administrative System (inter alia)

a) decline of sovereign-hierarchical modes of administrative action
b) rule of law, but pluralisation of legal sources
c) deterritorialisation
d) functional-institutional development according to the "dialectics of differentiation"
e) progressive weakening of career civil service
f) advance of entrepreneurial and market rationality

3.   Weakening of Traditional Forces of Integration

a) decline in the integrative capacity of public law
b) growing political heterogeneity
c) new challenges to co-ordinative and co-operative capacities
d) pluralisation of administrative cultures

4.   Constitutive Environments

a) externally and internally "delimited" liberal-democratic political system
b) internationalised market economy; post-welfare state paradigm
c) declining capacity of traditional intermediary associations

5.   Legitimatory Patterns

a) gradual erosion of functional-institutional autonomy as notion of common good is called into doubt; bureaucratic rationality is complemented (supplanted?) by entrepreneurial and market rationality; and professional career civil service perceived as anchronism.
b) disputed effectiveness of democratic structural and procedural principles, in particular as a consequence of Europeanisation

4.   Public Bureaucracy in Decline

Post-modernisation and Europeanisation have a profound impact on the internal features of the administrative system, integrative factors, the constitutive environment of public administration and its legitimisation bases (see Outline II). This paper restricts the analysis to internal features and integrative factors, before turning to the legitimisation bases in the subsequent section.

Turning first internal features, there is no lack of empirical surveys that document the current state of administrative development in Germany and discuss new trends. These surveys provide many examples of the gradual decline of the model of a hierarchical administration and of the "public bureaucracy state", even though the pace and, in particular, the direction of this development are the subject of much controversy. Key developments include:

A sovereign-hierarchical mode of action as a defining characteristic of public administration loses in importance. The more apparent the functional limits to a sovereign-hierarchical administration are, the more it relies on alternative decision-making procedures and forms of action. In German academic debate this development has been discussed with reference to the "co-operative administration" that relies on negotiation and mediation rather than command and prohibition to achieve its objectives [17]. Co-operation contains "structural, procedural and outcome-oriented aspects" [18]. In contrast to sovereign-hierarchical action co-operative administration requires that "the actors involved mutually recognise each other as having equal rights"; it demands "communication based on dialogue"; it is based on negotiation; and it aims at "voluntary agreement" and "a common decision recognised by all participants" [19]. Such administrative decisions are often not implemented through unilateral administrative acts, but through formal and informal agreements or private-law contracts. Public institutions do not simply relinquish their sovereign hierarchical instruments. Rather, as Hoffmann-Riem notes [20], they are employed in a more subtle fashion and jointly with other steering devices.

The subordination of administrative action under the rule of law is not questioned in principle, but the pluralisation of the sources of law changes the nature of the rule of law. Two developments deserve highlighting: the growing importance of private law, notably in the wake of privatisation and corporatisation; and the growing influence of supranational sources of law, especially European law. In both cases more is at stake than the rise in the number of relevant sources of law for public administration. What is more important are the potential conflicts between different sources of law and their consequences for the systematic principles of German administrative law. The influence of European administrative law on German administrative law has become increasingly obvious in recent years, in both as regards general and special administrative law [21]. This Europeanisation process affects not only "the law of administration. It also influences the structures of administrative action, the understanding of public administration and thinking about administrative law" [22]. Legal studies have only begun to analyse systematically the impact of European integration on the administrative law orders of the member states). Yet, some commentators speak of a "revolutionary impact of Community law" on the defining principles of German administrative law [23].

Territoriality as a central principle of administrative organisation and point of reference for administrative action loses in significance. The link between function and space as an ordering principle of public administration is not severed; but their traditionally strong connection is weakened. At least four trends contribute to this partial deterritorialisation. (i) In an integrating Europe the boundaries of the nation-state are no longer the boundaries of national administrative action. Domestic administrative action does not just have unintended "external consequences"; rather the purposive influencing of political, economic and social developments beyond national borders becomes an eminently important task of national administration. At the same time "extra-territorial" administrations intervene substantially in the national administrative process. (ii) Within the boundaries of the nation-state there is a growing awareness of the need for new forms of horizontal administrative co-operation, as the positive and negative externalities of public action become more apparent. In the Federal Republic this has given rise to attempts to institutionalise new forms of co-operation amongst the Länder [24]. (iii) New and improved means of information and communication imply that the close geographical link between the production and the consumption of administrative services is weakened. Similar to private service companies, many parts of public administration are increasingly able to use resources from outside their own geographical area of responsibility in the production of administrative services. (iv) Finally the notion of deterritorialisation points to the growing role of transnational enterprises for the production of public goods and services. As Dunleavy has noted, there is a growing "decoupling of public services production from a single-country context; (...) the direct implementation of tasks in the public services may cease to be organised in a single-country way, and come to be organised by private corporations operating on a much wider scale" [25].

Functional-institutional differentiation and specialisation continue to advance. However, as argued above, modernisation at the micro level translates into de-differentiation and de-specialisation at the macro level. German public administration has always relied on a diverse repertoire of organisational forms. In fact organisational variations, mutations and hybrid forms are so numerous as to defy comprehensive classification. This institutional differentiation within the German administrative system can to a large extent be understood as the result of functional specialisation. The same observation applies to the growing use made of organisational privatisation (corporatisation), i.e. the establishment of publicly-controlled enterprises under private law. Yet this "escape into private law", which is noticeable at all levels of the administrative system, constitutes another indicator of the decline of sovereign-hierarchical administration. At least from the perspective of many politicians and practitioners the advantages of a private-law, "deprivileged" form of public action seem to outweigh any potential disadvantages. The "constitutional costs" of organisational privatisation are rarely explicitly addressed in such cost-benefit calculations [26].

The gradual undermining of the professional civil service is a result of functional-institutional de-differentiation and de-specialisation. The "traditional principles of the career civil service" that are guarded by the German constitution presuppose a state that is functionally and institutionally clearly identifiable, oriented towards the common good and sovereign. The more the reality of the state deviates from these assumptions, the more the traditional civil service appears as an anachronism and an obstacle on the path towards an entrepreneurial administration. The state as an enterprise is an employer, not a *Dienstherr* to whom the civil servant owes special loyalty and responsibilities.

Entrepreneurial rationality and the rationality of the market become alternative guidelines for the administrative system. At the same time, as the internal features of the administrative system change, the forces that have traditionally helped to integrate the diverse parts of public administration are declining. This observation focuses on the declining integrative capacity of public law; growing political heterogeneity; the diversification of administrative cultures in the wake of institutional differentiation and the inter-penetration of systemic rationalities; and new challenges to co-ordinative and co-operative arrangements.

o The growing selectivity of public law is generally acknowledged amongst German academic lawyers. Suffice it to mention the studies by Grimm, whose work centres on the declining capacity of constitutional law for regulation and purposive steering [27]; or the studies by Hoffmann-Riem, Schmidt-Aßmann and others who focus on administrative law [28]. Schmidt-Aßmann emphasises that only law that is systematically developed is capable of responding to the demands for purposive steering to which contemporary administrative law needs to respond [29]. Yet this requirement is increasingly difficult to fulfil, as the traditional division between public and private law becomes eroded.

o The German political system is marked by growing political heterogeneity, most evidently in the party system. The German party system has become increasingly diverse over the past two decades, as a consequence of the consolidation of the Greens, the PDS in the new German Länder and extreme right-wing parties in some West German states. The centripetal character of the party system of the Bonn Republic is called into question by polarisation on the extreme left and right. Many commentators argue that two -arty systems are emerging within the Federal Republic. In his study of the 1994 Federal elections, the American political scientist Russell Dalton proposes that "the new Germany contains two different party systems and two distinct electorates. Although the party labels may be the same throughout Germany, the parties advocate and represent different political views across the regions and attract different bases of support" [30]. If this observation is true, it has far-reaching implications for intergovernmental relations.

o Research on administrative culture since unification has principally been directed towards developments in the new Länder [31]. It is not yet certain whether in the new Länder a specific east German administrative-cultural identity is taking root; but there is clear evidence of significant West-East differences which, as yet, show little sign of declining. However, in a longer-term perspective the reorientation of public administration towards entrepreneurial principles and the growing autonomisation of administrative institutions will probably pose a more fundamental threat to the integrative capacity of administrative culture. At heart, this is about the conflict between a bureaucratic organisational culture, on the one hand, and an entrepreneurial organisational culture, on the other. This pluralisation of administrative culture does not just create a substantial potential for conflict in inter-institutional relations within the public sector. Within discrete organisations cultural "misunderstandings" and disagreements are set to increase between personnel grounded in a bureaucratic culture and those with a manageralist and entrepreneurial outlook. Thus administrative culture is in danger of becoming a force of disintegration.

o Finally, traditional arrangements of inter-administrative co-operation and co-ordination are partially devalued as a consequence of the international orientation of the administrative system, but, in particular, because of the transition from "government" to "governance". As regards, first, the impact of European integration, the centrality of the national level of government in the member states has not, up now, been eroded as a result of intensification of EU regional activities. A "Europe of the Regions" is still a political demand rather than a governmental-administrative reality: "There has been no by-passing of the nation state in favour of a Europe of the regions" [32]. However, national co-operative and co-ordinative arrangements are becoming ever more closely tied into the EU multi-level system and EU-wide networks of co-ordination. As Wessels and Rometsch point out, "German civil servants at all levels have pushed and have been pulled into a growing EU system (...) For many German civil servants this 'multi-level game' is an addition to the game which they use to play inside the Federal Republic" [33]. Vertical and cross-boundary inter-administrative co-operation does not just necessitate substantial adaptation by national administrations. European integration also reinforces institutional fragmentation and the sectoralisation of policy-making at the national level [34]. European integration therefore tends to reinforce traditional co-ordination problems, while at the same time creating novel challenges.

Of no less importance are the new co-operation and co-ordination requirements associated with the transition from government to governance, notably through the transfer of public service responsibilities to para-public and private institutions. The classic instruments of steering and control in the relationship between the political executive and administration and in inter- and intra-institutional relations hardly apply for private actors. Only in exceptional cases can private institutions be legally obliged to co-operate and co-ordinate. For the Federal Republic the question of how public institutions co-operate and co-ordinate with their partners established under private law is only beginning to be investigated empirically; similarly the relations amongst private-law administrative institutions have not yet been the subject of any in-depth analysis. The experience of countries such as the UK does, however, suggest that such "interprivate" relations will become of particular importance in the system of intergovernmental relations.

5. The Legitimisation Challenge

Changes in the basic conditions of public administration and its internal features, integrative forces and its constitutive environment call into question the established premises of bureaucratic legitimacy. These challenges can be described as, first, the progressive erosion of bureaucratic rationality, and, second, the growing obsolescence of traditional patterns of democratic legitimisation, most notably as a result of Europeanisation. In short, the two main pillars on which bureaucratic legitimacy has long rested are crumbling.

From the discussion above, it should have emerged that the New Public Management has not yet comprehensively transformed German public administration; yet, outside the realm of the Federal ministerial administration, the signs of advancing privatisation, corporatisation and economisation are unmistakable. Organisational privatisation has already reached endemic proportions at the local level, and has also made deep inroads into the administrative systems of the Länder and into the non-ministerial administrative structures of the Federation [35]. Increasingly private-law "satellites" spread beyond the traditional enclaves of public service and infrastructural provision and perform classical core functions of the sovereign-hierarchical administration [36]. In the majority of cases organisational privatisation relies on tried and tested institutional models. To borrow an image of Hood [37], the species populating the German zoo of para-public institutions have remained fairly unchanged, but the animals are becoming ever more numerous and stronger, and they are increasingly roaming outside their traditional enclosures. At the same time economisation puts administrative authorities under pressure to redesign their structures, procedures and personnel systems in line with the organisational principles allegedly prevailing in the private sector. In line with this trend the

Federal Commission "Schlanker State" propagates a remodelling of classical administrative authorities in the image of "service enterprises" [38]. This is one of the basic ideas of the New Public Management, which calls for a "paradigm shift" from "administrative to entrepreneurial management" [39].

The less officials in "privatised" and "economised" parts of the public sector can plausibly maintain to act in the common interest, the less autonomy claims grounded in a special mission of public bureaucracy can be normatively justified. Perhaps more importantly, organisational privatisation removes many of the institutional barriers to the direct subordination of public administration under the will of politicians. Traditional public bureaucracy operates in a tight framework of legal programming through public law, budgetary provisions, audit controls and judicial review; this framework loses much of its force, if it is not altogether invalidated, as the state, by means of organisational privatisation, makes itself "invisible" [40]. Generalised rules decline in importance and are increasingly supplanted by formally - or informally - set performance targets; the scope for direct political directives and case-by-case interference widens. The loss in transparency as a consequence of privatisation further encourages such a development. Political authority may assert itself more freely and more directly as civil servants become employees, and as the institutional shields protecting the autonomy of officials become ineffective. Such an outcome is by means a foregone conclusion. What seems certain, however, is that traditional bureaucratic rationality will be less able to provide an effective safeguard either against political or economic rationalities.

The effects of Europeanisation on the democratic legitimisation of public administration, we find ourselves in largely uncharted territory, both in conceptual and in empirical terms. It scarcely needs elaborating that the Europeanisation of national statehood poses fundamental questions concerning the democratic legitimisation of the exercise of public power. As the "institutional backbone" of the modern state, public administration is inevitably affected by the legitimatory challenges facing state institutions as a consequence of Europeanisation. In fact, all of the traditional key tenets of the democratic legitimisation of public administration noted earlier - steering and control through democratically legitimated institutions and individuals; administration under the rule of law; subsidiarity; direct and indirect public participation in administrative decision-making through "integrative administration action" [41]; information requirements and the transparency of public administration - are directly and substantially affected by the integration process. Some brief remarks may suffice to underline this point. Thus, challenges to democratic steering and control are reinforced by Europeanisation. The chances for the competitive application of law by administrators increase as a consequence of the pluralisation of legal sources. At the same time, the scope for unilateral political-legal steering of public administration by national decision-makers decline. Moreover, control rights are increasingly shared between national and EU institutions, if they are not ceded altogether to the European level. As argued above, the principle of the rule of law is not called into doubt; but it is at least worth discussing whether the fundamental political, social and economic ideas underlying the German Constitution are readily compatible with the evolving European "constitution".

Subsidarity and decentralisation have a particular weight in German conceptions of administrative legitimisation. Well into the 1980s national principles of administrative organisation appeared largely unaffected by the European integration process. The European Community relied almost entirely on national administrations for the implementation of European policies and did not interfere with structures of national administrations. However, this traditional policy of non-interference is changing. It is not so much the transfer of administrative responsibilities to EU institutions that is of interest here. Rather the EU is increasingly engaged in establishing guidelines for the administrative organisation of the member states; at the same time, EU law substantially affects inter-administrative relations within the member states [42]. So far, there is no conclusive evidence to suggest that European integration substantially restricts the powers of the Länder, at least in their administrative competencies. But the Länder are "affected through the change and narrowing of the legal and practical framework for the decisions on administrative organisation" [43]. Opportunities for organisational choice and the diversity of administrative organisation at the Länder level are, thus, diminished.

For participation in administrative decision-making any assessment of the impact of European integration on citizens' participatory opportunities is highly dependent on the characterisation of the EU decision-making system and policy process. General descriptions are of little value. The participants in EU policy-making are too varied, and the differences between different policy sectors too distinct, to allow for authoritative generalisations. Moreover, the EU decision system is highly dynamic, since "the politics of the EU is also about constantly changing the 'decision-rules' of the system" [44]. Against this background, it is important not to prejudge the effect of integration on participatory rights and opportunities.

6.   Conclusion

Our preceding analysis has highlighted the profound changes in public administration associated with emergence of a post-modern and post-national statehood. It has been suggested that we are witnessing a transformation of the internal features of public bureaucracy, a weakening of traditional forces of integration and a reshaping of the relations between public administration and its constitutive environment. These developments call into doubt the dual legitimatory bases of bureaucratic authority. Increasingly, the functional-institutional autonomy of public bureaucracy is undermined as the notion of the common good is called into doubt; bureaucratic rationality is complemented (and often supplanted) by entrepreneurial and market rationality; and the professional career civil service is perceived as an anachronism in the context of managerialist public sector reforms. At the same time, Europeanisation calls into question the traditional arrangements for ensuring the effective democratic subordination of public bureaucracy.

Whilst this scenario serves to highlight the implications of administrative change for the legitimacy of administrative authority, it is certainly open to criticism. First, we have little systematic empirical knowledge of how the emerging Europeanised and (partly) economised public administration works. As was noted above, "Europeanisation" is, at present, a plausible empirical hypothesis rather than a well-researched and conceptually and theoretically well-understood reality. Equally, although there is an intensive discussion about the merits and demerits of corporatisation and economisation in the German public sector, little is known about the chains of command and control, steering and accountability that link parliament and the political executive with non-core administrative institutions. While, at the normative level, the shift towards a post-national and post-modern statehood undoubtedly calls traditional assumptions about bureaucratic legitimacy into doubt, it is an open empirical question of how much traditional arrangements designed to secure the legitimate exercise of administrative authority have, in fact, lost in effectiveness.

The second caveat points into the same direction. Even if it can be shown that there is a loss in the effectiveness of legitimatory arrangements, this does not necessarily imply that public administration does face a crisis of legitimacy in the eyes of politicians, officials and, most importantly, citizens. Put differently, what may, from a normative perspective, appear as a highly problematic development need not give cause for concern among the people. Citizens may well prefer a less accountable, but more efficient, effective and "customer-oriented" administration. Talk about a crisis of legitimacy is only justified if it can be shown that the post-national and post-modern administration is, in fact, judged to be less legitimate by the citizens than traditional public bureaucracy. So far, there is no conclusive evidence that would support such a verdict.

Third, even if the analysis is restricted to the normative level, it cannot avoid the question of whether traditional legitimatory patterns were, in fact, adequate and convincing. In particular, bureaucratic autonomy claims vis-à-vis "changeable political forces" could be said to owe more to pre-democratic traditions (and the self-interests of the bureaucracy) than to exalted notions of the public good.

Finally, it is important not to lose sight of the possibility that whilst traditional arrangements for balancing democratic subordination and functional independence may be weakened, novel and no less effective but, as yet, less well-understood patterns may be emerging in the context of a shift from "state authority to network state" [45]. Post-national and post-modern statehood not only poses a danger to the legitimacy of administrative authority; it may also create possibilities for novel forms of participation accountability whose legitimatory potential is only beginning to be explored [46].

References

[1]   See, for example, D. Czybulka, Die Legitimation der öffentlichen Verwaltung. Müller, Heidelberg, 1989; H. Dreier, Hierarchische Verwaltung im demokratischen Staat. Mohr, Tübingen, 1991; idem, Zur "Eigenständigkeit" der Verwaltung, *Die Verwaltung*, 25, **2** (1992) 137-156; M. Jestaedt, Demokratieprinzip und Kondominalverwaltung. Duncker & Humblot, Berlin, 1993.

[2]   Entscheidungen des Bundesverfassungsgerichts, Vol. 7, p. 162.

[3]   See, more recently, for example, W. J. M. Kickert (ed.), Public Management and Administrative Refrom in Western Europe. E. Elgar, Cheltenham, 1997; E. C. Page, Political Authority and Bureaucratic Power. Harvester Wheatsheaf, 2nd ed., Hemel Hempstead, 1992; B. G. Peters, The Politics of Bureaucracy. Longman, 4th ed., White Plains, N. Y., 1995; J. Pierre, Conclusions: A Framework of Comparative Public Administration. In: J. Pierre (ed.), Bureaucracy in the Modern State, E. Elgar, Aldershot, 1995, pp. 205-218.

[4]   K. H. Goetz, Ein neuer Verwaltungstyp in Mittel- und Osteuropa? Zur Entwicklung der post-kommunistischen öffentlichen Verwaltung. In: H. Wollmann, H. Wiesenthal and F. Bönker (eds.), Transformation sozialistischer Gesellschaften: Am Ende des Anfangs, Westdeutscher Verlag, Opladen, 1995, pp. 538-553; idem, Post-kommunistische öffentliche Verwaltung. Ostdeutschland und Mittel- und Osteuropa im Vergleich, *Yearbook of European Administrative History*, 7 (1995) 325-346.

[5]   G. Smith, West Germany and the Politics of Centrality, *Government and Opposition*, 11 (1976) 387-407.

[6]   M. G. Schmidt, West Germany: The Policy of the Middle Way, *Journal of Public Policy*, 7 (1987) 137-177.

[7]   K. H. Goetz, Kooperation und Verflechtung im Bundesstaat: Zur Leistungsfähigkeit verhandlungsbasierter Politik. In: R. Voigt (ed.), Der kooperative Staat, Nomos Verlagsgesellschaft, Baden-Baden, 1995, pp. 145-166; idem, Administrative Reconstruction in the New Länder: The Federal Dimension. In: C. Jeffrey (ed.), Recasting German Federalism: The Legacies of Unification. Pinter, London, 1999, pp. 85-115.

[8]   J. Pierre, *op. cit.*

[9]   See J. Hassard, Postmodernism and Organisational Analysis: An Overview. In: J. Hassard and M. Parker (eds.), Postmodernism and Organisations. Sage, London, 1993, pp. 1-22.

[10]   See R. Rhodes, Understanding Governance: Policy Networks, Governance, Reflexivity and Accountability. Open University Press, Buckingham, 1997.

[11]   S. Crook, J. Pakulski, and M. Waters, Postmodernisation: Change in Advanced Society. Sage, London, 1992.

[12]   W. Wessels, Staat und (westeuropäische) Integration. Die Fusionsthese. In: M. Kriele (ed.), Die Integration Europeas (PVS Sonderheft 23). Westdeutscher Verlag, Opladen, 1992, pp. 26-61.

[13]   K. H. Goetz, National Governance and European Integration: Intergovernmental Relations in Germany, *Journal of Common Market Studies*, 33 (1995) 91-116.

[14]   W. Hanrieder, West German Foreign Policy 1949-1963: International Pressure and Domestic Response. Stanford University Press, Stanford, 1967.

[15]   K. H. Goetz, Integration Policy in a Europeanized State: Germany and the Intergovernmental Conference, *Journal of European Public Policy*, 3, 1 (1996) 23-44.

[16]   A. Héritier *et al.*, Ringing the Changes in Europe. Regulatory Competition and the Transformation of the State. De Gruyter, Berlin, 1996.

[17]   See, for example, R. Voigt, Der kooperative Staat: Auf der Suche nach einem neuen Steuerungsmodus. In: R. Voigt (ed.), Der kooperative Staat: Krisenbewältigung durch Verhandlung?. Nomos Verlagsgesellschaft, Baden-Baden, 1995, pp. 33-92; N. Dose, Kooperatives Recht. Defizite einer steuerungsorientierten Forschung zum kooperativen Verwaltungshandeln, *Die Verwaltung*, 27, 1 (1994) 91-110.

[18]   A. Benz, Kooperative Verwaltung: Funktionen, Voraussetzungen und Folgen. Nomos Verlagsgesellschaft, Baden-Baden, 1994, p. 37.

[19]   *Ibid.*, pp: 38-39; A. Benz, Beyond the Public-Private Divide: Institutional Reform and Cooperative Policy-Making. In: A. Benz and K. H. Goetz (eds.), A New German Public Sector? Reform, Adaptation and Stability. Dartmouth, Aldershot, 1996, pp. 165-188.

[20]   W. Hoffmann-Riem, Verfahrensprivatisierung als Modernisierung, *Deutsches Verwaltungsblatt*, 111, 5 (1996) 225-232.

[21]   For the latter, see, for example, R. Steinberg, Probleme der Europäisierung des deutschen Umweltrechts, *Archiv des öffentlichen Rechts*, 120, 4 (1995) 549-594.

[22]   E. Schmidt-Aßmann, Deutsches und Europäisches Verwaltungsrecht, *Deutsches Verwaltungsblatt*, 108, 17 (1993) 924-936 (932).

[23]   G. Nolte, General Principles of German and European Administrative Law – A Comparison in Historical Perspective, *The Modern Law Review*, 57, 2 (1994) 191-211. For other contributions to the debate see, for example, H. W. Rengeling, Deutsches und europäisches Verwaltungsrecht - wechselseitige Einwirkungen, *Veröffentlichungen der Vereinigung der Deutschen Staatsrechtslehrer*, 54 (1993) 202-239; D. H. Scheuing, Europarechtliche Impulse für innovative Ansätze im deutschen Verwaltungsrecht. In: W. Hoffmann-Riem and E. Schmidt-Aßmann (eds.), Innovation und Flexibilität des Verwaltungshandelns. Nomos Verlagsgesellschaft, Baden-Baden, 1994, pp. 289-354; M. Zuleeg, Deutsches und europäisches Verwaltungsrecht - wechselseitige Einwirkungen, *Veröffentlichungen der Vereinigung der Deutschen Staatsrechtslehrer*, 54 (1994) 154-201.

[24]   F. W. Scharpf and A. Benz, Kooperation als Alternative zur Neugliederung? Zusammenarbeit zwischen den norddeutschen Ländern. Nomos Verlagsgesellschaft, Baden-Baden, 1991.

[25]   P. Dunleavy, The Globalization of Public Services Production: Can Government be 'Best in World'?, *Public Policy and Administration*, 9, 2 (1994) 36-64 (37).

[26]   W. Erbguth and F. Stollmann, Erfüllung öffentlicher Aufgaben durch private Rechtssubjekte? Zu den Kriterien bei der Wahl der Rechtsform, *Die Öffentliche Verwaltung*, 46, 18 (1993) 793-809.

[27]   D. Grimm, Die Zukunft der Verfassung. Suhrkamp, Frankfurt a.M., 1991; G. F. Schuppert, Rigidität und Flexibilität von Verfassungsrecht - Überlegungen zur Steuerungsfunktion von Verfassungsrecht in normalen wie in "schwierigen Zeiten", Archiv des öffentlichen Rechts, 120, **1** (1995) 32-99.

[28]   W. Hoffmann-Riem and E. Schmidt-Aßmann (eds.), Öffentliches Recht und Privatrecht als wechselseitige Auffangordnungen. Nomos Verlagsgesellschaft, Baden-Baden, 1996; W. Hoffmann-Riem and E. Schmidt-Aßmann (eds.), Innovation und Flexibilität des Verwaltungshandelns. Nomos Verlagsgesellschaft, Baden-Baden, 1994; W. Hoffmann-Riem, E. Schmidt-Aßmann and G. F. Schuppert (eds.), Reform des Allgemeinen Verwaltungsrechts: Grundfragen. Nomos Verlagsgesellschaft, Baden-Baden, 1993.

[29]   E. Schmidt-Aßmann, Zur Reform des Allgemeinen Verwaltungsrechts - Reformbedarf und Reformansätze. In: W. Hoffmann-Riem, E. Schmidt-Aßmann and G. F. Schuppert (eds.), Reform des Allgemeinen Verwaltungsrechts: Grundfragen. Nomos Verlagsgesellschaft, Baden-Baden, 1993, pp. 11-63.

[30]   R.J. Dalton, Unity and Division: The 1994 Bundestag Election. In: R. J. Dalton (ed.), Germans Divided: The 1994 Bundestag Election and the Evolution of the German Party System. Berg, Oxford, 1996, pp. 3-22.

[31]   See, for example, H. Damskis, Politikstile und regionale Verwaltungskulturen in Ostdeutschland, Deutscher Universitätsverlag, Wiesbaden, 1997; H. Damskis and B. Möller, Verwaltungskultur in den neuen Bundesländern. Peter Lang, Frankfurt a. M., 1997; H. Wollmann, Institutionenbildung in Ostdeutschland: Neubau, Umbau und "schöpferische Zerstörung. In: M. Kaase *et al.* (eds.), Politisches System, Leske und Budrich, Opladen, 1996, S. 47-153.

[32]   M. Keating and L. Hooghe, By-passing the Nation State? Regions and the EU Policy Process. In: J. J. Richardson (ed.), European Union: Power and Policy-Making, Routledge, London, 1996, pp. 216-229. Similarly, B. Kohler-Koch, Regionen im Mehrebenensystem der EU. In: T. König, E. Rieger and H. Schmitt (eds.), Das europäische Mehrebenensystem. Campus, Frankfurt a. M., 1996, pp. 203-227.

[33]   W. Wessels and D. Rometsch, German Administrative Interaction and European Union: The Fusion of Public Policies. In: Y. Mény, P. Muller and J.-L. Quermonne (eds.), Adjusting to Europe: The Impact of the European Union on National Institutions and Policies. Routledge, London, 1996, pp. 73-109. See also D. Rometsch, The Federal Republic of Germany. In: D. Rometsch and W. Wessels (eds.), The European Union and Member States: Towards Institutional Fusion?. Manchester University Press, Manchester, 1996, pp. 61-105.

[34]   R. Dehousse, European Integration and the Nation-State. In: M. Rhodes, P. Heywood and V. Wright (eds.), Developments in West European Politics. Macmillan, Basingstoke, pp. 37-54.

[35]   H. Bauer, Privatisierung von Verwaltungsaufgaben, *Veröffentlichungen der Vereinigung der Deutschen Staatsrechtslehrer*, **54** (1995) 243-286; F. Schoch, Die Europäisierung des Allgemeinen Verwaltungsrechts, *Juristen-Zeitung*, 50, **3** (1995) 109-123; L. Osterloh, Privatisierung von Verwaltungsaufgaben, *Veröffentlichungen der Vereinigung der Deutschen Staatsrechtslehrer*, **54** (1995) 204-242.

[36]   K. Lenk and R. Prätorius (eds.), Eingriffsstaat und öffentliche Sicherheit. Nomos Verlagsgesellschaft, Baden-Baden, 1998.

[37]   Ch. Hood, The Hidden Public Sector: The 'Quangocratization' of the World?. In: F-X Kaufmann (ed.), The Public Sector: Challenge for Coordination and Learning. De Gruyter, Berlin, 1991, pp. 165-187.

[38]   Sachverständigenrat "Schlanker Staat" (1997) Abschlußbericht. Bundesministerium des Innern, Bonn, 1997, pp. 113ff.

[39]   K. König, "Neue Verwaltung" oder Verwaltungsmodernisierung: Verwaltungspolitik in den 90er Jahren, *Die Öffentliche Verwaltung*, 48, **9** (1995) 349-358.

[40]   J. Isensee, Diskussionsbeitrag, *Veröffentllichungen der Vereinigung der Deutschen Staatsrechtslehrer*, **54** (1995) 303-307 (303).

[41]   H. Hill, Integratives Verwaltungshandeln - Neue Formen von Kommunikation und Bürgerbeteiligung, *Deutsches Verwaltungsblatt*, 108, **18** (1993) 973-982.

[42]   J. Oebbecke, Die europäische Integration und die Organisation der Verwaltung. In: J. Ipsen *et al.* (eds.), Verfassungsrecht im Wandel. Carl Heymanns, Cologne, 1995, pp. 607-622.

[43]   *Ibid.*, p. 622.

[44]   J.J. Richardson, Policy-making in the EU: Interests, Ideas and Garbage Cans of Primeval Soup. In: J. J. Richardson (ed.), European Union: Power and Policy-Making. Routledge, London, 1996, pp. 3-23.

[45] G. Lehmbruch, From State Authority to Network State: The German State in Developmental Perspective. In: M. Muramatsu and F. Naschold (eds.), State and Administration in Japan and Germany. De Gruyter, Berlin, 1997, pp. 39-62.
[46] For the local level see, for example, J. Bogumil (ed.), Verwaltungsmodernisierung und Demokratie: Risisken und Chancen eines neuen Steuerungsmodells fuer die lokale Demokratie. Nomos Verlagsgesellschaft, Baden-Baden, 1997; T. Klie, and T. Meysen, Neues Steuerungsmodell und bürgerschaftliches Engagement, *Die Oeffentliche Verwaltung*, 51, 11 (1998) 452-459.

The Fallacies of New Public Management - Can They Still Be Prevented in the Austrian Context?

Barbara Liegl [*]

1.   Introduction

The fallacies of New Public Management (NPM) do not only cover its tension laden relationship to the concepts of citizen and consumer, but also other problems which are indirectly related to this issue. As the state has to cope with many new and demanding trends - the globalisation of financial markets and industry, policy problems reluctant to sole national solutions, democratic pressure and the managerial revolution [1] to name but a few - it has to think about new ways of organising its executive branch, which does not only execute laws and regulations but has a major part in the preparation of these legal instruments. Most of the recent and current administrative reforms have counted on elements of NPM, especially the Anglo-Saxon and the Scandinavian countries have claimed an outrider position. Although there is no agreement on defining NPM, it is taken here to stand for ideas that were developed in the private sector and were then transferred to the public domain without adapting and changing them dramatically, whereby these ideas are underpinned by theories such as public choice, principal-agency, transaction-cost-economics and public management.

This chapter consists of three parts, the first one deals with NPM as a model, comprising its premises, policies and aims, which vary according to the political, cultural and historical contexts they are implemented in. The administrative system undergoes major changes when these new strategies are applied - increasing heterogeneity within the public sector, a different kind of relationship between the old style professionals and the new type of managers and the loss of institutional memory to name but a few. Taking these radical transformations into account one would expect NPM also to think about the new relationship between the administration, the state and society. What kind of state does the citizen and the administrator face? What kind of society is needed so that citizens can fulfil their new roles as consumers? How can solidarity be stimulated to overcome the fragmenting tendencies within this new movement? Unfortunately NPM does not answer any of these questions. The second section shows the weaknesses of the premises, requirements and consequences of NPM, of which some could be ameliorated by extending the model and adding new underpinning theories. These expansions should include perspectives of theories on citizenship and public goods as well as democratic models. The final part puts NPM in a historically and culturally totally different context - namely the Austrian one. Reforms at least claiming the aims of NPM on a broader basis have only appeared on this year's agenda. I'm going to concentrate on one reform which seems to be a halfway solution, as it neither totally reverts to the principles of NPM nor to the principles of the classical bureaucratic tradition.

[*] Barbara Liegl, Institute for Advanced Studies, Vienna, Austria

2.   New Public Management - A Theoretical Approach

NPM wants to reach three aims concurrently - namely the reduction of public spending, the enhancement of responsibility/accountability and of consumer satisfaction. The model of NPM implies to satisfy the distinguished standard of achieving all of these goals at the same time. Empirical evidence nevertheless shows that this request seems to be out of reach, as the three objectives appear to be cornerstones of a magic triangle.

2.1.   Aims, Policies and Underpinning Theories

The reduction of public spending and therefore the special stress on economy, efficiency and effectiveness sometimes shoves itself to the foreground, whereas the endpoints of the two other legs of the triangle - namely clear cut areas of accountability and responsibility as well as customer satisfaction - are only minor matters misused to legitimise drastic budget cuts. NPM wants to reach these three objectives by simultaneously modernising the internal structure of the administration, introducing market elements and mechanisms enhancing customer satisfaction.

The question of which tasks must be financed and fulfilled by the state itself and which can be at least executed by non-state institutions should always be taken into account before discussing special measures within the framework of NPM. This problem is not one which can be solved quite easily and readily, because it is of a flowing and amorphous state and therefore pops up, whenever administrative reforms are discussed. Within NPM "a split between a small strategic core and a large operational periphery" [2] of tasks is considered, whereby the state has to continue to guarantee rights and provide for regulations. Service production can be seen as a peripheral duty and can therefore be either privatised, contracted out or made available to competitive tendering. This formal model nevertheless shows some severe weaknesses, as it does not include criteria for the bottom line of state core activities. NPM wants to replace the service state and make it more of an economic and less of a political actor, nevertheless it is not at all clear whether the new kind of state is to become a regulator or more like an enabler/guarantor of administration.

Policies modernising the internal structure of the administration include measures like the abolition of multiple areas of responsibility, the separation of policy-advice and policy implementation as well as the provision of services and strategic management especially reverting to MbR and personnel management. The consequences of these strategies can be summarised as decentralisation and feigning the straightforwardness of administrative objectives. Concerning personnel management, measures to develop the skills and the knowledge of the staff are taken, new and sometimes worse working conditions arise and a new type of employee - the manager - emerges, which means that the relationship between the classical bureaucrat and the new public manager must be newly defined. Internal contractual management, using performance and results standards, enhances internal competition and sticks to monitoring, report and audit systems.

The market-oriented developments encompass the heightening of competition by quasi-markets and privatisations to enhance both the efficiency and effectiveness as well as the transparency of the administration, but it can also mean the devolution of tasks to society and the growth of the third sector. The contractor-provider model becomes prominent, where administrative tasks are made available to compulsory competitive tendering and therefore to external contract management. Many new kinds of organisations and agencies emerge within the public sector, which leads to its fragmented and heterogeneous structure and gives new non-elected élites the opportunity of gaining power.

Mechanisms guaranteeing customer satisfaction comprise both policies to harmonise the citizens' needs with administrative action and the modernisation of legal outline conditions. They all aim at making official channels more easily accessible and intelligible by the citizens and some of the measures even encourage citizens to participate to various extents. Which of these strategies is utilised in a more comprehensive way, very much depends on the cultural and historical context NPM is applied in and on the administrative level it is supposed to reform - federal, provincial or municipal. Customer satisfaction appears to play a very prominent role on the municipal level, whereas the modernisation of the internal structure gains more impetus on the federal or central level. NPM, where seriously practised, does not leave any of the administrative values unchanged and leads to major transformation processes, which do not only manifest themselves within the administration but also in its relationship to the state and society.

2.2. *Consequences*

So what are the consequences of the above described aims and policies of an administrative reform program of NPM? There are consequences on two differing levels, firstly those resulting from prerequisites of and assumptions within the model and its underpinning theories and those only becoming evident when NPM is actually realised. Reform programs under the wing of NPM create a totally new administrative culture differing in great degrees from the old traditional bureaucratic values. The following changes [3] are only the most obvious consequences of the changes caused by the introduction of NPM.

The replacement of rules as governance mechanisms by objectives and results makes efficiency and effectiveness as well as transparency the most important aims, but this strategy feigns the straightforwardness of administrative objectives although they are infamous for being quite hard to define, conflicting and opposing each other. The separation of policy-advice, policy-implementation, and financing goes hand in hand with the product-related organisation in the form of a process chain and leads to a quite fragmented, decentralised and heterogeneous structure of the public sector, which guarantees easier assessment, control of and co-ordination within these newly emerging areas but nevertheless it makes the public sector on the whole more difficult to overlook and control in political terms.

These processes of decentralisation and sometimes even devolution are underpinned by the decentralisation of personnel management and finance, seen to bring about new and sometimes even worse working conditions as well as worse quality. Pronounced hierarchies are substituted by contract management and along with it performance, results and quality standards become important concepts for personnel management, which has gained prominence due to the discovery that the civil servants themselves are the most important resource of the administration. When realised though, measures to develop the skills and the knowledge of the staff are usually not taken. Due to this managerialisation process a new type of employee appears, namely one that takes on the role of a manager, which is opposed to the traditional role of the professional among the civil servants. This change makes it necessary to think about the relationship between the classical bureaucrat and the new public manager. Another item is the replacement of producer dominance by customer orientation, which leads to a quite curtailed concept of the citizen as consumer and brings about the outsourcing of responsibility, whereby the costs of monitoring are externalised to the weakest link in the chain.

Contract management - another important consequence of NPM - must be seen as a twofold mechanism, firstly it is a device enhancing internal competition among the employees and secondly it increases external competition as new forms of quasi markets, contracting out and compulsory competitive tendering become prominent. New organisational forms emerge and many of them support the upsurge of new non-elected élites, a tendency which encourages debates on political accountability and the democratic deficit. Talking about accountability, the model of NPM differentiates three areas of accountability - political, managerial and qualitative [1] - but in reality only measures especially stressing managerial and sometimes qualitative accountability are realised, political accountability is badly neglected. Therefore the concept of democratic deficit is quite often associated with NPM, not only due to the lack of political control but also due to the abolition of multiple areas of accountability, where each agent only has one principal, which "could have potentially anti-democratic and illiberal consequences" [4].

On the whole it can be said that NPM introduces a broad range of new procedures and tasks alien to the traditional administration, whereby it causes a substantial loss of institutional memory. This can be interpreted as a strength of this strategy as it allows for reforms to break up the rigid structures and the standard operating procedures and gives the administration the chance of redefining its values and scope of duties. It should however also try to replace the old traditional values by new ones especially concerning the threefold relationship between state, administration and society. If the structure of one of these entities is transformed, it becomes quite evident that its position in relation to the others changes and that the others have to adapt as well.

3.　　Critique of New Public Management

The section above has already been suggestive of some of the critiques and uneasiness this model of NPM and its realisation bring about. These negative feelings are seen to come in on three different levels - namely on the one reverting to the premises of the model, on a second one concerning the requirements of the model and on a third one regarding its consequences. The first two points of critique discussed - the blurring of the differences between the public and the private sector and the differentiation of core and peripheral tasks - fall within the first range, the third one - the relationship of consumerism and citizenship - belong to the category of requirements and the fourth one - lack of political control - concerns the consequences.

The critique is not to suggest that all the aims and policies of NPM should be repudiated but rather that the model should expand the underpinning theories it depends on and rethink as well as redefine some of its premises. Reforming the administration on all levels is absolutely

---

[1]　I take this up in greater detail in section 3.4.

indispensable as it faces many new problems, which can no longer be adequately solved by classical and traditional bureaucratic means.

3.1.   Blurring of the Differences between the Public and Private Sector

There are two research strands giving evidence of the differences between the public and the private sector, which NPM appears to ignore. The first one looks at the different management processes and the second one at the different kinds of organisations that emerge in these two sectors. Within the first research strand [5] the public managers differ from their private counterparts, as they should rather be enablers than doers, who face much more ambiguity, and uncertainty as well as greater diversity. They have three tasks to fulfil - the first one aiming at enabling the political responsiveness to and government of the people, whereas NPM stresses efficiency and effectiveness rather than enabling the collective decision-making processes. The second task is to balance the functional and permeable boundaries of the organisations, but NPM indeed only emphasises one side by enhancing the flexibility and the external net-working. The final task is one not alien to NPM - namely organising the centre in a strategic and the periphery in a responsive way, but the customers within the concept of NPM are seen as much more passive and as only having ex-post voice.

The second strand [6] sees the differences in the organisational forms determined by the less stable context of politics, by the non-authoritative founding act of an economic enterprise and by efficiency not being a criteria for the persistence of a political organisation. So transaction costs and the market as decisive criteria for enhancing efficiency, as practised by NPM, are problematic in the field of politics, especially when marginalised and discriminated groups are the customers of an organisation. Another aspect of NPM, namely the emphasis on contractual agreements would require definite property rights, clearly definable objectives and secure as well as certain contexts, which the political environment cannot offer. So overall NPM ignores most of the differences between the public and the private sector mentioned above, which makes it difficult to accept this movement without demanding changes in its conceptions of public organisations and the public manager.

3.2.   Differentiation of Core and Peripheral Tasks

NPM does not provide for any normative criteria - as it only refers to those of transaction-cost economics - according to which administrative tasks could be classified into core and peripheral ones. It could rely on the theory of public goods [2] as an underpinning and supportive one to distinguish between genuine public, genuine private and a mixed form of goods. I want to assume that the provision of public security, social security, culture and environmental protection are among the long list of public goods. NPM would not deter from privatising institutions such as prisons, social services, state theatres and national parks.

In order to have additional, non-economic criteria, NPM should observe the assumptions of the theory of public goods [7] to have a bottom line for deciding for or against privatisation or contracting out. Especially in those areas, where public goods serve an internal and an external function (prisons provide internal security - namely safeguarding the inmates against

---

[2] I am grateful to two of our assistant Professors – Rainer Bauböck and Josef Melchior – at the IAS for pointing this idea out to me.

the violation of their basic civil rights - and external security - protection of the public, theatres not only provide for a politico-cultural mission to make art available to the public but the artists are also protected to choose which kind of art they want to present), the core of the civic rights is affected and the development of markets is more difficult and unlikely, so these are core public goods. Agencies providing them should not be privatised or contracted out, because the state has to guarantee the provision of these public goods and should not divest itself of this responsibility. The other kinds of public goods (national parks, social services) do neither interfere with "the hard core of fundamental and indispensable rights" [8] nor do they totally close themselves to at least contracting out, so that they could be classed with the mixed category. Within the category of genuine private goods falls only a minority of things like long distance train provision and the service of airlines, means of communication as well as the coal or steel industry and mining enterprises. Although the first two items mentioned can be seen as problematic depending on how the freedom of movement and the freedom of access to information are at least regarded as peripheral civic rights.

3.3.   *Consumerism and Citizenship*

The concept of the consumer is rather a reactive than a proactive one, as one can only act in reaction to the consumption of a service, which was delivered to one's satisfaction or dissatisfaction. Citizenship on the other hand side is a very active concept, ensuring both rights and entitlements as well as obligations for the holder of the office of citizenship [9]. Participatory democracy is not to totally substitute for representative democracy, but citizens could contribute to a more responsive and citizen-friendly administration at a much earlier stage than merely at the end of the chain, where policy is implemented. This could be accomplished by adding civic rights of participation to the model of NPM, so that citizens are not only granted ex-post voice but also ex-ante voice by giving them the chance of taking their stand before administrative procedures start.

A further problem is the status of consumers, which is very much opposed to the one of citizens, because they are always regarded as equals having the right to be equally and justly treated. Customers on the other hand side are usually assessed according to their surplus spending power, to their ability to pay and to their regularity of making purchases, all these being criteria closely related to the social status and disadvantaging those that are already marginalised or discriminated against. Services for these groups would not be offered by the market and these clients would not be seen as proper customers and would therefore be excluded from rights they are entitled to as citizens.

Summarising the problem of the curtailed concept of citizenship, it has to be said that both consumer rights and citizenship entitlements as well as obligations have to be expanded. In the first case product liability would enable the clients to take legal measures against the administration especially concerning quality standards and in the second one the customer should be given distinctive rights but also duties encouraging equal status and just distribution of services indispensable for liberal democracies based on the rule of law. NPM sees the citizen more in his/her economic dimension and as a tax payer and neglects the social and political dimensions of this concept.

3.4.   Lack of Political Control

The lack of political control and of democracy promoting elements is not necessarily due to the construction of the model NPM itself, but it is rather a consequence of its realisation, as managerial and qualitative accountability are paid more attention than political accountability.

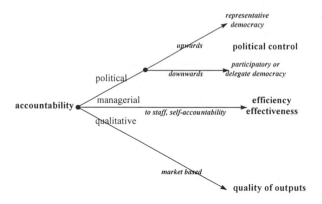

Graph 1: Political, Managerial, and Qualitative Accountability and their Mechanisms

I followed the distinction of Day and Klein [4] between the political and the managerial accountability and added a third one - qualitative accountability. Managerial accountability should however not only be productivity oriented, but should also be staff oriented, so that within this dimension staff accountability and self-accountability [2] could be two supportive mechanisms guaranteeing that personnel management is not forgotten. Qualitative and political accountability are as equally important as managerial accountability in the concept of NPM, but few measures are taken to ensure this when the model is realised. The first one should give the customers more say and is therefore rooted in market based mechanisms [2] and in the concept of "consumer rights" [4], it seems to shift most of the burden of quality control onto the consumers though without giving them active means of participation. Qualitative accountability must be balanced with political accountability - there is upward political accountability [2] concerning the flow of information both to the ministers and the MPs (model of representative democracy), and on the other hand side there is the opposite flow of information either including the local citizens (participatory democracy) or only comprising "a wider grouping of party members" [2] (model of delegate democracy).

NPM does not seem to offer new solutions to the problem of lacking political accountability. It only provides for a new quality in the lack of political control by balancing it with managerial and qualitative accountability and shifting the burden of control to new agencies in charge of reviewing performance contracts, employment contracts and contracts with external agencies as well as to the citizens responsible for the revision of quality standards.

I want to close the second section by summarising that NPM should stop ignoring concepts like citizenship, participatory democracy and the rule of law as well as the distinctness of the public sector, in order to ameliorate some of the problems mentioned above.

4.   The Reform of the Austrian Federal Theatres

The Austrian context is especially interesting as it differs greatly form the historical and cultural context of the Anglo-Saxon and Scandinavian countries, above all considering the tradition of the administration resulting from the Habsburg Monarchy and its therefore strict adherence to the rule of law [10] [11]. Administrative reforms have been on and off the schedule in Austria ever since the 1960s [12], they have taken place on two different levels - namely the administrative structures and the administrative personnel. Up to the late 1980s these changes were modelled on patchwork and single issue reforms, but then a global approach called – "Administration Management Project" - was adopted, which not only relied on experts from within the administration and active participation of at least the senior civil servants, but also on external ones especially from consulting firms. The main aim of the project was to reduce costs by 20% within four years, but the overall judgement of the project proved to be rather negative [3], as no overwhelming structural changes had taken place.

In 1997 the Austrian government decided to start a new attempt at reforming the administration - picking a catchy name for the project namely "Administrative Innovation Program" (AIP). The aims of the project read just like the ones of a prototypical NPM reform. The project can be said to have three crucial points: reforms of the tasks and of personnel management as well as the use of new technologies to modernise the administration. The reform to be discussed below - the reorganisation of the Federal Theatres - is launched within the frame of AIP and aims primarily at the managerialisation of the administration and a more efficient way of managing the administrative personnel. Other than that this reform unfortunately does not very well specify its goals so that it is hard to engage in ex-post evaluation of its success or failure. The aim of this act [3], which was introduced in July 1998, falls within the second category of the goals of the AIP project. The federal state had in mind to divest itself of another task, to make the administration more efficient and effective and to decentralise both budget and personnel management.

4.1.   *Elements of NPM*

The reorganisation of the Federal Theatres (see graph below) clearly adheres to the concept of NPM, as they are organised according to a concept very prominent in the private sector - namely the one of limited liability companies. Three theatres are organised in three companies with limited liability, a fourth company is one for service, which is responsible for the marketisation of tickets, for the maintenance work, the scenery, the scenic devices, the stage properties and the costumes. The Service Company is supposed to be prepared for the competitive market, as it is only guaranteed the purchase of its services by the other three companies till 2004 and at the same time it must offer its services solely to these other companies only till 2004, afterwards it is allowed to offer them on the free national and international market.

All these companies are overlooked by a Holding, which is owned by the federal state but which has lost its supreme financial control and the administration of the buildings to the four companies. Each of these companies is managed by two directors - an artistic and a commercial one, the artistic manager is not bound to instructions of the commercial director

---

[3]   Taken from : http://www.parlinkom.gv.at/pd/pm/XX/I/his/013/I01330_.html.

within his artistic competence, and in case of disagreement in a sphere of competence, where the two directors have to work together, the artistic director has the right to decide. The companies need not pay the federal state for the real estate they are using and the federal state pays a certain amount of money to the theatres every year, which is divided among them according to a ratio of distribution based on the budgets of 1996 and 1997.

The Bureau of the Federal Theatres, which is responsible for the civil servants, who are taken over by the newly founded companies, was founded for the purpose of decentralising the task of personnel management. They and the employees under contract must be employed according to their current contracts, only newly hired employees get different contracts. The Holding nevertheless has to pay the federal state for the civil servants and the employees under contract and it has to pay a share of their pensions as well. Taking decentralisation further into account the companies are allowed to negotiate collective and works agreements. Both the Holding and the companies are controlled by a supervisory board, which in the latter case consists of representatives of several ministries, of the works council and of the parliamentary parties declared as experts as well as one representative of the Holding. The supervisory board of the Holding encompasses representatives of the ministries and of the works council, one member of the Forum of the Audience and several experts.

The Forum of the Audience consists of 12 members and is elected for a period of three years. All members of the audience, who have the right to vote in national elections and who are either subscribers or regular theatre-visitors (must be able to produce tickets not older than six months), are allowed to cast a vote. If one wants to be eligible to election, one has to fulfil the same criteria as mentioned above, but in addition to that one has to be able to show 25 supportive signatures by participants in the election present. The Forum on the whole does not have the right to intervene in the sphere of artistic autonomy and freedom, but twice a year the Forum has to organise public audience discussions, where economic and organisational questions, the marketisation and sale of the tickets as well as the fulfilment of the politico-cultural mission [4] of the theatres are debated on.

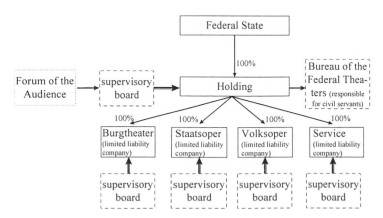

Graph 2: Organisation of the Federal Theatres

---

[4] The Federal Theatres are responsible for carrying out a politico-cultural mission, which the state is willing to guarantee by financially supporting the theatres.

So, taking all these re-organisational elements into account the reforms aim at enhancing the effectiveness and efficiency of the administration and at keeping the costs for the federal state as low as possible. Personnel and financial responsibilities are decentralised, the theatres gain autonomy and discretion. Profit making becomes important, as the institutions are allowed to keep the surplus and decide on its use. Competition is stirred further by making the Service Company fit for the free market. Managerialisation also gains prominence as the artistic directors are supported by commercial managers, which relieve them of some of their time consuming tasks. Financial controlling and planning are introduced and new employees are hired on completely different terms than the civil servants and the employees under contract. Customer satisfaction is also paid attention to by installing a Forum of the Audience.

4.2.   Critique

The organisational reform of the Federal Theatres seems to contain several drawbacks inherent to the concept of NPM. The re-organisation aims at reducing profit-making and costs, which are rather unfortunate and delicate goals relating to performed art. Enhancing the effectiveness and efficiency of this kind of administration could cause an extreme qualitative loss and could encourage the theatres to engage in extremely populist programs neglecting current, innovative and pluralistic trends. So this kind of art seems to be a public good which is hard to privatise and to make profit with.

Besides the new organisational structure does not really seem to cut administrative costs but it rather expands the administrative personnel and encourages the formation of "inner circles" [2] by multi-board membership. The number of directors increases as well, although the separation of artistic and commercial director does not always have to prove disadvantageous. Problems could be nevertheless caused by the newly to define relationship between the two, although the artistic directors have a say in the choice of the commercial director.

As new employees are hired according to different contracts than the ones taken over from the old organisational structure, competition and discrimination could be among the consequences of this strategy. The new employees being cheaper than the old ones could be forced into working more extra-hours than their civil service colleagues, so they could be much worse off concerning working conditions and pay.

When thinking of the Forum of the Audience the model of the Finnish municipal service commitment board comes to mind, where customers are represented to have a say in quality control. This idea however is not transferable from the municipal administration to the administration of performed art on the federal level. Although it seems to be legitimised by way of its democratic election, it is not guaranteed that non-political and non-interest group members are elected to this institution. Besides it is very hard to define quality in this context and it can definitely not be decided on by 12 members of a Forum which is only elected by a very tiny minority of the Austrian citizens.

5.   Conclusion

Most of the administrative reforms adhered to in the late 80s and early 90s were in accordance with NPM ideas, although they varied according to the political, cultural and historical context they were implemented in. So in the first section of this paper I tried to comprise the premises, the aims and policies of the various NPM strands and looked at them from a theoretical perspective. Taking NPM as a model, I distinguished consequences on two different levels - namely the ones based on inherent assumptions and those coming to the foreground when the model is translated into action. It has been shown that the model tries to follow several conflicting goals at the same time and that its implementation brings about major changes for the classical traditional bureaucracy. These consequences can be seen as advancing the grounds for reform, as they break up these old structures, but there are also several dangers inherent to this model, some of which are only seen when NPM strategies are realised.

The second part looked at the weaknesses of the premises, the requirements and the consequences of NPM from the perspective of the theories of public goods and of citizenship as well as of models of democracy. It has been highlighted that many of its fallacies could be wiped out by extending the model of NPM and by adding new underpinning theories. The ideas of NPM are not on the whole to be regarded as having a totally negative impact on the administrative system and the public sector, but that it should include concepts like democracy, citizenship, the rule of law and the distinctness of the public sector into its premises and requirements as politics and administration are two inseparable systems that both take place in the public sphere and are to enable collective decisions of the community. NPM should also think about its consequences for the concepts of the state and society, as the position of the administration in relation to these two is changed by NPM reforms.

The third part took up a historically and culturally totally different context than the Anglo-Saxon and Scandinavian countries present - namely the Austrian administrative system and public sector. Up to 1998 NPM has not been broadly discussed and only few reform steps encompassed elements of this trend, but the AIP clearly points into the direction of NPM. Considering the strict adherence to the rule of law and the history of the Austrian administration there are several contextual factors that might hamper reforms in this wake. The reform of the Federal Theatres seems to be only a halfway solution - neither totally reverting to the principles of NPM nor to the principles of the classical bureaucratic tradition.

References

[1]   V. Wright, Reshaping the State: The Implications for Public Administration, Special Issue of *West European Politics* **17** (1994) 102-137.
[2]   E. Ferlie *et al.*, The new public management in action. Oxford University Press, Oxford, 1996.
[3]   F. Naschold, New frontiers in public sector management: trends and issues in state and local government in Europe. Walter de Gruyter, Berlin, 1996.
[4]   J. Boston *et al.*, Public Management: the New Zealand Model. Oxford University Press Australia, Melbourne, 1997.
[5]   St. Ranson and J. Stewart, Citizenship and Government: The Challenge for Management in the Public Domain, *Political Studies* **XXXVII** (1989) 5-24.
[6]   T. M. Moe, The Politics of Structural Choice: Toward a Theory of Public Bureaucracy. In: O.E. Williamson (ed.), Organization Theory. From Chester Barnard to the Present and Beyond. Oxford University Press, Oxford, 1990, pp. 116-153.
[7]   M. Olson, Die Logik des kollektiven Handelns: Kollektivgüter und die Theorie der Gruppen. Tübingen, 1985.

[8]   R. Dahrendorf, The Changing Quality of Citizenship. In: B. van Steenbergen (ed.), The Condition of
        Citizenship. Sage, London, 1994, pp. 10-19.
[9]   B. van Steenbergen, The Condition of Citizenship: an Introduction. In: B. van Steenbergen (ed.), The
        Condition of Citizenship. London, 1994, pp. 1-9.
[10]   B. Liegl and W.C. Müller, Senior Officials in Austria: A First mapping Exercise. In: E. Page *et al.*, The
        Role of Senior Officials in the Service State. Oxford University Press, Oxford, 1998 (forthcoming).
[11]   B. Liegl, Civil Servants and Politics in Austria, *Revue Française d'Administration Publique* **86** (1998)
        195-204.
[12]   W.C. Müller, Approaches to the modernisation of the Austrian Central Administration: From Citizen-
        Friendliness to Marketisation. In: Y. Mény *et al*, La riforma amministrativa in Europa. Il Mulino,
        Bologna, 1994.

The Consumption of Best Practices
How to Understand New Public Management

Tarja Saarelainen *

1. Introduction

In this paper I ask how best practices can be consumable for others when we are developing our administrative practices by adding the customer or client perspective to that of the citizen. The stage or space for this research is the Internet and the Best Practices databanks. The aim of the work is to describe the new public management by using Best Practices as binoculars, describing the context of networks where Best Practices are consumed, and respectively constructing the actor-network where practices become the Best Practices for public administration. The value of these practices lies in their use by citizens, customers, and public managers and by making their judgements of each other visible to the other parties involved.

Two trends are apparent in public management: the wish to increase the primacy of politics over bureaucracy; and the tendency to introduce more businesslike management into government [1]. The reform of the government sector has obviously transformed public management. Understanding this revolution in public management means analysing through three issues: the basic ideas of reform, the connections between the reforms and governmental processes, and the linkage between the processes of reform in the structures of governance [2] [3]. I see the world of the public administration reform analyst as a set of articulated links between actors, as in the actor-network theory.

The actor-network theory refers to the methodological choice for studying the mobilisation of administrative reforms. The networking activity of interpretations that link - in one continuous chain of representations - politics and the world of scientific discovery, creates mixed narratives. The interpretations of academics or practitioners are as much networks as any other combination of elements [4]. Actor-network theory is concerned with how power is constructed. It also fills in other starting points of practice-theories, of which five are particularly noteworthy [5]. Analysing Best or Good Practices provides the means to understand how everyday administrative practices are transmitted into the wider processes of development projects. It points out how public services are constructed in these projects, rather than assumed to be a property of them. Like performance, Best Practices are not objective realities waiting to be measured, evaluated and consumed. Instead they are socially constructed realities that exist in the minds of people. We could name them "ex post satisfying" or "collaborative advantages" as they are the outcome of good partnership. Our space, the Internet, is also "people" behind computers and networks. "It is a network of people without geographical boundaries, acting globally, and interacting almost in real time" [6]. The ANT study indicates that the process of public services' construction in the roles of clients, customers, citizens and other partners, requires constant effort. The study demonstrates how public administration and management are constructed through the processes of translation,

* Tarja Saarelainen, University of Lapland, Faculty of Social Sciences, Finland

association and alliance, strengthening particular positions of practices at the expense of others [7].

The study has two parts. First is the actor-network, which constructs new public management and its ideas to make public services more economically efficient and effective. The NPM concentrates on hierarchical control, value for money, the clear distribution of authority and responsibility. In our space, this means turning the Internet databanks of Best Practices into a consumption of Best Practices, as a name-place giving those practices meaning by human intervention in our project [8]. This displacement story refers to the ways in which actors organise and structure the movement of materials, resources and information. More recently the Organisation for Economic Co-operation and Development (OECD), and especially its Public Management Committee (PUMA), has provided the basis for this displacement (http://www.oecd.org/puma). Its publications, forums and data banks have become important sources of knowledge about managerial change in member countries. We can agree with the multifaceted role of the OECD as both central and marginal to the network of reforms. The OECD both disseminates information about reforms and gathers it from various countries. The second part points out how Best Practices (http://web.bham.ac.uk/l.montiel /government/best.htm) are transmitted into the construction of administrative reforms and the NPM. The relationship between the NPM movement and network management or governance seems to characterise the study of public administration and constitutes its identity. The purpose of this study is to establish an interpretation with a view to understanding how the content and identity of discourse on administration are constructed by consuming Best Practices. Consumer orientation could be realised by defining the role of material and non-material goods, through experiences, in Best Practices networks.

2.   Consumer orientation

There is also support for the statement that consumer orientation is the way for increasing the power of citizens in relation to public administration. Consumer orientation means the rational use of markets under well specified conditions. The core element of all internal public sector modernisation programmes is the introduction of the new administrative steering model. The new steering systems are to be considered as less a rational basis for decision making than as a suitable basis for collective, binding learning and the processes of experience. The problem is that the context where consumer orientation is constructed for public administration is not the same in every country. First, there are different constitutional arrangements. Secondly, the neo-liberal arguments are clearly political; the use of market mechanisms as administrative instruments is not an idea free of ideological belief. It seems that convergence toward markets, both for service delivery and in respect of the labour market for civil and other public servants, would require an ideological commitment. Thirdly, there are different cultural attitudes toward the role and nature of the state [9] [10].

There must be negative and positive impacts from the adaptation of consumer orientation in public services. As Kettl [11] says: on the one hand, the reforms build smaller and more efficient governments, driven by market-based incentives and sometimes staffed by managers with significant private sector experience and, on the other hand, the job of managing government is more than just a function of production. In public administration the important question to be asked is: can we make Best Practices consumable for one another by considering different constitutional arrangements, ideological beliefs and cultural attitudes?

The presumptions detailed below are important in studying the relation of NPM and inter-organisational action. There are many reasons for a network-like situation. Governments often seek to execute their efforts via structures of interagency collaboration and the role of non-profit organisations is extensive and growing. The frequency and variety of links to for-profit firms is impressive, and government contracting is a growing industry [12]. Kickert, Klijn and Koppenjan [13] examine the consequences of the existence of policy networks for governance and public management. They state that public management differs from governance by focusing on the consciously and deliberately undertaken actions by public actors to influence societal processes. The internal action of public organisations is the central focus in perspectives of NPM. Governance in networks requires a different perception of public management that is more geared to the external action of the public sector.

> *"One of the criteria for participation was that women should actively take part in the planning process. The six municipalities had to undertake, by political decision, to implement planning processes which made sure that the women's perspective was taken care of in municipal plans."*
> *(Best Practices for Human Settlements).*

They continue that these observations have consequences on our perception of governance and public management. One of the major challenges with which public management as a form of governance is confronted is to deal with interdependencies. Public management should therefore be seen as network management. This idea of public management as network management is in conflict with the ideas of NPM. The ideas of new public management are concerned with managing networks [14]. So, to talk about public management is to talk about the process of governance and the way we use, for example, Best Practices. The user's perspective has connection to consumers' (the person or authority demanding good/service) or clients' (the person or authority financing the provision of a good/service) perspectives. The reform of the civil service has been a part of the package for most public management reforms. The reforms have sought to transform the culture of public organisations, which includes encouraging employees to think about citizens as customers to be served instead of clients to be managed. The changes have required technical reforms, including the development of output and outcome measurement systems and strategic planning to guide them [15].

When network management refers to a process which involves the collaborative relations and structures of private, public and voluntary or non-profit or third sector, it then depends on support from the internal functioning of organisations. If the basic idea of public management reform is managerialism (better customer services) by letting the managers manage ideas, then the development of NPM depends on how it supports these desirable ideas. If the idea of public management reform is to support participation of citizens, we could ask whether the element of NPM builds on the philosophy of continuous improvement. Perhaps the quality of network management and the question of the life or death of the NPM depends on how successful linkages will be constructed between the NPM reform processes and the participating structures of network management or governance. It has been argued that if the NPM takes the progressive approach to public management, it assumes that there is "one best way" to handle every situation, and that way can be captured in a book of rules. The other way is to emphasise an organisation's capacity to learn, adapt, and innovate under constantly changing conditions, knowledge and technology. This means an active role of citizens and the fact that the citizens have learned to demand services tailored to their specific circumstances. Could these databanks be the arenas where learning takes place for both citizens and public managers?

> *"The co-operation and communication between citizens, the local government, social organisations and businesses is based on accessibility of all necessary information and participation for all. The information is made available by producing and widely spreading several reports with statistics, conclusions about basic quality, results from survey etc. Communication takes place on several organised platforms at frequently held meetings, visits, etc. in the neighbourhoods." (Best Practices for Human Settlements).*

Theoretically the spread of communication technology has provided opportunities for citizens to take a more meaningful role in deciding and running their own public affairs and becoming more involved in governance. By consuming Best Practices we build one interpretation of NPM and governance. An independent international committee of technical professionals identified 105 submissions as Best Practices and twelve were selected by a jury to receive the Tokyo and Dubai Awards for "Excellence in Improving the Living Environment" at a special ceremony during Habitat II. Among the lessons learned from this process were the following:

> *"- there is a tremendous demand for Best Practices information, experience and expertise;*
> *- the Best Practices database is primarily a networking tool; and there is a need*
> *to deepen our understanding of what makes a Best Practice work;*
> *- the lessons learned from Best Practices should be transferred and widely disseminated using modern information and communications technology wherever possible." (http://www. unhabitat.org/blp/index.html.) See also "Best Practices Databases" Website (http://web. bham.ac.uk/l.montiel/government/best.htm).*

As Menzies [16] has claimed, the tools for computerised communication have not just become the new tools of production. They are also new tools for various other functions. These functions could include distribution, consumption, learning, sharing and healing, research and knowledge adjudication. The tools are redefining work, and the power relations involved.

3.   Consumption and being consumable

How are Best Practices transferred from space to space, how are these practices applied to different cases, what makes them Best Practices and finally how do we consume these practices, and are they consumable? I would like to raise this question: How are those Best Practices consumable, one for another? What, also, is their value for others? From the citizen perspective, citizens are partners in projects where they are expected either to act like consumers or to consume public services. From the perspective of this study public managers face situations where they are expected to use databanks, they are the consumers of this data. The role of public managers is no longer so regulated. They are also consumers of different kinds of Best Practices, in which they have to deal with managerial or economic, legal and political accountability. By doing this they also define the roles of the customer, client and citizen. This politicisation of public administration is a prominent feature of the NPM. Perhaps there are two sides to the coin, one that supports the NPM and the other that opposes the construction of the NPM. If the partnership arrangements have effects which change the role of citizens by developing more agencies for government programs, then such partnerships are not without problems for both parties. Citizens as social sector partners lose their autonomy, which is contrary to the primary purpose in sharing power [17].

Dowding and Dunleavy [18] have noticed transformations in the commodification processes which lie at the heart of contemporary global change. Our space is moving in the context of post-Fordism; dematerialization can point to at least four different social developments. Firstly, non-material goods play an ever greater role in the economy and in consumption. Secondly, even material commodities appear to have a greater non-material component. A more general sense of this dematerialization is indicated by the fact that, whereas people used to talk about the consumption of goods and services, we now tend to talk about product experiences. Thirdly, part of this increasingly non-material composition is attributed to the mediation of goods; that is to say, we encounter objects and services, experiences and activities that have become objectified as commodities increasingly in the form of representations. Fourthly, the dematerialization of consumer goods is closely related to the equally non-material nature of producer goods, above all the commodity labour-power [19].
The question of empowerment arises in the context of public services. What is the government's role as the provider or producer of services? Does empowerment mean that people need fewer material services from the government? The common citizens, like public managers, can also be consumers of Best Practices thereby gaining their own empowerment.

> *"The city's administration faces the constantly changing and increasing expectations and demands of citizens. Confronted with scarce resources, pressure on its units has grown to re-set priorities and critically examine the tasks and duties to be performed. Whilst not every demand for public services can be responded to, performance must be measured against that of other service suppliers." (Best Practices for Human Settlements)*

However, there are different levels to consider: on one level there is the consumption of experiences and ideas and at the other level there are the various roles of the consumer. The role of the consumer is taken by both public managers or citizens. Without these two levels consumers would not be involved in the decision-making processes. Usually, commerce is a metaphor for the social - the free exchange not only of goods and services within a monetary economy but also of ideas, conversation and opinion within a free public sphere. It could be argued that consumer culture, like mass society, is one of several terms that comes to replace the idea of civil society and indicates the degeneration of the ideal of voluntary association in which free and equal women/men enter into commerce and communication with each other. Consumer culture is often identified with the idea of mass consumption because it exemplifies the generalisation of commodity consumption for the entire population [20].

The characterisation of modernity as a mass identity crisis connects with consumer culture in several major ways. Firstly, the metaphor of individual choice dominates our sense of the social. Modern identity is best understood through the image of consumption or the consumption of Best Practices rather than the progressive one-way practice. Behn [21] argues that the advocates of the new public management do not respect the bureaucratic ideal that seeks to base the implementation of policy on impersonal rules. Ironically, they do not completely reject scientific management; but rather than search for the one best way, they look for today's best practice. Second, identity itself can be seen as a saleable commodity. We have to produce and sell an identity to various social markets in order to have relationships and social standing. The consumption of Best Practices means that we have to produce and sell an identity of public management of networks for different actors. Thirdly, the resources through which we produce and sustain identities, increasingly take the form of consumer goods and activities through which we construct appearances and organise our time and social encounters [22].

The consumer focus in the NPM can justify the view of the new public managers, who, analogous to their private-sector counterparts, consider themselves more capable of getting closer to their customers than traditional politicians whose jobs have been to represent and articulate the needs of the precustomerised public. Cheung [23] writes that this consumerist paradigm in public-sector reform is easily susceptible to manipulation by the public managers and would be used by them to strengthen and legitimate their institutional power versus that of politicians, producers and consumers. While market-type reforms are based on the service user as a customer, there is also concern for the role of citizenship and rights. One aspect of customer orientation is the attempt to make existing services more accessible, in many cases by making a single access point to a range of services. Under the new public management paradigm administration can be connected with politics or policy. Civil servants are empowered to make decisions. They are instructed to be responsive to individual citizens and encouraged to develop new, innovative approaches to solving public problems.

A second way of reorienting organisations to consumer orientation is the establishment of an internal market. Databanks can create common internal markets for administrators. The commodification processes in public services have already been changed by NPM techniques. An inherent consequence of NPM strategies is that citizens will interact increasingly with service providers and not with purchasers. The argument is that service providers are not in a market relationship with their end-users who have no choice of provider and are dependent on the state for the service [24] [25].

4.   Public management reforms as an actor-network

A text is only strong if its components have force at the point where the text is received and they are recognised as having been properly borrowed. First, the reform need or the basic idea of reform must be identified. This means the identification of citizens (clients, customers), the role of the state, and also the role of the reformers, the practitioners, the different organisations, the NGO and so on. After this problematisation, the other actors will be locked into the roles proposed for them in the programme of reform [26]. Both the evidence for globalisation in public management and the notion of a new global paradigm may be questioned. Indeed, a careful review of the evidence may suggest the policy analyst is best served by adopting a sceptical view, considering that the case of an old paradigm or model never really existed. For example, Hood [27] argues that it is more doubtful that there is such a thing as a new global paradigm. While there are several key-concepts that appear to have a global application, namely those relating to markets, individualism and measurable performance indicators, accepting this set of criteria as a new paradigm is hard. Furthermore, to speak of a global shift from one paradigm to another is to assume that there is a single old paradigm and a single exit route from it. Which paradigm succeeds depends on the mobilisation of the actor-network. Whether there is change or not could be problematised by asking whether change makes public administration more responsible and accountable to the citizens.

The theory of public management is neither coherent nor neutral; it represents a different political perspective not only on the structure and functioning of public organisations but also on the political basis of the public sector itself [28] [29]. Rhodes [30] comes to the conclusion that traditional public administration has three pillars: a distaste for theory, the study of institutions, and criticism or administrative engineering. Public administration is multi-theoretic and characterised by methodological pluralism, so there is no dominant paradigm. Cheung [31] asks in his article whether the changes observed in the public sector across countries constitute an inevitable convergence of public management principles and practices on a global level and if so, how should such global developments be understood and interpreted.

In spite of different variations, most writers have identified a set of dimensions in changes that most countries follow. If there was no convergence between countries, perhaps we could find general tendencies within countries. Klages and Löffler [32] hypothesize that differences in national administrative cultures and traditions are diminishing and differences in researching modernisation strategies at the nation state level will be less useful than looking for local differences in approach from which to learn; this implies that comparative country studies through binoculars will become irrelevant. Instead, limiting the analysis of micro-level strategies to one part of a political system, which allows the use of the microscope, will be more profitable. These arguments present problems for methodology and presentation. If the hypothesis by Klages and Löffler (that there is both convergence between countries and diversity within them) holds true, then the nation state may not be a relevant unit or object of analysis (see also [33]). Could the transfer of Best Practices and databanks be a relevant unit of analysis? Best Practices in the Internet seem to become a place through which different Best Practices applications are arranged. These applications are also indicators for the hypothesis that the nation state may not be a very relevant unit or object of analysis for NPM.

Our place is a changing learning centre where reforms in public administration are being lead by the ideas of new public management and network management. Thus, the notion of visibility is central to understanding possibilities for sharing. The first important thesis implicit in the consumption view is sharing goods always involves exclusion. If the shared practices of good public management are understood to be good network management or governance, then an actor's everyday consumption involves exclusion of other practices. So the question is about learning and self-organising. It also becomes natural to exclude some matters from discussion. In this research only some problems count as problems [34]. The construction of new, good or best practices could marginalise and overlook some questions in providing public services. The practices being followed could construct a world in which inclusion or exclusion could occur. This is why studying how these Best Practices change from country to country is important. Do they support the function of public management in the direction where people are able to participate in public administration?

In problematising and redefining their identity, general practitioners are internal network builders. Politicians, citizens, and public administrators themselves have found it necessary or expedient to declare that administration is distinct from, and subordinate to, politics and involves mere management or execution of policies developed in other institutions of government with greater perceived legitimacy. Theorising, as opposed to building a theory, may be quite sufficient if we could agree on what we hope for or what we believe the practice and praxis of public administration should be in a democratic era [35]. We could illustrate the processes of persuasion and identity-construction by looking at how the user of Best Practices and their spokespersons attempt to attribute a particular sort of identity to ordinary people, to the network itself and to public administration. This endeavour is tied in with an attempt to legitimate science-in-general and incorporates particular versions of things such as the state, the citizen and democracy, responsiveness and accountability.

Michael [36] shows how power and the power of the state is concerned with persuasion and that this is interwoven with the production of identities. Then he considers some techniques by which such identities are set in place. He looks at how scientists and their spokespersons attempt to attribute a particular sort of identity to ordinary people in trying to legitimate science-in-general, and by implication, a particular version of democracy and the state. He considers the way that "the public" has been constructed by the scientific establishment and uncovers the use and some identities purveyed to the public in an effort to gain their consent.

According to Klages and Löffler [37], the NPM is still at a pre-theoretical stage, from a theoretical point of view. It cannot be expected that a paradigm offers a body of theory; rather, a paradigm has to be understood as "an extended family of ideas" [38] that are somehow interrelated but there is no obvious hierarchy of ideas, no single key principle from which all the others can be deduced. What is the connection of those ideas in the NPM and the Best Practices database? NPM builds on the basic economic premise that private-sector management and economic principles are transferable and functional in the public sector. This means that private-sector enterprise becomes the reference model for public organisations.

As mentioned earlier, the NPM paradigm was fruitful in focussing attention on intra-organisational problems of public organisations, such as the inefficient production of goods and services, autocratic leadership and the ineffective use of information technology. However, the NPM paradigm needs to be taken one step further to focus on emerging problems. Klages and Löffler [39] offer the promising approach of a macromanagement perspective because it allows us to go beyond the public organisation as a research object and to return to a systemic perspective of administration as a subsystem of the political system. Furthermore, the macromanagement perspective also enriches the conventional focus on intra-organisational problems.

What is the place of Best Practices and their relationship to public management in that actor-network world? In this study, I understand that Best Practices and learning from them construct the roles of state, public management and the citizens. The current discussion about NPM often oversees three main arguments that were put forward in the article of Klages and Löffler [40]: 1) The implementation of NPM does not take place in an ideal-type Weberian bureaucracy but in very different administrative systems that all have a history of administrative reforms. From the perspective of this study, we are interested in how the consumption of Best Practices will become an agency in an actor-world. 2) The NPM is not just an organisational reform but a long-term learning process within public administration. Therefore, focusing it on implementation strategies is important, rather than on abstract models. A presumption of space could be made on where the implementation of the NPM takes place. These places are built by people who learn to use these practices. 3) The NPM always has a political dimension that goes beyond the issues of steering and political accountability. Could these networks which are built by the actors who are involved in Best Practices at a certain time act as a better intermediary than politicians?

As a result of the reforms undertaken, the following assumption could be made: increased self-organisation may lead to increased network building and create new organisational forms which are something between public and private. Best Practices take their place in implementation strategies and give meaning to relationships. Best Practices databanks are places for arranging, ordering and naming public management. An important part of this ordering process is naming, because it constitutes a place for differences. Perhaps some spaces become obligatory points of passage through which places are ordered by the agents associated with those spaces (See [41]).

> *"The general guidelines of the method used consist of five steps which are as follows: 1. Problem recognition - to identify all problems in the neighbourhood; 2. Agreement - to discuss the results together; 3. The solution - how the recognized problems can be solved; 4. The responsibilities - who is responsible for carrying out the solution; 5. The agreement - are individuals and organizations in agreement with the solutions. " (Best Practices for Human Settlements)*

The advocates of public management modify a new paradigm: "Don't hold us accountable for process; hold us accountable for results." To create a new theory of democratic accountability, the advocates of the new public administration paradigm need to answer the essential question [42] of who decides what results are to be produced. The answer offered by the advocates of the new public management is practical, not theoretical, and they accept that civil servants do make policy decisions. So, they need a new political theory that explains why and how this is consistent with democratic accountability. As noted by Behn [43], they need a political theory that answers four interrelated questions about how empowered, responsive civil servants can make innovative decisions in a democratic government.

5.   Identity for public administration

The phrase "the hollowing out of the state" suggests the British state is being eaten away [44]. The limitation of discretion for public servants through the NPM raised the threat of a policy catastrophe (privatization, decentralization, agencification and new limits on public intervention are also mentioned). If "the hollowing out of the state" means a state with an increasingly weak core executive, three logical hypotheses follow [45]:

> *"1. The core executive is losing or conceding capacities to societal actors;*
> *2. The core executive is losing or conceding its capacity to control other state actors;*
> *3. The core executive is losing or conceding capacities to supra-state entities."*
> *"To prevent a gap developing between professionals and volunteers, particular attention is paid to joint training." (Best Practices for Human Settlements)*

Saward's main contention is that the state is being redefined, or reshaped, not hollowed out, at least on this internal dimension. However, changes in the instruments of policy making should not be misunderstood as shifts in the substance of policy control. For Richardson [46] less government may mean strong government rather than hollowed-out government. As Western economies have shifted broadly from Fordist standardised mass production to new manufacturing strategies that emphasise productive flexibility, so their public sectors have been shaped in a way that might also be called flexible specialisation [47].

Rhodes [48] writes that there are several difficulties with Saward's analysis of internal hollowing out. First, the centre's motives for getting rid of a function are not the point at issue. The centre can no longer do something it used to do. It may have more control but it may be more control over less. Second, Saward's analysis of internal hollowing out does not distinguish clearly enough between intentions and outcomes. Third, Saward's evidence can be interpreted as a loss of control. Hood [49] argues that much of the appeal of Osborne and Gaebler's [50] collection may precisely lie in the way that they combine incompatible elements of hierarchism (the emphasis on steering and leadership), individualism (the stress on market-type consumerism) and egalitarianism (the ideas of empowering local collectivities). Empowerment, however, means different things to people with different world views or local agendas.

All consumption is cultural. This statement signifies several things. Firstly, all consumption is cultural because it always involves meaning; in order to have a need and act on it we must be able to interpret experiences and situations and we must be able to make sense of various objects, actions, resources in relation to these needs. Secondly, consumption is always cultural because the meanings involved are necessarily shared meanings. Thirdly, all forms of consumption are culturally specific. They are articulated within, or in relation to, specific meaningful ways of life [51]. We hypothesize that Best Practices function like an intermediary and change the interpretation of public administration.

The Best Practices programs represent the success stories of the connections between the processes of reform in the structures of governance. The citizens' participation in the networks of Best Practices is a critical point in producing good governance. If the most significant feature of the reforms is their instrumental and utilitarian nature and their comprehensive scope, it perhaps neglects marginal issues (see [52]). The actor-network theory differs from traditional or conventional network analysis (see [53]) and both work on abstractions belonging to different realms. The interest of this study is how a new practice progressively develops by inserting itself within already established practices. This is the story of displacement.

References

[1]   Aucoin, P., Administrative Reform in Public Management: Paradigms, Principles, Paradoxes and Pendulums, *Governance: An International Journal of Policy and Administration* **2** (1990) 115-137.
[2]   Ch. Hood and M. Jackson, Administrative Argument. Dartmouth, Aldershot, 1991.
[3]   D. Kettl, The Global Revolution in Public Management: Driving Themes, Missing Links, *Journal of Policy Analysis and Management*, 16, **3** (1997) 446-462.
[4]   B. Latour, *We Have Never Been Modern*. Harvester Wheatsheaf, Hemel Hempstead, 1993, p. 10-11.
[5]   N. Thrift, Spatial Formation. Sage, London, 1996, p. 23.
[6]   L. Montiel, The Internet as a research and learning tool: A review of its use for the study of local government and decentralisation in Latin America, 1998, p. 2. Http:www.bham.ac.uk/IDD/lenislas.htm. (1998).
[7]   N. Thrift, *op. cit.*, p. 23.

[8]   K. Hetherington, In Place of Geometry: the Materiality of Place. In: K. Hetherington and R. Munro (eds.), *Ideas of Difference. Social Spaces and the Labour of Division.* Blackwell Publishers/The sociological Review, Oxford, 1997, pp. 183-199.

[9]   N. Flynn and F. Strehl, Introduction. In: N. Flynn and F. Strehl (eds.), Public sector management in Europe. Prentice Hall, London, 1996, pp. 1-22.

[10] F. Naschold, New Frontiers in Public Sector Management. Trends and issues in State and Local Government in Europe. Translated by A. Watt With Case Studies by R. Arnkil and J. Virkkunen in Cooperation with M. Lehtonen and C. Riegler. Walter de Gruyter, Berlin, 1996, p. 8-9.

[11] D. Kettl, *op. cit.*, p. 454.

[12] L. O'Toole, Treating Networks Seriously: Practical and Research-Based Agendas in Public Administration, *Public Administration Review*, 57, **1** (1997) 45-52.

[13] W. Kickert, E.-H. Klijn and J.F.M. Koppenjan, Introduction: A Management Perspective on Policy Networks. In: W. Kickert, E.-H. Klijn and J.F.M. Koppenjan (eds.), Managing Complex Networks. Strategies for the Public Sector. Sage, London, 1997, pp. 2-3.

[14] W. Kickert *et al.*, *op. cit.*

[15] D. Kettl, *op. cit.*, p. 452.

[16] H. Menzies, Whose Brave New World? The Information Highway and the New Economy. Between the Lines, Toronto, 1996, pp. 1-15.

[17] J. Shields and M.B. Evans, Shrinking the State. Globalization and Public Administration "Reform", Halifax: Fernwood Publishing, Halifax, 1998, p. 77.

[18] P. Dunleavy and K. Dowding, Production, disbursement and consumption: the modes and modalities of goods and services. In: S. Edgell, K. Hetherington and A. Warde (eds.), Consumption Matters. The production and experience of consumption. Blackwell Publishers, Oxford, 1996, p. 39.

[19] D. Slater, Consumer Culture and Modernity. Polity Press, Cambridge, 1997, p. 49.

[20] D. Slater, *op. cit.*, pp. 23-26.

[21] R. Behn, The New Public-Management Paradigm And The Search For Democratic Accountability. Http://www.willamette.org/ipmn/research/papers/salem/index.htm., 1998.

[22] D. Slater, *op. cit.*

[23] A. Cheung, Understanding public-sector reforms: global trends and diverse agendas, *International Review of Administrative Sciences* **63** (1997) 435-457.

[24] N. Flynn and F. Strehl, *op. cit.*, p. 18.

[25] P. Dunleavy, The Globalization of Public Services Production: Can Government be "Best in World"?. In: A. Massey (ed.), Globalization and Marketization of Government Services. Comparing Contemporary Public-Sector Developments. MacMillan Press, Ipswich, 1997, p. 40.

[26] J. Law, Editor's Introduction: Power/Knowledge and the dissolution of the sociology of knowledge. In: J. Law (ed.), Power, Action and Belief: A new sociology of Knowledge? Routledge & Kegan Paul, London, 1986, pp. 15-16.

[27] Ch. Hood, Contemporary Public Management: A New Global Paradigm?, *Public Policy and Administration* 10, **2** (1995) 104-105.

[28] Ch. Hood, Beyond "Progressivism": A New "Global Paradigm" in Public Management?, *International Journal of Public Administration* 19, **2** (1996) 151-177.

[29] A. Massey, Search of the State: Markets, Myths and Paradigms. In: A. Massey (ed.), Globalization and Marketization of Government Services. Comparing Contemporary Public-Sector Developments. MacMillan Press, Ipswich, 1997, pp. 4-9.

[30] R. Rhodes, Understanding Governance. Policy Networks, Governance, Reflexivity and Accountability, Open University Press, Buckingham, 1997, p. 167.

[31] A. Cheung, *op. cit.*, p. 435.

[32] H. Klages and E. Löffler, New public management in Germany: the implementation process of the New Steering Model, *International Review of Administrative Sciences* **64** (1998) 41-54.

[33] N. Flynn and F. Strehl, *op. cit.*, p. 6.

[34] R. Munro, The consumption view of self: extension, exchange and identity. In: S. Edgell, K. Hetherington and A. Warde (eds.), Consumption Matters. The production and experience of consumption. Blackwell Publishers, Oxford, 1996, pp. 248-273.

[35] G. Wamsley, A Public Philosophy and Ontological Disclosure as the Basis for Normatively Grounded Theorizing in Public Administration. In: G. Wamsley and J. Wolf (eds.), Refounding Democratic Public Administration. Modern Paradoxes, Postmodern Challenges. Sage Publications, California, 1996, pp. 351-401.

[36]   M. Michael, The Power - Persuasion - Identity Nexus: Anarchism and Actor-Networks, *Anarchist Studies* **2** (1994) 25-42.

[37]   H. Klages and E. Löffler, *op. cit.*, pp. 41-42.

[38]   M. Barzelay, Breaking Through Bureaucracy. A New Vision for Managing in Government. University of California Press, Berkeley and Los Angeles, 1992, p. 116.

[39]   H. Klages and E. Löffler, *op. cit.*, p. 45.

[40]   *Ibid.*, p. 52.

[41]   K. Hetherington, *op. cit.*, p. 184.

[42]   R. Behn, *op. cit.*

[43]   Ibid.

[44]   R. Rhodes, The hollowing out of the state: the changing nature of the public service in Britain, *Political Quarterly* **65** (1994) 138-151.

[45]   M. Saward, In Search of the Hollow Crown. In: P. Weller, H. Bakvis, R.A.W. Rhodes, (eds.), The Hollow Crown. Countervailing Trends in Core Executives. MacMillan Press, London, 1997, p. 20.

[46]   J. Richardson, Doing Less By Doing More: British Government 1979-1993, *West European Politics* **17** (1994).

[47]   M. Saward, *op. cit.*, p. 25.

[48]   R. Rhodes, 1997, *op. cit.*, p. 208.

[49]   Ch. Hood, 1996, *op. cit.*, p. 156.

[50]   D. Osborne and T. Gaebler, Reinventing Government. How the Entrepreneurial Spirit Is Transforming the Public Sector. Penguin Books, New York, 1992.

[51]   D. Slater, *op. cit.*, p. 132.

[52]   M. Cartner and T. Bollinger, Science Policy Reforms: The New Zealand Experience. *Social Studies of Science* **27** (1997) 775-803.

[53]   M. Strathern, Cutting the Network, *The Journal of the Royal Anthropological Institute* 2 (1996) 517-535.

REPORTS OF THE PERMANENT STUDY GROUPS OF THE EGPA

Informatisation in Public Administration:
Re-Territorialisation in a Framework of De-territorialisation?
Geographic Information Systems in Public Administration

Wim van de Donk & John Taylor [*]

Introduction

EGPA's permanent study-group on informatisation in public administration convened for its XIIth meeting during the annual conference in Paris (September 1998). At the beginning of this meeting professor Ignace Snellen, who founded and chaired this group, announced that he had accepted the invitation to become EGPA's next president. Consequently he passed the chair on to the study-group.

On behalf of the group, Wim van de Donk recalled the important role of Ignace Snellen for this group's work and expressed, on their behalf, appreciation and esteem for the way he has inspired and challenged researchers in the field of informatisation to work together in this group in the past. His successors, Dr. Wim van de Donk (Tilburg University) and Prof. dr. John Taylor (Glasgow Caledonian University) will try to maintain the productivity, quality of the work and the amicable way in which the group has worked together. In this report, we present some of the highlights of the sessions in Paris.

Geographic Information Systems

In Paris, the group focused its attention on an interesting and intriguing application of information and communication technology (ICT) which is finding its way into many of the organisations and processes of public administration: Geographic Information Systems (GIS). A GIS is, essentially, a "database" containing spatially referenced data emanating from sources inside and outside an organisation, amenable to interrogation and capable of being presented in various modes (maps, graphic, 3-D). A further vertical and horizontal integration of different information sources within and between various organisations, fuelled by more or less explicit information policies, can be seen as a sub-stratum for the further development of these systems in public administration.

It became clear in many of the contributions and interventions during this meeting, that GIS has much potential, making it interesting for public administrators, policy makers and politicians. GIS would appear to be a useful tool in all stages of the policy process (e.g. agenda setting, analysis, decision-making, implementation, and (especially) monitoring.

Ignace Snellen, in his contribution, has showed the strategic potentialities of these systems by indicating their ability to:

---

[*] Dr. Wim van de Donk, Tilburg University, The Netherlands & Professor John Taylor, Glasgow Caledonian University, United Kingdom

a) visualise the spatial distribution of social entities and their characteristics;
b) to combine these with the geographical spread of other social entities and their characteristics;
c) to register and present the dynamics of these entities and their characteristics, and
d) to establish correlations between dynamics of entities and characteristics and to follow the relative accumulation in spatial terms of social opportunities and problems.

These abilities were demonstrated to the study group by both Jim Owen (Fort Wayne, United States) and Louis Smith (Rotterdam, the Netherlands) in their discussion and presentation of GIS which is used in the local governments they represented. The Rotterdam "City-Map" in particular has the analytical power to represent these systems. By integrating (and updating regularly) the many administrative databases of different administrative bodies of the Rotterdam Municipal Government, many kinds of questions about welfare, social, educational and cultural facilities in the city can be answered and presented in various types of maps. Owen also presented other systems which had been especially developed for the management and monitoring of public infrastructure (such as roads and sewerage systems).

Anticipating more systematic research in this field, Snellen observed that four key-developments in this field make GIS all the more important. Firstly, there has been a shift in the kind of data that is fed into these systems (from land data only to various administrative data about social entities). Secondly, the initial focus on registration is widening out to include other functions (analysis, monitoring, simulation, supporting planning procedures, presentation, manipulation, mapping etc.). This development is encouraged by the ability to transcend administrative and sectoral borders. By enabling the integration of data of different sectors (e.g. social welfare, labour, demography, housing conditions, health conditions); of different kinds of participation (e.g. sports, churches); and of education (e.g. drop outs), GIS becomes more and more important to policy makers and politicians who, as in the case in the Rotterdam system, can produce maps where they can easily see how many variables correlate. Fourthly, GIS is here to stay. At first GIS was not user-friendly; mainly static and used for one-shot registrations in restricted domains. Now, the early technical problems have been solved and new technologies encourage its integration within regular administrative transaction systems (e.g. social allowances, school registers, register of police data).

A further dissemination of GIS in and around public administration will, moreover, be encouraged by developments in the cultural and policy environment of public administration. The desire to reduce uncertainty and the renewal of political ambitions towards the quality of society, on the one hand, and the further development of governmental information policies (aiming at an efficient standardisation of data), on the other, seem to pave the way for a further extension of the domains where GIS can be developed and applied. Pollard (UK), Bekkers en van Hout, Lips, Boogers & Weterings (the Netherlands) and Dayre & Miellet (France) have showed that, alongside these policies, new infrastructures, institutions and policy-networks arise that pose new questions about the commodification, accessibility, co-ordination and availability of governmental information.

GIS: Monitoring Society?

The "monitors" (welfare monitor, police monitor, racism monitor, depreciation monitor) found in the Netherlands by Snellen will be followed by many others, it seems. Politically, these and other GIS are becoming more and more interesting, as Jim Owen has showed by illustrating how the use of GIS has supported the successful annexation strategies in American local government. Examples from France have illustrated that a successful integration of all kinds of data at a regional level has critically supported a renewed role of some governmental bodies that, like the phoenix, are making a comeback in the politico-administrative arena.

GIS: De- or Reterritorialisation?

The assumption that the GIS-phenomenon could contribute to a reinforcement of the notion of territoriality in policy-making and politics is provocative when set against the more general observation that informatisation is fuelling de-territorialisation and, indeed, is representing a more general threat to the major foundations of the modern state. This claim was presented to the study-group by René Trégouët, member of the French Senate. Trégouët presented his extensive report on the meaning of informatisation with the provocative title *Des pyramides du pouvoir aux réseaux de savoir* (*From pyramids of power to networks of knowledge*) to the study-group. On the basis of an analysis of historical and contemporary technologies, he showed how information technologies challenge the existing institutional foundations of the modern state. Hierarchy and hierarchical power is challenged by virtualisation, interactivity and transparency. Informatisation represents a whole new set of questions to fuel debates about the design of public administration and democracy in an information age. As Taylor rightly observed, the transparent pyramid in the courtyard of the Louvre can be seen as a metaphor for the new relationships and problems that arise in the information society. Meyer, in his contribution, has shown how the use of information systems challenges traditional notions and procedures about accountability and responsibility.

Future Projects

A more extensive presentation of the research on the GIS-phenomenon will be presented in a special issue of Information Infrastructure and Policy, authored by the members of the group and some other authors from the United States.

Future projects to be developed by the group will concentrate on informatisation in parliaments. Both in Athens (1999), and in Glasgow (2000), the group will focus on informatisation developments within and around parliaments.

Interventions and Contributions

The programme in Paris consisted of various interventions, debates, most often on the basis of written contributions. Most of them can be downloaded from the home-page of the study-group (URL: http//cwis.kub.nl/~frw/schrdijk/CRI/people/wimdonk/contact). In due course these and other contributions will be found in a special issue of the journal Information Infrastructures and Policy.

Interventions

Sénateur René TREGOUËT, Des pyramides du pouvoir aux réseaux de savoir.

Jim OWEN, GIS Applications in an Urban Setting: Innovations in Record Keeping, Program Analysis and Policy Making.

Louis SMIT, Presentation of GIS in the Municipality of Rotterdam (Head of the Department of Geographic Information Services, Public Works, Municipality of Rotterdam).

Jaap VAN DER VEEN, Large-scale Base Map of the Netherlands, organisation, use, current developments. (Dutch Partnership for the Large Scale Base Map).

Papers

Ignace SNELLEN, Territorializing governance and the state. Policy Dimensions of Geographic Information Systems.

Barbra BARDSKI/ John TAYLOR, You can't get there from here: the obsolescence of geographicality as a defining concept in the Emerging digital landscapes.

Frank HENDRIKS, The post-industrialising city: political perspectives and cultural biases.

Miriam LIPS, Marcel BOOGERS, Rodney WETERINGS, Reinventing territories in Dutch local government: experiences with the implementation of GIS in the Amsterdam-region.

Philippe MIELLET, GIS in planning procedures: a French perspective.

Pascal DAYRE, Presentation of a GIS and some experiences using it in strategic decision making processes regarding l'aménagement du territoire. (Direction Départementale de l'Equipement de Seine Saint Denis).

Pauline POLLARD, What is an Effective Approach to Developing the Sharing of Geographic Information to Enable complex organisational decision making? A UK Perspective.

Eelco van HOUT, Victor BEKKERS, Transitory Policy Making and Virtual Organisation. The Case of the National Clearing House for Geographic Information.

Albert MEIJER, Why did you build that road just there?

William WEBSTER, Surveying the Scene: Geographic and Spatial Aspects of the Closed Circuit Television Revolution in the UK.

Personnel Policies

David Farnham, Annie Hondeghem & Sylvia Horton *

The Study Group on Personnel Policies (SGPP) has been in existence for over 10 years. The aims of the SGPP are: (1) to study personnel policies in public organisations in European countries; (2) to disseminate information on developments and research in this subject area; and (3) to create a network of experts on public personnel policy. The central theme which the Group studied at this year's conference was "Human resources flexibilities in European public services". This was the third year that the Group has been investigating this topic, following its successful completion of the "New Public Managers in Europe" project in 1996.

The main purpose of this year's meeting was to receive papers from colleagues on key human resources flexibilities in their own countries and some thematic topics. This was prior to submitting the papers for publication as a book to the Macmillan Press early in 1999. The Group also discussed possible themes for next year's conference. The Group held two days of well attended meetings, where 10 papers were presented. It has also set up a website to update members of its activities and publicise its work to a wider audience. Following the Group's earlier meetings at Budapest in 1996 and Leuven in 1997, seven papers were presented on generic, national studies of human resources flexibilities in these countries, including one on leadership and performance management, and three papers examined thematic flexibility issues.

The country studies

Building on papers presented over the past two years, there were national studies of current human resources flexibilities in Belgium, Finland, France, Germany, the Netherlands and Spain. A wide range of new flexibilities was identified within and across these countries including: part-time employment; fixed-term appointments; temporary employment; variable working hours; temporary employment pools; changes from civil service status to contractual status; career mobility; decentralised collective bargaining; pay flexibilities; and performance related pay. What flexibilities were being introduced in particular countries depended on a number of factors. These included what was driving flexibility, the legal status of public servants, at what level public employment was organised (i.e. central, regional or local level) and the attitudes of trade unions and their members to such changes. In the Netherlands and Spain, for example, the prime motive for reform and introducing human resources flexibilities was to reduce public expenditure and cut employment costs. In the Netherlands, it was also policy to shift responsibility for managing human resources issues to the lowest organisational level in public organisations. In Germany, it was reported that most innovations in personnel management had taken place at local government level and that the German trade union for public servants had shown a positive attitude to the introduction of more flexible, human

* Professor David Farnham, University of Portsmouth, United Kingdom, Professor Annie Hondeghem, Catholic University of Leuven, Belgium & Professor Sylvia Horton, University of Portsmouth, United Kingdom

resources management techniques (HRM). In Germany, financial constraints, demographic changes and career mobility were driving the new trends.

The country where human resources flexibilities appeared to have penetrated deepest was Finland. Here 12 sets of flexibilities were identified. Research by the Personnel Department of the Ministry of Finance had indicated that nine of these flexibilities were being used by over half of all government agencies. The main ones included: fixed-term appointments; carrying over vacation allowances to future years; contracting work out; part-time work; overtime; and combining pension arrangements with part-time employment. It was also noted that in Finland there were examples of partially decentralised collective bargaining arrangements in the public sector. From initial surveys of leadership culture and the impact of results-orientated management systems in some public agencies, it was apparent in Finland that changes in employee commitment to work and their organisations appeared to be independent of changes in performance management systems.

In Belgium, the central question being posed was how could state regulations governing employment practices in public organisations accompany flexible arrangements in HRM? Here a number of flexible personnel practices were identified in federal ministries, state ministries in Flanders, other public bodies and local government. A general conclusion was that increased autonomy of public institutions was leading to variations in personnel practices in different organisations, which was an innovation compared with past experience. In the Netherlands too, human resources flexibilities are expanding. This was particularly true regarding labour relations, staff mobility and working hours. Mobility and employability were important targets in the Netherlands. These were being actioned through changes in conditions of employment, mobility banks and interdepartmental mobility. It was also noted that in the mid-1990s about 20 per cent of central government staff and 27 per cent in local government were working part-time in the Netherlands. Some use was also being made of internal, temporary employment pools, whilst education and training were helping some staff to become more flexible and mobile.

In France and Spain, in contrast, there were fewer human resources flexibilities. In France, for example, there were problems associated with part-time and non-tenured employment and career mobility. But there was some flexibility in the collective bargaining system. Ways had been found to add bonuses, adjust scales and rebalance reward packages for civil servants. The unions, however, would not abandon national pay determination and there was little discretion to reward individuals at local level. Developments have been limited but some changes are taking place. Although the Spanish system of public administration has changed considerably in recent years, with the creation of autonomous regional authorities, it was observed that the central administrative system remained largely centralised in terms of employment and work organisation. The two main strategies being used by the authorities to facilitate some degree of flexibility were removing the managing of human resources from the corps and trying to get some autonomy at regional level to avoid public law regulations regarding employment.

The thematic studies

The three thematic papers presented to the Group covered a comparative study of flexible working patterns in member states of the European Union (EU), pay flexibilities and flexibility in HRM policies in international organisations. Research on flexible working patterns in Europe highlighted three main issues. First, it is clear that all member states in the EU have central rules and regulations enabling public servants to do part-time work. Some countries even provide financial incentives to people to encourage them do part-time work, by giving them higher remuneration. Second, regarding length of working life it appears that it is possible in many European civil services to retire early. Some governments, however, place restrictions on schemes that are relatively expensive to implement. Third, the most striking form of contractual flexibilities are fixed-term contracts for senior civil servants, with managerial responsibilities. More and more civil servants seem to be moving in this direction, with their employment contracts specifying the results they have to obtain over target periods of time.

The evidence on pay flexibilities indicates that a variety of arrangements exist. There is no single model and large differences remain amongst countries and even between sectors in different countries. Elements of pay decentralisation can be detected in many countries but degrees of variation persist. Three observations stand out. First, at one extreme, highly centralised systems are being loosened to allow some variations locally. Second, at the other extreme is the wholesale fragmentation of pay determination to departmental or agency level, with local managers being given powers to appoint staff at their market value. Third, individualisation of pay and limitation of trade union power appear to be more common in northern Europe than in southern states.

The examination of personnel and HRM policies in international organisations highlighted the special contextual features of such bodies. Whilst examples of staffing and pay flexibilities exist within them, it is also clear that the problems associated with flexibilities in national systems are not posed in the same ways in international organisations. This is because in international bodies the drive for HRM reforms does not take the same form as in national systems. Such reforms cannot be driven from the top of international organisations.

Conclusion

The Group came to four main sets of conclusions, following the national and thematic studies. (1) It was agreed that understanding human resources flexibilities is a complex task and that using comparative frameworks and analyses is a very useful conceptual tool. (2) Some similarities and some differences were noted amongst the different national systems but that further observations were needed to arrive at definitive conclusions. (3) It was noted that despite variations in human resources flexibilities within each country, differences were particularly apparent between northern European countries and southern ones. This raises some important theoretical issues, which hopefully can be addressed in the book being written by members of the Group. (4) It was recognised that there was a need for further empirical research to identify and analyse the effects of human resources flexibilities on civil servants and public employees.

No decision was taken about next year's theme but three possibilities were discussed. These were: (1) the changing nature of the personnel function in the public services; (2) competencies in the public services; and (3) staff representation, involvement and empowerment in public services. The final topic will be decided by members of the Group, through a process of consultation, early in 1999.

Finally, the Co-ordinators of the SGPP would like to thank all those who presented papers, participated in our discussions and attended our meetings for their support. We look forward to meeting them again next year, where we expect the discourse to be equally stimulating, productive and enjoyable.

Productivity and Quality in the Public Sector

Geert Bouckaert & Petri Uusikylä [*]

Permanent Study Group on *Productivity and Quality in the Public Sector* has been active since 1986. During these years several issues in the field of public management have developed dramatically. Most of the OECD-countries have established performance management systems and there are already comparative analyses available on the experiences of the performance budgeting, management, contracting out and decentralised personnel policy and the overall impacts of the public management reform on societies. Also, this study group has - during intensive and systematic work - managed to develop and elaborate new public management theories and concepts and has, in deed, been able to accumulate knowledge on performance management during its period of work. In addition to its academic achievements the group has also managed to build a well-functioning bridge between academic world on the one hand and world of practitioners on the other hand. There has always been a well matching mix of these two groups in the study group.

This year the group had chosen a special theme on performance contracting. The group heard altogether seven well prepared and high quality presentations that covered a broad range of topics from performance contracting and contracting out practices to accountability talks and country evaluations on performance contracting and management. These papers and presentations (from the UK, Belgium, the Netherlands, Northern Ireland, and Finland) covered the whole cycle of policy making starting from the preparatory stages of policy-making moving then to analyse and theorise the contractual relations between public sector organisations as well as the relations between public and private organisations. Also individual relations between management and employees were studied from the point of view of the accountability and trust building mechanisms. Implementation and evaluation of the public policies were assessed from the perspective of the broader societal-level accountability structures. Papers discussed the new problems arising from decentralised and deregulated managerial settings. These problems of asymmetric information, moral hazard and adverse selection have their theoretical foundations in the agency theory. The main problem is that of how political (or administrative) principals can become convinced of the compliance of their agents in a situation where traditional control mechanisms (i.e. regulations, detailed budget control, centralised administrative structures) do not exist in the old sense any longer.

One partly solution to the problem is to increase openness and transparency of the public administration. This refers both to policy outputs and outcomes as well as to administrative processes. This, however, is possible only if we have sufficient number of clear indicators demonstrating how economic, efficient and effective the work of our administrations have been. Papers and the discussion in the group indicate that the measurement problems arise in every stage of the policy cycle. There are problems of identifying relevant policy objectives, problems of operationalising them into measurable indicators, including these measures in performance contracts and finally evaluating the net-effects of government policies.

---

[*] Professor Geert Bouckaert, Director, Public Management Institute, Catholic University of Leuven, Belgium & Petri Uusikylä, Senior Advisor, Ministry of Finance, Finland

To avoid too cynical a view, it has to be said that, much improvement has happened during recent years in most of the countries that have established performance management systems. The common lesson has been that there can never be perfect indicators but one has to start from something and develop these measures persistently and systematically. Perhaps an even more worrying finding is that given all the indicators constructed there seems to be relatively little utilisation of this performance information at the parliament level. In many countries the problem is how to aggregate this information and report it back to governments and parliaments.

The group had a long discussion on the relationship between performance management structure on the one hand and changes in management culture on the other hand. The general conclusion was that in most OECD-countries the public management reforms have been mainly tool and technique driven (i.e. introducing new structures and procedures) rather than introducing real cultural changes. These changes naturally take much longer time and therefore are much more difficult to implement. Nevertheless, governments still have not paid enough attention to introduce sufficient incentive mechanisms into public sector. Public sector employees need more independence and responsibility and certainly there needs to be more direct feedback-loop connecting their performance and the rewards given. However, the group was quite unanimous in agreeing that performance pay systems are not sufficient incentive mechanisms in the public sector due to their marginal and technical nature. A much more efficient way to motivate people is to introduce open career systems with objective selection criteria. As far as effective performance related pay schemes are concerned collectively shared productivity gains seem to produce better results at the organisational level. In order to create real performance culture it is very important that the results of the organisation and each individual are systematically evaluated and openly discussed within the organisation.

Even if performance evaluation is important at the organisational level, one should always bear in mind that the main function of the public organisations is to prepare and implement government policies. If the focus is too much on intra-organisational behaviour one looses the sight of the whole. We can have an efficient and dynamic public administration producing simply bad policies as one member of the group reminded. This brings us close to the overall theme of the conference namely the citizens' perspective to public management and policy-making. The overall success of the public administration lies behind the question: can public administration transform abstract political objectives (that reflect - at least in theory - the values of the majority of the citizens) into good public policies and services as economically, efficiently and effectively as possible. The real challenge for public managers is to find the right kind of indicators that measure also the external efficiency., i.e. effectiveness of their performance. The final judgements of the administrative performance is not made by the top-managers but instead by the politicians and citizens – the principals of public administration.

Public Finance and Management

Mihály Hõgye [*]

In preparing and discussing papers in the Paris conference, the study group continued its activities in the field of the management and organisation of tax administration. Earlier this topic had been analysed from the view of national systems of tax administration in an international comparison. Last year in the Leuven conference issues of tax compliance and ethics in tax administration has been added. This year call for paper has been devoted partly to continue studying questions of management tax administration, but to extend it towards other national systems and other levels of tax administration. Another target has been to discuss the participation of citizens in formulating local and intermediate government financial policies including the institutional settings for exercising policy implementation.

The following papers were presented in the study group:

- Arthur Midwinter & Murray McVicar, "Council Tax Collection in Scotland";
- Katarina Ott, "Tax Administration Reform in Transition: the case of Croatia";
- Hugo Van Hassel, "Methodological Problems in Comparing and Adopting Fiscal - Administration";
- Mihály Hõgye, "Tax Administration at Intermediate Level in Hungary".

The first paper deals with the collection of the main local tax - the Council Tax - in Scotland. The mechanics of local taxation have undergone considerable reform during the last decade. In 1989, the Thatcher Government abolished the long-established local property tax and replaced it with the community charge (or poll tax) which was a head charge levied on all residents. The unpopularity of this tax partly contributed to the downfall of Margaret Thatcher and to her replacement by John Major whose administration instituted a reformed system of property tax - the Council Tax.

Although seen as a great improvement on the poll tax, the execution of the council tax has not been problem-free. Cuts in financial support from central government and perceived difficulties in collecting the tax have led to pressure on local authorities to increase the rate of collection. The Accounts Commission for Scotland, the independent auditors of Scottish local government, have undertaken a study of council tax collection rates and practices in authorities across Scotland. The Commission's report concludes by offering advice and "priorities for action" for councils failing to achieve acceptable levels of collection.

This conference paper asserts that the assumptions under-pinning the Commission's techniques are inappropriate and its conclusions over-estimate the scope for extra revenue potential. The authors examine the historical context of local tax collection in Scotland, and offer a discussion and critique of the Accounts Commission's findings, and present an alternative approach that better explains variations in collection rates.

---

[*] Professor Mihály Hõgye, University of Economics, Budapest, Hungary

In the Croatian paper, the analysis of the contemporary trends in reforming tax administration concluded that modern tax administrations are concerned with a stronger focus on taxpayers, specialisation of personnel, independence from the ministries of finance and privatisation of those areas that could be better performed by the private sector. In order to accomplish the above mentioned goals, many countries have set in motion tax administrations reforms aimed at solving some of the key problems such as low salaries and the connected problem of attracting high quality personnel, corruption among tax administration personnel and complex and incomprehensible tax laws. Most reforms stress functional organisation of tax administration, organising a special customer service unit and separate departments to deal with the largest enterprises. This should also reduce tax revenue collection costs and help to prevent tax evasion.

The extent to which Croatia, as a transition country, a small country and a country carrying out reform of its fiscal system including tax administration reform, fits in with the processes described above has been discussed in detail. Suggestions for further improvement of tax administration in Croatia have been also given.

For example, as far as the question of customer orientation concerns, it is difficult to estimate the extent to which in practice the Croatian tax administration is focused on taxpayers, which is one of the elementary conditions of its effectiveness and efficiency. Such focusing is not indicated at all in the Law on Tax Administration. In its further development, the Croatian Tax Administration should, therefore, pay special attention to the following: (1) requiring in an official act polite and prompt communication of Tax Administration officers with taxpayers, (2) during the study Course in Taxation, special attention must be paid to educating students in the spirit of democratic principles and good relations with the public, and (3) organising special customer service unit at least on the level of the Central Tax Administration Office.

The issue of independence of the tax administration from the ministry of finance is not only of technical, but also of political nature. Croatian Tax Administration is neither independent, nor particularly autonomous. It is a part of the Ministry of Finance, does not have the status of legal body and is financed from the budget. The salaries of its employees are restricted by the budget, which makes it difficult to attract and keep high quality experts and impossible to stimulate adequately their better performance at work.

Complex and incomprehensible tax laws have been an increasing disease of modern taxation systems. Although one of the basic criteria in Croatian tax reform was simplicity (Rose and Wiswesser 1995), the new system is still rather complex, vague and imprecise.

The practice of other countries has shown that establishing special service for the largest enterprises can achieve excellent results in collection and inspection of taxpayers who bring in the major part of revenue.

Focus on taxpayers, reducing tax evasion, increasing tax administration effectiveness and efficacy must be accompanied by a precise and detailed knowledge of both compliance and administrative costs. The majority of developed countries try their best to reduce these costs, increasingly due to the complexity of taxation systems, to some reasonable, acceptable level. No precise calculation of these costs exists in Croatia as yet.

In the paper of "Methodological problems in comparing and adapting fiscal administration" the author pointed out that this study group is concerned with tax administrations that operate in different social, economic and cultural systems. Organisational structure and behaviour of the actors will be different and that difference has to be identified in the analysis and in eventual, subsequent proposals concerning the modernisation of the taxation systems. The analysis of taxation systems will be conditioned by the people involved, by their perceptions, their values, skills and culture, by the structures the actions build, by the actors' behaviour, by the power they can generate and use, and by their economic development. Also the overhead system in which tax administration operates, is important, since the former and the latter are both probably important for the way tax administration functions and might possibly adapt as well.

The problem of equivalence is remaining with comparative studies, and when research is done in different systems. Do the concepts have everywhere the same meaning? Are the tax administrations in the environment with their specific decision structures and their social meaning not divergent in the countries that are studied? There can be a problem of acceptance of a change process and of a transplantation of structures of a piece of new technology, or managerial process from one to another tax administration since perception of the actors are different or the openness for change and for self adaptation in the administration are not present.

Comparing and adapting fiscal administrations in Central and Eastern European transition countries present major methodological problems not so easy to master.

The first problem is that tax administration as part of system of governance, must be studied in different institutional, social, economic, cultural and political environments. The common denomination of those systems is in fact that they all belonged to a very distinct world, as parts of a relatively short living empire of several centralised and bureaucratised forms of socialist state capitalism. Although geopolitical elements of that time kept them together as well, these elements also allowed for some differentiation.

Historical and cultural factors also were important for each of them, influencing their way of institutionalisation, depending on the way they culturally perceived the world and this would refer to their own identity. This explains how some of them engaged in change very early, while others went on very slowly, when adaptation seemed to become unavoidable as the system went out of balance in more than one perspective.

Local government in Central and Eastern Europe generally was marked by centralised governmental structure without historical democratic traditions and later by the communist centralism. The development of the local self-government in this region is not a simple process. Technical expertise, skills and attitudes, not only have to be developed at the local level with regard to the agents, but to the citizens as well.

Another difficulty lies with the introduction of new management and organisational concepts, that start to be applied in European fiscal administrations and that are alien to centralised bureaucratic systems of uncontrolled state capitalism. To measure or find out a certain openness towards these innovations is hard to be done in a rather short research project. It has to be done in further in depth, checking not only the existing available knowledge in the administration on this matter, but also attitudes and that type of behaviour that learns, accepts and implements change.

In the paper of "Tax Administration at Intermediate Level in Hungary" the author summarises the findings of a survey that has aimed to position local, intermediate and central administration and to give information that enables to integrate data resulting out of other more technical questions on fiscality. It has focused on the management in tax offices where the taxpayer meets the tax officer, let it be either a local government tax office, or a local tax office or even an intermediate tax office as part of central tax administration.

In Hungary, the Tax and Financial Control Office (TFCO) is an office with a national scope of authority. The TFCO is and independent institutions not part of the Ministry of Finance. In general, the Government appoints the President of the Office for 4 years and only the government can replace the president. The Minister of Finance carries out the supervision of the Office. The Ministry of Finance elaborates fiscal policy and tax legislation with certain input from the TFCO. All taxes and tax procedures are enacted by the Parliament. The TFCO performs the tasks of registration, control, accounting and enforcement to ensure collection of the central taxes (personal income tax, value added tax, excise tax and corporate income tax) which are the most important with regard to revenues.

The TFCO now has a two-tier organisational structure, with headquarters in Budapest, while the second level is comprised of 19 directorates operating in the counties (one in each) and four directorates operating in Budapest. The territorial competence of the county directorates is within the county borders. The TFCO has fully merged tax operations (implementation) at the county level. It has been organised along functional lines with activities.

All county tax authorities are responsible for their own tax decisions. In most cases the County Tax Authorities look to the National Tax Board for guidance to solve difficult legal problems. Each authority also has its own legal department to offer advice to the tax offices.

There is no particular central (government) task imposed on the county directorate but specific features and conditions for the county in some fields like agricultural export subsidies are taken into consideration. It should be noted that this type of emphasis is not a central directive. However, the Headquarters of the APEH sets new and new exact objectives towards the county directorate in every year according to the actual governmental policy. Thus, for example, if the fight black economy is a priority of the politics the number and efficiency of tax audits must be increased. Beside operational objectives a strategic plan is under development in the Headquarters containing rather general purposes.

The Headquarters applies certain administrative and performance related management and control tools towards county directorate. There are no standardised systems in these fields. Sometimes exact performance indicators are required but it is rare. Two tasks are really claimed by the centre:

– an action plan must be elaborated in the beginning of the year;
– there is an evaluation system consisting of 18 performance indicators on the basis of which the Headquarters compares the performance of county directorates.

The director of a county directorate has an overall responsibility for his office, but from the point of view of the whole tax administration his rights are limited. For example, the director has right to employ people, but it is within the limits set by central "statuses".

The discretion of directors is also limited because of the strong functional lines. It means that the main departments in the Headquarters can order and instruct not the director of the county directorate but the departments directly concerned there. For every professional questions an instruction is sent to the county departments along the functional lines.

However, beside the central instructions related to uniform policies and means the implementation of policies is county specific work. This characterises mainly taxation functions like registration, assessment, and collection. In fields of control and audit a decentralisation trend could be seen since 1991. The county directorate can form and elaborate its own policy in close co-operation and in sometimes serious discussion with the Headquarters. For example, taxpayers are selected for audit purposes by the county directorate; no central selection is made.

In principle the deconcentrated central tax administration can adapt to the local needs of the tax process only with the consent of the central office but own initiatives can often be accomplish except some main significant changes.

Co-operation in Continuing Education, Training, Research and Consulting Between Eastern and Western Europe

György Jenei [*]

The Permanent Study Group participants examined the hows and whys of East-West cooperation in the context of its impact on the average citizen in Central and Eastern Europe. Six papers were discussed in four sessions. The discussions were based on a hierarchy of cooperation ranging from informal contracts to institutionalized partnership which was developed in an earlier work of György Jenei and Lance T. LeLoup [1]. This paper discusses the participants conclusions regarding the level and the dynamics of cooperation.

Levels and Dynamics of Cooperation

Going from the lowest level to the highest level of cooperation a five level hierarchy was defined in the terms of its direct and indirect impacts on citizens. The result was as follows:

Exchange of Contacts and Information: Collaboration often begins with meetings, contacts, and mutual exchange of information. This can be useful since partners may not be well informed about each others needs and interests.

Systematic Exchange of Knowledge and Experience: As partners get to know each other better, the relationship can expand to meaningful dialogues, visits, initial exchanges, and exploration of collaboration.

Joint Action: The third stage of collaborative relationship is marked by the identification of projects and activities. The product can be a library, a teaching program, internship, formal exchange relationships and/or joint research activities.

Mutual Cooperation: As the collaboration becomes more extensive and regular, a truly mutual cooperative relationship can exist, characterised by coordinated activities and programs based on and agreed upon strategies which meet the needs and interests of both partners.

Institutionalized Partnerships: Finally, the highest level of collaboration consists of institutionalized partnerships where the relationships are on-going and continuing, rather than dependent on particular individuals. Perhaps the most important characteristic of these relationships is that they are self-sustaining in terms of funding and organization on both ends.

---

[*] Professor György Jenei, Deputy Chairman, University of Economics, Budapest, Hungary
[1] György Jenei and Lance T. LeLoup, East-West Cooperation in Public Policy Programs: Lessons from Experience. In: Van Hassel, Högye and Jenei (eds.), New Trends in Public Administration and Public Law: EGPA Yearbook, Budapest, 1996, pp. 340-355.

In the model a crucial issue is the dynamics: how to go from one stage of cooperation to another level. The primary hypothesis of these discussions was that the impact of cooperative programs depends on the key elements of cooperation and level of collaborative relationships. To examine this hypothesis, we identified possible outcomes of cooperation on the public, including social, economic, and political outcomes.

In terms of our hierarchy of cooperation, our conclusion was that the more advanced and institutionalized forms of cooperation are most likely to have a positive impact on the average citizen rather than just the individuals who are directly involved. That is not to say that informal or even systematic exchanges are not valuable, but rather that more extensive mutual cooperation and institutionalized partnerships are more likely to have the staying-power to affect citizens as a whole. In several cases studies we found that a temporary reversion in the level of cooperation has to be accepted. To overcome regression in cooperation of institutions cooperation between individuals is imported. As said in the paper of Renger Afman: "Generally speaking, technical assistance works, in many situations due to strong personal involvement".

Future research into the question should begin by expanding on the list of potential economic, social, and political impacts that public administration reforms might have on the general citizenry. Although it is difficult to establish direct causal relationships between East-West cooperation in public administration reform and changes in the lives of citizens, it is likely that clearer links will be seen as successful programs persist over time.

Differences in the Cultural Context

At the same time, we agreed that the impact of cooperation differs among countries. We examined some key cultural differences between the nations of Western and Central and Eastern Europe. We distinguished between state administration and public administration and their role in civil society and between societies in citizens were seen as "clients" or " citizens".

Western influences emerging from cooperation have less potential impacts in nations where the concept of public administration itself has been alien. Administration in some countries can more accurately be thought of as *state administration* rather than *public administration.* Social groups have nothing to do with public affairs. The fundamental notion of citizenship is different as well, more along the lines of *client* rather than *customer* which has become more prevalent in public administration reform today. The client in this tradition is dependent, unable to articulate his or her own interest, and therefore needs patronage from the state.

Reform of public administration is difficult in Central Europe after decades of Soviet domination. Many of the reforms of the public sector that are based on the citizen as customer run into the cultural tradition of the citizen as client. Although it is difficult to measure with precision exactly how these historical and cultural traditions vary among the nations of these regions, we believe that it is still useful to keep these factors in mind when examining the possible impact of East-West cooperation on average citizens.

The Potential Impacts of Cooperation on Citizens and their Limits

It must be recognized that East-West cooperation at any different level, even the most permanent and institutionalized forms cannot by itself change certain fundamental aspects of society. History shows that democracy cannot be forced on a country from the outside. In some instances, reform efforts and cooperation even run the danger of creating false expectations among citizens. Reform efforts designed to change the lives of citizens may be subject to certain characteristics of the political system that remain unsatisfactory.

We raised the question of whether cooperation must be limited to technical issues and whether it can result in any meaningful changes in the value orientation of the society? Our answer was that cooperation does not lead to transfer of values. However cooperation may lead to reflection on the values in the home-situation. Such a process of reflection can result in changes of values. We found out that one can build a gradual, step by step process that fosters a climate for meaningful change. Cooperative reform efforts can be fruitful and effective when they begin with an understanding of the cultural and political context, then proceed with a realistic needs assessment. Reforms that are successful are more likely to be *practice-oriented,* rather than value-oriented. In the long run a more pragmatic approach is the one that may ultimately have the greatest impact on changing values from the grass-roots up, and therefore have a greater impact on the average citizen.

Given these limitations, the next question was what are the possible impacts on citizens that might emerge from cooperative programs to reform public administration? To begin with one could distinguish between economic, social, and political consequences from a more "reformed" public administration. Greater wealth and economic security for the people is a desirable goal for the citizens of Central and Eastern Europe. Usually, however, we thought of this outcome as stemming from the transition to a market economy and privatization of state-owned industries rather than from reform of public administration. But reform of public administration and bureaucracy could have potential effects on the economic well-being of average citizens. *Deregulation and the elimination of burdensome bureaucratic rules and procedures* can be one possible benefit to citizens. We agreed upon that there is a stronger need for reforming public administration. Public administration (national, regional and local) has to adapt itself to a role and function which is congruent with a market economy.

We pointed out that another potential impact on citizens of public administration reform emerging from East-West cooperation can be found in terms of tax administration and collection. At first glance, *more effective tax collection agencies and compliance* may seem to make citizens worse off, making it harder to avoid taxes or shield income from the gray economy. However, reforms of this nature are likely to benefit those on the lower end of the economic scale more than those who are already well off and make it possible for governments to lower tax rates. We agreed upon that tax-collecting is highly related to the democratic right of budget. Without an effective tax- collecting system, any democratic system is in danger. There are several historical examples (the history of English parliament in the fifteenth century the Dutch revolution in the sixteenth century, the American revolution in the eighteenth century) which proves this point.

In the social realm, reform of public administration could have other important consequences. Encounters with the state and bureaucrats were often unpleasant experiences under the communist regimes. Citizens perceived their relationship with government antagonistically as "us against them". Government agencies were often involved in spying on average citizens, encouraging others to inform on them, creating severe social mistrust. Reform of public administration and the introduction of western-style reforms has the potential to change some of these social dimensions. Training in terms of treating citizens more as customers than as clients has the potential to *improve citizen contacts with bureaucrats and reduce dehumanizing nature of those contacts.* Reforms to restructure domestic security agencies and police can affect average citizens by *reducing social mistrust.* Reform of public administration can also increase justice and fairness by *reducing bureaucratic discretion and arbitrariness.*

East-West cooperation in public administration also has potential to have political effects on the average citizen. Perhaps the most important is *greater citizen participation in governance.* Although this is a long-term process and most citizens remain inactive in political cultures with an absence of traditions of participation, changes can filter down to the mass citizenry. To the extent that public input in policymaking increases, all citizens may benefit from policies that are *more responsive to real citizens' needs and desires.* This can extend from the local agencies to the national government and may lead to laws that affect the lives of all citizens through more effective delivery of local services.

Despite the limitations of public administration reform and the fact that most instances of East-West cooperation are among political and educational elites, there is still potential that such reforms could have a positive impact on the mass public.

The Influence of West European Models

There were discussions about the influence of the three West European model (Weberian, managerialism and coproduction) on Central and Eastern European countries. In the Central and Eastern European democracies the rule of law is fragile. The first conclusion was that the role of the Weberian model is crucial. Without an existing Weberian model the impact of managerialism and coproduction are dysfunctional. But, that does not mean that East-West cooperation should be limited to the Weberian model.

Non-governmental organisations and other actors of the public service should be involved in the cooperation as well. In that case managerialism and coproduction can be useful as well because the public sector in these countries can only be improved on the basis of a combined strategy in which different components (weberian, managerialism, coproduction) are involved.

The conclusion are based on six papers:

György Jenei (Budapest University of Economic Sciences) - Lance T. LeLoup (Washington State University Pullman, USA), "East-West Cooperation in Public Administration: Does It Impact the Citizens of Central and Eastern Europe?"

Frits Van Den Berg (AO, Adviseurs voor organisatiewerk, Dribergen, The Netherlands), "Illustrated Consideration in the Theme Citizens Participation in Eastern-Western Cooperation and its Practical Consequences".

Svetlana N. Khapova (Stavropol State Technical University, Russia), "A Case Study of the Citizen in the Context of Cooperation between Eastern and Western Europe".

Gábor Zupkó (Budapest University of Economic Sciences, Hungary), "Influence of Western European Reform Patterns on the Modernization of Hungarian Local Governments".

Renger J. Afman (CMG, The Netherlands)", Some Experiences in Technical Assistance for Central Banks".

Dr. Simeon Gelevski (University "St. Gyril and methodins", Skopje, The Former Yugoslavian Repulic of Macedonia), "Relationships between the Citizen-Administration in the Context of Governance".

Contractualisation in the Public Sector since 1980

Yvonne Fortin & Hugo Van Hassel *

In 1998, the permanent Study Group selected the following research topic: "The impacts of new public-sector contract management on the citizen".

In addition to in-house contract management practices and public sector-private sector partnership contracts, the study group's focus during both 1996 and 1997 included quality control contracts (quality charters, quality agreements, quality compacts). The concepts of public service quality, efficiency and costs for the taxpayer were used as the cornerstone of the analytical work, even though they were far from being the only concepts receiving significant attention from the group's participants. Yet, throughout this work, the citizen was most often considered in his capacity of service user, customer, consumer or taxpayer. His economic dimension tended to conceal his political and social dimensions.

The general topic of the 1998 annual conference, structured around the "citizen", incited the study group to undertake a detailed evaluation of this recurrent term which, despite its common usage, has proved difficult to define with precision on the basis of previous studies and which has been showing signs that any potential definition would have already been modified. The term "citizen" had come to primarily, if not exclusively, embody an economic connotation.

The issue raised then could be summarised as follows:

Would this revised version of public-sector management based on a contractual framework, which was originally designed and intended by economists as a means of extending a macroeconomic policy of curbing public spending, be merely confined in practical terms to incorporating a new - and economically-oriented - dimension into the notion of citizenship, positioned alongside its deeply-rooted and universally-recognised political attributes as well as its more recent and more limited social attributes. Or, on the other hand, could this new dimension actually be impacting the political and social attributes of citizenship? and, if so, how and to what extent?

The fields examined by the participants who gave a paper are quite varied; they encompass State-municipality joint financing contracts in France, police and public prosecution services in England and Wales, employment services in the Netherlands, the United Kingdom, Australia and New Zealand, the contracting of a variety of public services in Sweden and Denmark, the contracting of both water supply and wastewater services in Portugal, and, lastly, the impact of contracting practices on public law in the United Kingdom.

---

* Dr. Yvonne Fortin, Chargé de recherche au CNRS, GAPP, France & Professor Hugo Van Hassel, former President of EGPA, Catholic University of Leuven, Belgium

The work conducted, which was comparative to a certain extent, by both practitioners and academics specialised in different disciplines represents the result of in-depth, field-oriented studies.

The quality of the papers presented, the diversity of the services being contracted, the variety of the disciplines involved and the methodologies employed, and the array of countries represented (nine in all) make the findings which emanate from an initial reading of these reports all the more surprising.

These findings reveal that while the terms "contract" and "contracting" do wind up appearing regularly throughout the text, the use of "citizen" or "citizenship" is much less frequent and at times extremely rare, with one exception (the report presented by Karin Bryntse and Carsten Greve). This tendency is even more startling given that not only the title of the topic but the drafting of the specific study program itself had heavily emphasised "citizen" and "citizenship" as well as the concepts related to these two terms.

In short, the term "citizen" is not one that gets employed easily. Its presence is disturbing.

Other glaring voids in the papers delivered: the word "rights" as in the expression "citizens' rights", and the word "democracy". The overall tone would suggest that the act of contracting had also served to delete these words from the literature.

Lastly, the expression "public interest" also tends to appear less frequently.

"Searching for the lost citizen" could aptly sum up the approach adopted on the part of the study group's members whose objective was to stalk the citizen, this entity which has been bestowed certain, and mainly political, rights (the right to vote in the election of their representatives on the basis of a given political platform, the right to exercise controls over State-run services from a broad perspective, participation in the decision-making process or in the implementation of decisions taken, etc.).

Contracting practices: Debates and political platforms

Karin Bryntse and Carsten Greve have observed that contracting out public services incites more widespread and more open political debate in Denmark than in Sweden, where the need for finding rapid solutions to a severe economic crisis has left little room for political debate. In Denmark, however, such debate has been ongoing with very few interruptions ever since the beginning of the 1980's at both the national and the local authority level.

In Denmark, with respect to local authorities, the defining line between public services managed by an in-house agency and those managed by private entities or companies via contracting out corresponds to the distinction that separates the grip on local government power between, on the one hand, the Conservatives, whose liberal economic stance is favourable to contracting out public services and, on the other, the Social Democrats who prefer an in-house management approach. The boundary between contracting out practices and political ideology tends to get blurred.

Another characteristic of the Danish situation: the State's core activities and the policy-making process are both considered as beyond the scope of contracts entered into with external entities or organisations. Along these lines, the authors have underscored that: "Citizens here are protected exactly as citizens and not as customers". As regards issues of authority, all talk of "customers" ceases and the citizens' identity gets emphasised.

Contracting practices modify the functions being performed by elected representatives and serve to loosen the link between politicians and citizens.

In both Denmark and Sweden, the issue of redefining the functions assigned to elected representatives as well as their relationships with citizens, users or customers has been raised by the authors in most pertinent (or perhaps impertinent) terms: "If many public services are regulated by contracts, what then should politicians be doing with their time?".

Luis Ramos and Julio Pereira, in basing their assessment on the Portuguese experience, emphasise the fact that contracting out public services widens the gap between citizen and elected official.

While in the past these same services had been under the direct and permanent authority of elected officials, who themselves had to answer to citizens/users/voters, contracting out has had the impact of creating a barrier between elected officials and citizens. Such a barrier is first erected by interposing a third party and then reinforced over time (since the length of the contractual period does not necessarily coincide with the electoral calendar). A legal barrier is ultimately introduced inasmuch as the user, who has become the customer of a private concern, very often gets cast in the role of a third party with respect to the contract that bonds a local authority to a private company.

These authors have gone on to highlight that citizens may still be quite receptive to the service being provided by private companies and, by utilising their influence as users/voters, could exert pressure on elected officials to delegate a particular service which had heretofore been managed by a public agency. Such is the case whenever contracting out appears as the only solution for overcoming the inadequacy of public financing sources, thanks to private-sector financing and the development of new services or the improvement to existing services, depending on the wishes of the citizens-turned-users. A great risk would thereby be incurred of creating inequalities in public service provision, according to whether or not the geographic / human parameters allow the contracted private companies to project the attainment of a satisfactory level of profitability. Another risk encountered by the participants had to do with the gradual degradation of the "contracted" service, associated over the long run with a sizeable price increase passed on to the "customer", who is often left with no alternative.

It would thus appear that public service contracts, entered into between a local or regional authority and a private company, have increasingly tended to transform the user-citizen into a customer. This latter term captures most accurately both the economic and legal reality of the situation. The relationship between the private service management company and the service "recipient" is definitely a mercantile one, which falls within the scope of private commercial law. The individualism that dominates these types of relationships between private entities acts to suppress the room left for "public interest", which then surreptitiously gets pushed aside.

Contracting practices: Public participation and building social bridges

In France, the State-municipality joint financing contract ("contrat de ville") studied by Raphaëlle Fabre-Guillemant is intended to recreate, by means of public participation, a social bond or a sense of citizenship which has been undermined to a great extent by the country's economic crisis. Inciting public participation in the local authority's decision-making process within economically-depressed neighbourhoods has been designed as a kind of social therapy. The State-municipality contract is based on a joint financing scheme which reflects the necessity of combined intervention on the part of local-level authorities and the State. The primary obstacles encountered in laying out such a contract pertain first of all, in certain extreme cases, to the complete disappearance of a social bond, a condition which renders any kind of collective action very uncertain. Other obstacles include the complexity of the procedures required to finance a project, the inherent procedural delays and inflexibility, and the imposed budgetary rules, chief among which is the preparation of budgets on a yearly basis. Moreover, differences in party affiliation among the elected representatives involved in setting up these financing schemes, as well as among local associations and local elected officials, slow down this process in terms of both general budget allocation and oversight of actions conducted in the field.

More generally, experience has shown that the political (or presumed political) focus on the part of associations (non profit organisations or formal groups of citizens) is often denounced and used against them, in much the same way as are their lax handling of public funds and their lack of transparency; these do get cited as reasons for removing associations from the public action arena.

Furthermore, the contracting out of public services tends to exclude users from the public policy-making process even when they have been traditionally affiliated at the local level, as demonstrated in Sweden for example. The drop-off in "associative" participation might thereby be explained by the mercantile nature of the contractual relationships considered which, due to this inherent mercantilism, would not leave any room for third parties in the contract.

Yet, contracting in and of itself is not incompatible with participation.

Mark Considine has pointed out the originality of the contractual procedure adopted by the Netherlands for developing and implementing their policy to curb unemployment, which has been based on the set of three-party agreements reached between the State, the employers' unions and the trade unions. In the Netherlands, trade unions include the unemployed in their representation, thereby serving to strengthen the social bond.

Contracting practices: Public action and transparency

The progress in transparency that the "New Public Management" has allegedly provided in the areas of operating costs and performance, as evaluated from the standpoint of output, efficiency and quality of service, thanks to the development and publication of performance measures, was expected to benefit the taxpayer, the user and the citizen. A glimpse of reality would suggest strongly tempering such optimism.

Along these lines, Barry Loveday has demonstrated how in-house management contracting, in combination with the appropriate performance measures, has within England's Police and Public Prosecution Services led, as the result of certain skewed effects (reclassification of felonies and misdemeanours, etc. in order to reach the objectives set by the in-house annual management contract), to considerably impacting not only the way in which justice is rendered but the very mission of justice in the first place.

As regards the contracts signed between a local-level authority and a private company for the provision of a public service, despite containing at times a "Users' Charter" or a "Customers' Charter", the guidelines on business secrets (e.g. technological processes, financial issues, etc.) dictate however that all clauses or at least certain clauses related to such secrets not be made available to the public at large.

Within the scope of contracting practices, transparency has proved to be a legitimising factor of at least an ambiguous character.

Contracting practices and jurisdictional control over public action

The contract, which remains above all a legal means of action and type of relationship, throughout its different legal variants, should logically lend itself easily to a judge's oversight. Such is simply not the case.

In his paper, Gavin Drewry has analysed the current confrontation raging in England and Wales between the New Public Management contracts and legal precepts. He shows that contracting practices have had the impact of creating, from a legal standpoint, "gray areas" in which it is difficult to establish a clear distinction between the State and the private sector. For English judges, these boundaries, owing to their lack of precision and state of flux, are difficult problems to resolve. The concepts employed turn out to be poorly adapted to a public policy that explicitly considers the law as an obstacle to economic performance, or moreover as a risk that needs to be eliminated. He goes on to note that: "... the fragmentation and diversification of post-modern public administration has tended to frustrate the development of a solid administrative law of jurisprudence". Those contracting practices which constitute the primary factor of this fragmentation thus serve to restrain the control of citizens' influence on public action. This diminished jurisdictional control has not been offset by a broadening of the responsibilities assigned to the "Parliamentary Commissioner for the Administration", who was and has remained powerless in this particular area. The contracted management by private companies of services formerly provided by a public agency has reduced even further the Commissioner's range of oversight authority.

This detour via the law has helped strengthen the analyses based on other fields of investigation; contracting does in fact lead to creating gray areas where the standard defining lines tend to get blurred. Herein lies the uncertainty which may partially explain the hesitation encountered in using the term "citizen".

A significant portion of the discussions was devoted to exploring these gray areas, by relying in particular on the legal rights bestowed upon "citizens as members of a governed society" and then upon "citizens as public service users", as developed during the 1960's, 1970's and 1980's. The different types of management contracts selected for the papers presented were subjected to a battery of tests, such as the following:

- the ombudsman test;
- the access to official information test;
- the test to justify administrative decisions (the bounded duty for officials to give the reasons for their decisions);
- the means of redress test and the so-called "locus standi" test; and
- the legal aid test.

This approach enabled drawing up an initial diagnosis, which consists of the following: The contracting of services has indeed acted to steadily scale back these rights, which reflected above all else a political conception and, to a lesser extent, a social conception as opposed to any kind of economic attributes - at least with respect to the term's current individualistic interpretation - of the citizen and of his role in a democratic society.

Such an approach also reveals that contracting practices exert a powerful reactive influence when used for analysing the impact of the new public management on democratic institutions.

The work conducted by the Study Group has demonstrated not only that the "citizen's" economic dimension is becoming increasingly dissociated from its political and social dimensions, but also that it is indeed replacing these two other dimensions. Such a statement is hardly surprising at all. The change in both the values and rationale underlying public action gives this very impression. Nonetheless, it was an important point to be made. A refinement to the analysis of the way economic rules and democratic rules interact still needs to be carried out, as does an assessment of the magnitude of the changes being observed and their various implications for democracy.

This is exactly what the members of the Study Group have projected to accomplish in 1999 in Greece. Now that a Pandora's box has been opened, they would like to extend this inventory and enrich the initial observations drawn in 1998. In order to do so, they have proposed that the topic of their 1998 work be: "Contracting and justice", with emphasis put on access to justice. Each of these three terms is to be interpreted from a broad perspective.

The time has come to cast judgement on the reforms at democracy's finest hour and, if necessary, to sound the warning bells before democracy disappears altogether into "the purple shroud where the gods rest in peace", according to Ernest Renan in "Prayer on the Acropolis".

Reports presented at the 1998 annual conference:

Karin Bryntse / Carsten Greve: "Contracting out in Denmark and Sweden: A comparative perspective on implementation of policy and outcome for citizens".

Mark Considine: "Contracts, targets and reflexivity: Comparing Employment Service Reform in the UK, the Netherlands, New Zealand and Australia".

Gavin Drewry: "The Citizen and the New Contractual Public Management: The quest for new forms of accountability and a new public law".

Raphaële Fabre-Guillemant: "Contrat de ville et démocratie locale".

Barry Loveday: "The impact of New Public Management on Criminal Justice Agencies in England and Wales with reference to the Police and Crown Prosecution Service (CPS)".

Luis Ramos / Julio Pereira: "Les collectivités locales et la contractualisation des services publics: le cas de la Région Nord du Portugal".

ABOUT EGPA

The European Group of Public Administration

The European Group of Public Administration (EGPA) was set up in 1974 as a working group of the International Institute of Administrative Sciences (IIAS) to strengthen contacts and exchanges among European scholars and practitioners. EGPA is now a regional group of IIAS.

- **Its objectives**

  * to organise and encourage the exchange of information on developments in the theory and practice of public administration;
  * to foster comparative studies and the development of public administrative theory within a European perspective;
  * to facilitate the application of innovative ideas, methods, and techniques in public administration; and
  * to include young teachers, researchers, as also civil servants in its activities.

- **Its activities**

  To achieve its objectives, EGPA, whose primary function is to serve as catalyst and intermediary, uses the following means:

  * *organises and sponsors conferences and small scale study meetings*

    The annual conference is the core activity of EGPA. It is held in a different European country every year. It is normally hosted by a member organisation. Each year, the theme selected for the conference is a topic of major concern for public administration in Europe.

  * *sets up study groups*

    Each Study Group is managed by a Director and a Chairperson, and is necessarily comprised of academics and practitioners. Papers contributed by members are country studies or comparative studies, which are discussed in the meetings of the groups during the annual conference. The work of each group is geared towards a publication or series of publications.

    EGPA has six Study Groups, which develop the following topics:

    - Informatization in Public Administration;
    - Personnel Policies;
    - Quality and Productivity in the Public Sector;
    - Public Finance and Management;

- Co-operation in Permanent Education, Training, Research and Consultancy between Eastern and Western Europe;
- The Development of Contracting in the Public Service since 1980

* *sponsors publications*

- The EGPA Yearbook published annually;
- Scientific studies resulting from the study groups' research;
- The International Review of Administrative Sciences (IRAS) to which EGPA contributes;
- The IIAS Newsletter to which EGPA contributes.

- **Its address**

European Group of Public Administration, c/o IIAS, rue Defacqz 1, box 11, B-1000 Brussels, Belgium (Tel.: 32-2-538.91.65, Fax.: 32-2-537.97.02, e-mail: geapegpa@agoranet.be, web site: http://www.iiasiisa.be/egpa/agacc.htm)

Publications of EGPA

Books

* *Les responsabilités du fonctionnaire*. Paris, Cujas, 1973, 223 pp.

* *The Public's Servant*. Finnpublishers, 1981, 160 pp.

* *Développement industriel régional; centralisation ou décentralisation - Regional Industrial Development; Centralization or Decentralization.* Brussels, International Institute of Administrative Sciences, 1981, 426 pp.

* *Consultative Mechanisms of Central Government - Les organismes consultatifs de l'Administration centrale.* Hugo Van Hassel & Jozsef Varga. Brussels, International Institute of Administrative Sciences, 1985, 130 pp.

* *Changing Agriculture in Europe : Policy making and Implementation - L'agriculture européenne en mutation : l'élaboration et la mise en oeuvre des politiques.* Bernard Hoetjes & Carlo Desideri. Brussels, International Institute of Administrative Sciences, 1987, iv & 318 pp.

* *New Trends in Public Administration and Public Law*. Hugo Van Hassel, Mihaly Hogye & György Jenei (Eds.). EGPA Yearbook. Annual Conference, Budapest 1996. Budapest, European Group of Public Administration & Center for Public Affairs Studies Budapest, 1997, 449 pp.

* *Ethics and Accountability in a Context of Governance and New Public Management.* Annie Hondeghem (Ed.). EGPA Yearbook, Annual Conference, Leuven 1997. , IOS Press. Amsterdam/Oxford/Tokyo/ Washington D.C.: IOS Press (ISBN 9051994192, xiii & 299 pp).

Occasional Papers

Series in which 23 papers were published from 1983 to 1988. These papers were specially prepared for the series or discussed during EGPA meetings. They were selected for the series by an editorial board headed by Jan Kooiman, Netherlands.

1/83 **KASTELEIN**, J., *Management and Organisation in Central government*. 22 pp. + ann.

2/83 **McMAHON**, Laurie & al., *Power Bargaining and Policy Analysis. What Prescriptions for Practitioners*. 33 pp.

3/83 **KIVINIEMI**, Markku, *Research on Structural Changes in Public Sector Organisation: Findings and Perspectives*. 25 pp.

4/83 **SMITH**, Brian C., *Access and the Reorganisation of Local Government in Britain*. 47 pp.

1/84 **DERLIEN**, H.-U., *Programme Evaluation in the Federal Republic of Germany*. 21 pp.

2/84 **KLINKERS**, Leo & **GUNN**, *Lewis, Survey among European Experts of Training and Education in Public Administration*. Final Report. 20 pp. + ann.

3/84 **MAARSE**, Hans, *Some Problems in Implementation Analysis*. Final Report of the workshop on « Methodological Aspects of Policy Implementation Analysis ». EGPA Conference on Policy Implementation with Special Reference to Agriculture. Dublin: 3-5 September 1984. 17 pp.

4/84 **AQUINA**, Herman J., *Implementation and the Strategic Use of Evaluation*. 19 pp.

1/85 **HANNEQUART**, A., *Production publique et Science de l'Administration publique*. 43 pp.

2/85 **KIVINIEMI**, Markku, *Local Government Reforms as Related to Structural Changes in the System of Public Administration*. 40 pp.

3/85 **WILLIS**, David, *Distributional Coalitions and Functional Interest Representation in the EEC: Problems, Diagnoses and Cures*. 72 pp.

1/86 **PEETERS**, C., **VERBEKE**, A. & **WINKELMANS**, W., *Effective Public Policy Formulation: The Belgian Inland Navigation Case*. 27 pp.

2/86 **WASS**, Douglas, Loyalty, *Neutrality and Commitment in Career Civil Service*. 23 pp.

3/86 **SPANOU**, Calliope, *Fonctionnaires et groupes de pression: le cas du ministère de l'environnement en France*. 31 pp.

4/86 **BODIGUEL**, Jean-Luc, *Les relations entre Administration et Partis politiques dans la France contemporaine*. 21 pp.

1/87 **HELANDER**, Voitto & **STAHLBERG**, *Krister, Corporatism and Bureaucracy*. 26 pp.

2/87 **BRESSERS**, Hans & **HONIG**, Mac, *A Comparative Approach to the Explanation of Policy Effects*. 28 pp.

3/87 **HANNEQUART**, A., *Evaluation and Public Policy. A Conceptualisation of the Case of Industrial Policy in Belgium*. 16 pp.

4/87 **AF URSIN**, Klaus, *Ethically Questionable Phenomena in Central Administration*. 29 pp.

1/88 **HOULIHAN**, Barrie, *Managing with Less: the Changing Roles of Professional Officers in the Local Policy Process*.

2/88 **HERWEYER**, *Michiel, Hard Cuts and Soft Spoils*. 16 pp.

3/88 **POLLITT**, Christopher et al., *Improved Organisational Performance: Dream and Reality in Health Service.* 36 pp.

4/88 **VAN DE DONK**, W. and **SNELLEN** I., *Knowledge-based Systems in Public Administration.* 28 pp.

International Review of Administrative Sciences

The members of the Group collaborate to the International Review of Administrative Sciences (IRAS), the journal of the International Institute of Administrative Sciences (IIAS), published quarterly, in French, English and Arabic. The French version is published by E. Bruylant and the English version by Sage publications.

Books published by the EGPA Permanent Study Groups

* I. Th. Snellen, W.B.H.J. van de Donk & J.-P. Baquiast (Eds.), 1989, *Expert Systems in Public Administration. Evolving Practices and Norms.* Amsterdam/New York/Oxford/Tokyo: Elsevier Science Publisher (ISBN 044488038, viii & 323 pp.)

* P.H.A. Frissen & I.Th.M. Snellen (Eds.), 1990, *Informatization Strategies for Public Administration*, Amsterdam/New York/Oxford/Tokyo: Elsevier Science Publishers (ISBN 0444888004, viii & 193 pp.).

* P.H.A. Frissen, V.J.J.M. Bekkers, B.K. Brussaard, I.Th.M. Snellen & M. Wolters (Eds.), 1992, *European Public Administration and Informatization*, Amsterdam/Oxford/Washington/Tokyo: IOS Press (ISBN 9051991118, 636 pp.).

* W.B.H.J. van de Donk, I. Th. Snellen & P.W. Tops (Eds.), 1995, *Orwell in Athens. A Perspective on Informatization and Democracy*. Amsterdam/Oxford/Tokyo/ Washington D.C.: IOS Press (ISBN 905199219X, xii & 289 pp.).

* J.A. Taylor, I. Th.M. Snellen & A. Zuurmond (Eds). *Beyond BPR: Institutional Transformations in Public Administration. Ideas, Cases and Opportunities*, Amsterdam/Oxford/Washington/Tokyo: IOS Press (ISBN 9051993099, xi & 258 pp.).

* D. Farnham, S. Horton, J. Barlow and A. Hondeghem (Eds.), *New Public Managers in Europe: Public Servants in Transition*. Macmillan, 1996. 308 pp.

* I. Th. M. Snellen & W.B.H.J. van de Donk (Eds.), *Handbook of Public Administration in an Information Age*, IOS Press. Amsterdam/Oxford/Tokyo/ Washington D.C.: IOS Press (ISBN 9051993951, xix & 579 pp).

Author Index